# 100 Nasty Women of History

# 100 Nasty Women of History

## Hannah Jewell

HODDER &
STOUGHTON

First published in Great Britain in 2017 by Hodder & Stoughton
An Hachette UK company

5

Copyright © Hannah Jewell 2017

A CIP catalogue record for this title is available from the British Library

Hardback ISBN 978 1 473 67125 6
Trade Paperback ISBN 978 1 473 67126 3
eBook ISBN 978 1 473 67127 0

Typeset in Iowan Old Style by Palimpsest Book Production Ltd,
Falkirk, Stirlingshire

Printed and bound by CPI Group (UK) Ltd, Croydon, CR0 4YY

Hodder & Stoughton policy is to use papers that are natural,
renewable and recyclable products and made from wood grown in
sustainable forests. The logging and manufacturing processes are expected
to conform to the environmental regulations of the country of origin.

Hodder & Stoughton Ltd
Carmelite House
50 Victoria Embankment
London EC4Y 0DZ

www.hodder.co.uk

*For my friend Sylvia Bingham, who was bold and brilliant and unlike anyone else.*

# Contents

# Introduction

In the final debate of the 2016 US presidential election, Donald Trump leaned into the microphone as Hillary Clinton spoke about social security, twisted up his small, wrinkled mouth, and called his opponent 'such a nasty woman'. The phrase has stuck around since he first uttered it. It's been whacked on T-shirts, it's been put in Twitter bios, and it's come to mean something more than either a smear of Hillary Clinton or a defiant rallying cry for her supporters. In this book, a nasty woman is one who has managed to piss off a man for not behaving as she was expected. Or for having unladylike ideas. Or for murdering him.

When dear Donald became president, it was hard to know what to do to feel better if you weren't a Donald fan, beyond perhaps a cathartic scream, or drinking to oblivion. So here's a suggestion: what better time than the present to look back at the difficult women who came before us? What can we learn from them about how to live our nastiest lives?

Often when learning about history, when you get to hear about women at all, their lives are made to sound decidedly un-nasty. As if they spent their entire time on Earth casting woeful but beautiful glances directly into their glittering futures, calmly rebuking those that would stop them from achieving their goals.

'But you're a woman!' a powerful man says to the imagined

Bold-Yet-Morally-Irreproachable Woman of History. 'Shh, I shall overcome this difficulty,' she replies heroically, turning to face the audience. 'Because I am a strong, empowered woman, and I will never stop believing in the power of my dreams! Live, laugh, love.'

Well, that isn't how life works, and it never has been. There are no unrelentingly noble people. When you hear the story of a woman who lived a life that was 100% pure and good, you're probably missing the best bits. The nasty bits.

Maybe she got her tits out. Maybe she slept around. Maybe she stole. Maybe she betrayed someone, or was betrayed. Maybe she *was* pure and good, but made mistakes. Maybe she fought against one injustice, but ignored another. Maybe she was shot by Nazis. Maybe *she* shot a Nazi, or perhaps a tsar, or some twat come to colonise her country.

These are the types of stories in this book. Please take these women's names and commit them to your brain. Clear away the likes of Jack the Ripper, who was literally just a murderer, and John Hancock, who, let's face it, is only famous for having a swirly signature, and make room for these names instead. They're better. They're lady names. They're the names of women too brave and too brilliant and too unconventional and too political and too poor and not ladylike enough and not white enough to be recognised by their shrivel-souled contemporaries.

Take these stories and tell them to your friends. Because these women shouldn't only be known by a few historians. They should be so well known that their names would make terrible passwords. So well known that Netflix commissions a miniseries about their lives. (Or at least we get a Channel 5 documentary.)

These women should be so well known that lazy eight-year-olds, when tasked with a history project about a famous person from history, say, 'I don't know, there are like eight books in the library about Phillis Wheatley, let's just copy from them and call it a fucking day.'

So well known that people dress up as slutty versions of them for Halloween, and don't have to explain them. 'Oh, I get it, you're slutty Septimia Zenobia, warrior queen of 3rd-century Syria,' your friends say when you enter the party. 'Didn't Jill come as that too? Awkward!'

So well known that not one, but two members of your weekly pub quiz team will be able to instantly recall their names in the history round, despite being quite drunk.

So well known that people incorrectly assign great inventions and achievements and conquests to them, when really the story was more complicated than that, or actually she was only one of a group of people, who maybe even included a few forgotten men. So that the conversation goes like this:

*Person A*: 'Emmy Noether invented all of mathematics.'
*Person B*: 'Yeah that sounds right, I remember learning some-
    thing about her in school. She's very well known.'
*Person A*: 'Well that settles that, let's get tacos.'

That well known.

Beyond fear and bewilderment, since Trump's election you may have found yourself in your day-to-day life as a 21st-century gal developing an overwhelming desire to climb into a womb. Any womb.

This book is my womb. I feel most warm and most foetal when sitting in a library, absorbing stories of long-dead women as if through an umbilical cord, having promise and possibility pumped into me like so much nutritious amniotic fluid. As a foetus floats in a womb and sets about growing fingers and toes and guts and eyeballs and a brain, I have been suspended in my book-womb growing these stories one at a time.

Reading about cool women from history just feels good. It feels like a relief. Sometimes it feels like coming up with the perfect retort for an argument you had many years ago. 'SEE,' you'll want to say. 'LOOK AT HER! THAT PROVES . . . MY POINT!' It can feel bittersweet – which, by the way, was an emotion first expressed in history by a woman. Keep reading to find her. There will be a test.

I am not a historian. This isn't to talk myself down. I am, like all women, very clever and funny. I just don't have a PhD. Instead, think of me as a fangirl and a journalist, who's been travelling across space and time in search of women who may make you feel better for a moment, suspended in goodness, totally relaxed and exempt from life's troubles, and most of all relieved to find that it's really OK – in fact, it's encouraged – to be nasty. Because the people who don't like nasty women, today and in the past, generally turn out to be the bad guys.

So join me! Come share my womb! Crawl inside it, there's plenty of room. Where there are mistakes, forgive me. I have done the best I can, and it turns out there is a *lot* of history out there which I have shoved into my eye sockets, processed through the lukewarm innards of my brain, and squeezed through my fingers. It's inevitable that some things will have gotten lost on that perilous, squidgy journey. Should you have any complaints about the need for a book such as this at all, however, kindly write your concerns on a piece of paper and deliver them directly into the sea.

There will be no more mentions of Donald Trump in this book, because frankly I can't be bothered. So just forget he exists for a while. It will be like a nice little vacation. His tweets can't find you here. Unless you're reading this on an iPad. In which case, you can't be helped.

Read these stories and bask in the warm, tingling sensation that comes from learning for the first time about a woman from history who gave zero fucks whatsoever. It's a healthier pastime than drinking to oblivion, and just as satisfying as a cathartic scream – not to mention less alarming to your friends and neighbours.

And finally, pick your favourite woman from this book and pass her story on. Tell it to your friends, shout it at your enemies as you froth at the mouth, write her name in skywriting, or have a bit of a Google to find out more about her life – there's so much I missed.

Enjoy.

Wonderful ancient weirdos

# 1

# Hatshepsut

c. 1507–1458 BC

Barely had civilisation begun when women first started to forget their place in it. It all started in the 15th century BC with those great lovers of cats and triangles, the ancient Egyptians, when Queen Hatshepsut looked upon her people and said, 'Are you saying that just because I'm a *woman* I can't be king of Egypt? Wow.'

Hatshepsut had already been queen, the wife of the pharaoh Thutmose II, and then after his death (RIP) ruled Egypt as the regent for his infant son. But by 1473 BC, Hatshepsut had had enough of pretending some shitty baby would make a better pharaoh than she was, and so she took power for herself, ruling under her own name and exercising the full sovereignty of a strong, empowered pharaoh who didn't need no man.

Hatshepsut ruled in her own right from 1473 until 1458 BC. (Remember that before Jesus, time went backwards.) She wasn't the first female ruler of Egypt, as a few had served as regents before her, but she was the longest-reigning and most important until Cleopatra's 21-year reign beginning in 51 BC. She emphasised her kingly power by depicting herself in portraits with a beard and male pharaoh regalia, just to drive the point home to any haters. Hatshepsut's reign was a very successful one, marked by lucrative trade, successful military campaigns, the construction and restoration of grand temples, and all that other ancient Egyptian stuff.

It's not clear how Hatshepsut managed to convince everybody that it was chill for a girl to be pharaoh, but she certainly benefited from a close and loyal cohort of advisers. Foremost among them was Senenmut, her chief adviser, tutor to her only daughter, and *possibly* Hatshepsut's lover. It can be hard to work out who did or didn't bone thousands of years ago, or indeed last weekend, but for now let's say it happened. This is my book, and everyone gets laid.

After Hatshepsut died, Thutmose III, who was no longer a shitty baby but a shitty man, took over and ruled for 33 years. Towards the end of his life, he took it upon himself to try and wipe any memory of Hatshepsut from the historical record, destroying her statues and monuments and removing her name from the official list of kings they kept stuck to the fridge. Perhaps it was in order to make the succession from Thutmose I to II to III perfectly uncontested, or perhaps it was just because he was a bit of a dick.

Hatshepsut's most impressive construction project was also her final place of rest, the Dayr al-Bahri temple. You can still visit the monument today, and have a sit in the sun and think about the fact that Hatshepsut ruled Egypt a cool three and a half millennia ago, but, you know, the US just isn't ready for a female leader. Maybe soon though! People need time to adjust to crazy new ideas.

# 2

# Brigid of Kildare

?–524

St Brigid of Kildare died around 524 AD. It's not known when she was born, 'cause I guess being born wasn't a big deal in those days. When you die you're a whole person, but when you're born you don't even bother to remember it. You don't even have any friends when you're born, but when you die it's a whole big thing.

Anyway, whenever it was, Brigid was born in County Louth in Ireland. Her father was of noble stock, and her mother a slave – she and her mother were both sold to a druid. She was a virgin and an abbess, the most popular career for an ambitious lady of 6th-century Ireland. She founded the first nunnery in Ireland, but this isn't the best thing about her.

When you apply to be a saint at the Department of Saints, you have to prove you did lots of miracles. Brigid proved that she should be both sainted and remembered as an absolute lad when she once turned water into beer for an entire leper colony. Sorry, Jesus, some people just prefer beer. Another time, she created enough beer for 18 churches' worth of legends from one beer barrel. Today she is one of Ireland's patron saints, and also now yours, you absolute bantersaurus. Anywhere you know that's called Kilbride is named after her.

One time, Brigid was hanging out with a church official and he went into a trance and accidentally made her a member of the clergy. So she was also a bishop for a while.

Now, buzzkills might contend that Brigid didn't actually exist, and rather, she's been conflated with a Celtic goddess of the same name. But whatever the buzzkills might say, we can at least all agree the following tale is pretty great:

Brigid, being a charitable type, wanted to build a convent, so she asked the King of Leinster, who, I dunno, was some fucking guy, if she could please have some land for it. They were in a nice spot, with a nice forest, a nice lake, and nice fertile ground – everything a girl could ever want for her convent. But, alas, the King of Pricks said no, and he laughed at her. Laughed! At the virginal Brigid. Imagine.

So Brigid, not being one to crumble in the face of a roadblock like the King of Pricks, had a bit of a pray and a think. And she had an idea! She said, hey, kingo, how about you give me as much land as my girly little cloak can cover? And he was like, lol OK. Yeah, have at it.

Brigid and her three gal pals then each took a corner of the cloak and walked in opposite directions, when, SURPRISE, BITCH the cloak extended for many, many acres.

At this point the king, to be fair, was like, well, shit, God is real, and fell at her feet and gave Brigid and her gal pals lots of gifts and supplies, seeing them to be holy AF. He even became a Christian and stopped being a dick to the poor.

Is any of this true? That's between you and your God and your giant, magical cloak.

# 3

# Sappho

c. 640–570 BC

The ancient Greek poet Sappho's sexuality has been the subject of debate for more than two and a half thousand years, such is the anxiety of civilisation after civilisation over the idea that some women may have no interest in men, despite men being so endlessly interesting. Sappho wrote passionately about her desire for women, but it is also said that she once threw herself off a cliff due to heartache over some guy with a boat. However, we must not discount the possibility that she was merely trying to get away from him, and his boring boat too.

Nearly nothing is known about Sappho, her parents, her day job, or what she looked like – according to competing histories she was either 'beautiful' or 'very ugly', which is true of most people depending what time of day it is, or what angle the selfie is being taken from. With so little information available about her, it would be irresponsible to assume something about Sappho as wild as the idea that she was straight.

Sappho was born in 640 BC and lived long enough to complain about her knees in a lyric poem. She lived in Mitelene, the capital of Lesbos, an island long associated with women who are just good friends, and nothing more. Sappho's world was one of pitched political battles between clans, and she may have run some kind of school for educating (Greek) chorus girls, or she may not have. But whatever job Sappho did to pay the ancient Greek electricity bill, in her spare time she busied herself with becoming one of the most gifted poets of all time.

Sappho was greatly celebrated in her day, admired by Aristotle and Plato, and considered on a par with Homer. Scholars in Alexandria listed her among their Top Nine Lyric Poets You Have To Read Before You Die, and compiled nine full papyrus scrolls of her works, which were like old-timey books but harder to read on the beach. Her completed works comprised perhaps 10,000 lines of lyric poetry altogether. (Lyric poetry is poetry intended to be sung, perhaps accompanied by someone jamming out on a lyre.)

While the fruits of male genius such as Homer's *Odyssey* and *Iliad* survived to the present day so that bored year 13 students can pretend to have read them for their A Level English class, nearly all of Sappho's work has been lost to the floods, fires, and fanatics of time. Whether or not the early Christian church had a hand in her works' destruction is yet another unknown in the story of Sappho, but at least one Christian critic called her 'a sex-crazed whore who sings of her own wantonness,' which also happens to be my Tinder bio.

What remains of the works of the greatest woman artist of antiquity is about 650 fragments, containing only 70 complete lines. This means that while we can read lots of people's opinions about her work that she was the Gosh Darn Best, only tiny pieces of her work have made it all the way to the 21st century – though every now and then, a new fragment pops up on a freshly discovered scrap of ancient papyrus. Reading her work can feel like trying to make a phone call when there's terrible signal, and also the person you are calling died thousands of years ago.

Here is a taste of her intense love poetry, which was perhaps written to be performed by a chorus:

*He seems to me as lucky as the gods,*
*that man who sits on the other side*
*from you and listens closely while you speak*
    *sweetly*
*and laugh wonderfully – truly, it sets off*
*my heart trembling in my breast;*
*when I glance for a moment at you*
*no words come:*
*but my speech is in pieces, and at once*
*a thin fire comes creeping under my flesh,*
*and my eyes see nothing*
*while my ears whir*
*with noise.*
*Sweat pours down all over me, fear*
*seizes me completely, I am greener*
*than grass, and I feel like I'm nearly dead ...*

*But everything can be endured, for even a poor man ...*

And then NOTHING! What about that poor man?? What happened? Is he OK? *When is the next episode?*

In another scrap of surviving work, Sappho invented the concept of bittersweet love:

*Eros, the limb-loosener, once again shakes me up*
*a sweet-bitter pathetic creature*

Next time you feel something bittersweet, be angry but also happy at Sappho and her gal pals.

It's a terrifying prospect for a writer: that of all your life's work, only 70 lines will remain. What if the 70 lines that sum up your life were part of an angry tweet thread complaining to Ryanair about a delay? Well, it could also be a comfort to think that someday the Internet will be destroyed in a colossal fire, taking every last embarrassing thing with it.

What I'm saying is, Sappho was a lesbian, so get over it, and always back up your work.

# 4

# Seondeok of Silla

?–AD 647

Korea's first female sovereign was Seondeok, who ruled the Kingdom of Silla from 632 until 647 AD, which as everyone knows was a solid time in Korean history. There are many legends surrounding her, the first of three Korean queens from the Silla period, a time when female heirs could succeed to the throne as well as male ones.

Once, when Seondeok paid a visit to a temple, a young admirer named Jigwi travelled to wait for her arrival and catch a glimpse of the beloved queen. But before she arrived, he fell asleep under a pagoda and missed her entire visit. Classic Jigwi! Luckily for him, Seondeok was pretty chill, and left a bracelet on his chest as he slept. When he woke up and discovered the bracelet, as the legend has it, his heart was set so ablaze that the pagoda literally burned to the ground, which is pretty romantic but also a bit of a health and safety nightmare. That was somebody's pagoda! Men have no respect for other people's property. They think that just 'cause they're in love they can burn down anybody's pagoda they like.

Beyond setting hearts aflame, Seondeok's 15-year reign laid the foundations for the eventual uniting of the kingdoms of Korea into one, thanks to her careful diplomacy. She was an open-minded, logical, and compassionate ruler, who revealed her wisdom to her people in three key prophecies, the first of which will make you say 'Hmm.'

When the Tang emperor Taizong sent her family peony seeds

from China, Seondeok apparently said, 'Oh that's nice, shame they won't have a smell though,' and people asked her, 'BUT HOW DO YOU KNOW?'

She replied, 'Well lads, the picture on the packet doesn't show any bees attracted to the flowers.' And when the peonies grew and didn't have any scent, she was like, 'Told you fucken so.'

Hmm.

Her second prophecy was a more militarily significant one (unless you're a bee I guess). One winter, the Jade Green Pond at Yeongmyosa Temple was chock full of frogs croaking their little hearts out at the totally wrong time of year. The people were like, 'But why?' And Seondeok was like, 'Enemies are near.' She sent troops at once, who discovered enemy forces in the valleys surrounding the capital. 500 of her foes were killed, and Seondeok was like, 'RIP.'

For her third trick, Seondeok predicted the date of her own death, despite being in perfect health at the time, and requested to be buried in a place that many decades later proved to be prophetic in Buddhist tradition. So that was pretty cool.

In her years of rule, Seondeok promoted culture and welfare in her kingdom. She built important Buddhist temples and the pagoda of Hwangnyongsa, which was nine storeys tall and 80 metres high, for a time the tallest wooden structure anywhere in the world. Only its foundation stones remain today, presumably because some guy's heart was set ablaze in its vicinity, burning it to the ground. Ugh, men.

# 5

# Khayzuran

?–AD 789

Born in Yemen, Khayzuran was captured as a slave and brought to the palace of Caliph al-Mahdi in Baghdad, the seat of the Abbasid Empire that ruled the Islamic world from the 8th century until 1258, when the Mongols conquered the city. If you don't know much about Baghdad other than what you've heard on the news in recent years, wipe your mind free of those perceptions and begin again in the year 775, as al-Mahdi came to power, the third Abbasid caliph.

Baghdad in this time, and for centuries after, was lit.[1] Well-regulated markets offered trade from India, China, and basically everywhere else. People came from all over and shared scientific and literary knowledge. Baghdad has from its start been book-obsessed. Educated Baghdadi citizens frequented libraries and bookstores and read works from around the world translated to Arabic in one of the translation schools of the city.

Now forget what you think you know about harems. If you have vague memories of the word or paintings of women lolling about half-naked, know that these images come from the minds of horny white European men, the kind of men who nowadays visit a Middle Eastern country for a week and thenceforth hold court in all social

---

1. Hello there! If you don't know what this means, please refer to the Old People Glossary, which I have included at the back of this volume for your convenience.

gatherings about the *mysteries of the Orient*. In reality, the harem was the private sphere of women in an imperial court, and was a highly political place. Throughout this book we'll meet quite a few powerful women who started out as slaves in the harem but ended up ruling empires through the work of their own wits, their alliances, their education, their skill at political intrigue, and, sure, their beauty.

When Khayzuran was brought to the palace at Baghdad, her impoverished family came with her, and their fate would be altered beyond their wildest imaginings. Khayzuran became the wife of al-Mahdi, and manoeuvred their sons to be named his heirs in spite of an earlier marriage. As the wife of the caliph, Khayzuran was an active and public face of state affairs, and arranged excellent positions in government for her much-elevated family.

When al-Mahdi died in 785, Khayzuran's two sons were away from Baghdad, but she acted quickly to assert her family's claim to power. To quell any unrest in a sudden power vacuum, she disbursed two years of pay to the army. You wouldn't be interested in a coup if you'd just received two years' salary, would you? Khayzuran called back her sons, and arranged for dignitaries and power brokers to swear allegiance to the elder son, al-Hadi.

Unfortunately for all involved, al-Hadi turned out to be a garbage son. (There's one in every family, and if you don't know who yours is, it's you.) He was also jealous of his younger brother, who was obviously less of a shitbag and better liked than he. Al-Hadi felt very threatened by his mother, who had cultivated a powerful network of advisers and officials who visited her regularly in the palace. 'It is not in the power of women to intervene,' he had the nerve to say to his own mother who birthed him, 'in matters of sovereignty. Look to your prayers and your prayer beads.'

Well, instead of looking to her prayer beads, Khayzuran *may* have gotten involved in murdering her trash son instead. Was it her who did it? Who's to say! Whoever it was, they *may* have sent sexy ladies to his bedroom to girlishly smother him with pillows, putting a sexy end to al-Hadi's rule after just over a year.

It seems that al-Hadi had probably been plotting the deaths of his mother and brother. Once, he sent his mother food with instructions for her to 'eat it up because it's sooooo soooo yummy!' but she fed it to her dog first, who promptly died. So better to get in there first when you're playing the murdering game, I suppose.

And so Khayzuran's second son, Harun, who didn't suck, came to power. Khayzuran continued managing her own affairs of state just fine, and Harun trusted his mother for advice in matters of policy. He happily divided responsibilities and power with her, and presided over a glorious court.

The moral of this story, children, is to listen to your mother, or you'll end up dead.

# 6

# Subh

?–999

Subh was born some time in the 900s AD. It's not clear exactly what year she was born, and it's not polite to ask. She was captured as a slave in the Basque region during battles to consolidate the western branch of the Umayyad Empire's control of Andalusian Spain. Her name was originally Aurora, and Subh has the same meaning in Arabic – the dawn. As we saw with Khayzuran, the way women exercised power in a caliph's palace was through working her way up the ranks of the harem, marriage, and the installation of garbage sons who were easily manipulated and/or murdered. You know, your standard princes and princesses fairy tale stuff.

Subh married the caliph al-Hakam, who was a nerd. Like all nerds with money, al-Hakam spent vast fortunes on books, collecting and copying and rebinding them, and, presumably, putting them in a large tub and swimming in them. In the days before Kindles, this meant sending out emissaries across the world to seek out books and purchase them for enormous sums. Also because he was a nerd, al-Hakam destroyed all the wine in Cordoba (boo), encouraging his people's pursuit of learning, poetry and science instead of getting wasted all the time, which is pretty solid life advice to be fair. He built up the University of Cordoba to be perhaps the greatest in the world, ranking quite high on the league table based on student satisfaction.

Subh had captured al-Hakam's attention not just for being a

babe, but for her witty wordplay and her knowledge of history and religion. As al-Hakam got older, he just wanted to chill with his bathtub full of books, and left matters of state to Subh instead. Which is fair enough; ruling a massive empire isn't for everybody.

Busy with her political machinations and the management of the empire, Subh took on a secretary, Ibn Amir, who was 26 years old, hot, smart, and helpful. At this point he and Subh may have had a thing. How old was she? Wow, that's a really rude thing to ask, leave her alone already. But anyway, did they or didn't they? It could just be a rumour spread by Subh's enemies. Or was there even a three-way thing going on? Or a four-way thing including the books? We just don't know, but in any case, why should only men get to sleep with their secretaries? Girls, we won't have full equality until everyone's sleeping with their hot male secretaries.

Ibn Amir, as well as being a sexy side piece, was also ambitious. Like career girls in every film that has ever been made about career girls, he wanted to work his way to the top, and that he did, becoming *hajib*, or chief adviser. Meanwhile Subh had managed to change the laws of succession to ensure her son Hicham, who was either nine or eleven when al-Hakam died (it's rude to ask) would become the next caliph instead of al-Hakam's brother, and she could rule as his regent while he was still a child. Subh ruled publically, and not behind the scenes from the harem. The young Hicham, ever his father's son, was also a nerd, so Subh and Ibn Amir encouraged his nerdiness and his study of mystical religious things, all the better to carry on ruling Cordoba themselves.

But soon enough, things got sticky between Subh and her side boo, Ibn Amir, as these things always do. He wanted to break the glass ceiling that had so long held back male secretaries, and rule the empire himself. The power struggle between the two colleagues and/or tumultuous lovers reached a fever pitch. Ibn Amir convinced

Hicham to sign a document which said 'I'm just a little nerdy nobody, I can't rule a thing!' or thereabouts, and assumed power himself. It was the first time in the Islamic world that a non-caliph ruled, (though not in the sense of being totally awesome.) Subh had kind of set a precedent for this, by normalising her role as regent. What I'm saying is, don't trust hot men.

After ruling Cordoba for two decades until her boo betrayed her, Subh disappeared from political life, and spent her later years much the same way many old ladies do, commissioning large infrastructure projects. She directed the construction of bridges and mosques and hospitals and more. In the end, she died in 999, probably looking great for her age, whatever that was.

# 7

# Hildegard von Bingen
### 1098–1179

Hildegard von Bingen was a 12th-century polymath, composer, and dirty nun. OK she was actually very religiously conservative and really into virginity and all that, but everybody loves a naughty nun, and she at least *wrote* some dirty things, so let's start with her description of the female orgasm:

'When a woman is making love with a man, a sense of heat in her brain which brings forth with it sensual delights communicates the taste of that delight during the act, and summons forth the emission of the man's seed, and when the seed has fallen into its place, that vehement heat descending from her brain draws the seed to itself and holds it.' Heyoooo! That's what *she* said!

Hildegard had plenty of time to contemplate, if not experience, the summoning forth of the emission of a man's seed, as a nun's life in 12th-century Germany was by its nature cloistered from the distractions of the world. Hildegard was born in 1098, and was given away at age 14 to a convent. That was the rule with children. It's a bit like a loyalty card in a coffee shop. Have nine kids, give the tenth to God. Wrap them in a shroud, give them a fake funeral, and hand 'em over to the lil' baby Jesus, never to be seen by sinful society again.[2]

The strict regimen of the convent demanded that each day the nuns have eight hours' sleep, four hours' prayer, four hours' study, and eight hours of manual labour, which entailed, I dunno, putting up retaining walls and stuff. But at least on Sundays they got to watch reality TV. Everything was rumbling along just fine for Hildegard, going about her nun life, doing nunny things, and thinking nunny thoughts, when what should happen but she should be struck by an intense vision:

And it came to pass when I was 42 years and 7 months old, that the heavens were opened and a blinding light of exceptional brilliance flowed through my entire brain. And so it kindled my whole heart and breast like a flame, not burning but warming, and suddenly I understood the meaning of expositions of the books.

It sounds very much like the female orgasm according to Hildegard's contemplations on that topic above; however, her *sudden understanding of the meaning of expositions in the books* was really about Jesus stuff. It would take a bit more time, though, before Hildegard

---

2. Parents would often give away their girls in order to avoid paying their dowries if and when they got married. If you had loads of girls, paying a dowry for each one would be incredibly expensive, so it was off to the convent with them instead. Of course parents could also save money by spending less in posh coffee shops, couldn't they? Some people.

would finally run out of fucks to give about what people thought of her and so become an international celebrity genius. Because even having received a direct vision of God, which is pretty cool, Hildegard still suffered imposter syndrome:

'Although I heard and saw these things,' she explained, 'because of doubt and low opinion of myself, and because of diverse sayings of men, I refused for a long time a call to write, not out of stubbornness, but out of humility,' which just goes to show that nobody should listen to the diverse sayings of men.

Hildegard eventually got over her self-doubts and took her show on the road, or, at least, took her visions on the road by writing them down, interpreting and sharing them, while remaining cloistered in the nunnery. In this way she became an ecclesiastical mega celeb, receiving envoys from popes and dishing out blessed advice to whomever needed it. She even set up her own monasteries, like the strong empowered career woman that she was.

But Hildegard didn't let her spiritual fame distract her from her many other talents. Hildegard is most famous nowadays, among classical music fans at least, for her work as a composer. You can hear her music either by going online or by suddenly encountering a chorus of angels in a moment of religious ecstasy. In fact, one of her most famous works is the *Canticles of Ecstasy*. Old Hildy loved a bit of ecstasy.

But no, having a direct line to God, dishing out political advice to 12th-century power players like popes and clergymen, and producing a vast quantity of medieval music wasn't enough to fill Hildy's regimented four hours of study each day. She's also considered one of the founders of natural sciences and medicine, based on her time in the convent's gardens and observations of illnesses and their cures.

In her medical book, *Causes and Cures*, we find many helpful remedies that may well cure our modern ailments. For example, if you are struck by excessive horniness, the best thing to do is to get in a sauna with some lettuce. That'll sort you right out.

If you should come down with 'jaundice', by which she means an STI, there's only one cure according to Hildegard: 'A bat, knocked senseless, tied to the loins of a human and left to die, is guaranteed to cure that person's jaundice.' Guaranteed, or your money back!

Anyway this is why the average life expectancy of a person in medieval Germany was minus 25. And for bats it was even shorter! But we cannot fault her: Hildegard was at the cutting edge of 12th-century medicine and science.

I hope Hildegard's description of female pleasure was based on a bit of personal experience, perhaps courtesy of a fellow naughty nun, as some historians and Hildegard fans believe was the case, because boy did she deserve a break from her career of writing books on science and medicine, keeping her dream journal of visions, writing poetry, composing 77 songs, advising popes, and, of course, tying bats to diseased dicks.

# 8

# Margery Kempe

c. 1373–1438

The mystic Margery Kempe lived from 1373 until 1438, which, as every little girl and boy knows, was a chaotic time in the religious life of England. See, the Roman Catholic Church in England was having all kinds of drama with heretics, those great troublemakers of history. Margery was about to make much more trouble for them than most.

Margery was living a perfectly normal life as a 14th-century gal, pottering about what is now King's Lynn and enjoying her well-off status, when who should turn up at the foot of her bed but Jesus H. Christ himself, looking like a cool drink of water. While seeing Jesus Christ in your bedroom would be a bit of a shock to anyone, no matter your religious beliefs, for Margery he'd turned up just in the nick of time.

See, Margery was having some trouble with demons. She'd just given birth to her first child, and was stressing about some sins she hadn't confessed. Naturally, she feared she might die and go straight to the fiery pits of hell. (It's not clear what the sin was that she was so worried about, so let's just assume it was something kinky.)

So there she was, being tormented by demons telling her she should burn in hell for all eternity, when Jesus pops along and reassures her, 'It's chill, I haven't forsaken u,' then flounces off back to heaven. Margery was like, 'Awesome,' and that was that for 15 years.

Margery carried on her life, giving birth to a casual 13 more children with her boo, John Kempe. It wasn't until her 40s that Margery started to experience more visions, and that her career of religious weeping would really kick off, proving that you're never too old to get famous for crying. This time, the visions were more intense than ever, with encounters with Jesus in which he'd ravish her soul, and then some. According to my pal Tim who knows all about sexy medieval mystics, 'women were seen as more inclined to sensuality and "fleshiness" back then and therefore given to particularly emotional, physical expressions of spirituality. But this also gave them a special connection to Christ who had taken on human flesh.' Hot.

Margery, ever the keeno, started to wear a ring and say that she was actually married to Jesus. And not just *nun* married. *Married* married. In her visions, she'd feel the pain of his crucifixion, and it sucked. She'd also have conversations with Mary, God, and other such Christian celebrities. This was the real deal, and Margery knew it was time to make changes in her life. She stopped eating meat, and also made a pact with her pre-existing, non-Jesus husband that they wouldn't have sex any more. (A PACT LIKE GETTING MARRIED, AMIRITE FELLAS?!) Anyway, she was married to Jesus now, and things were going great.

Margery began to preach – which women weren't meant to do at the time – and speak about her sometimes-horrifying visions. She saved her extra good crying for holidays like Palm Sunday and Good Friday, and set out on a grand tour to take her weeping on the road. She travelled across Europe, and went all the way to Jerusalem. It was like *Eat, Pray, Love*, but mostly Pray. Although she apparently loved a good dinner party, so there was also plenty of Eat. And, of course, further ravishings by Jesus. So yes, it was exactly like *Eat, Pray, Love*.

Margery travelled in groups, as you did in those days, but faced trouble on account of being really fucking annoying, constantly telling people off for their various unholy actions, and, of course, weeping. Her travelling companions were also irritated that she'd dress in white, suggesting she was a virgin, when they knew her to have 14 children. And so they were total jerks to her, not letting her eat with them, stealing her money, and ditching her. But in the end, we're not sitting around talking about *A History of Jerks*, so sucks to be them, really.

To make her pilgrimage more difficult and therefore more on brand, Margery would give away her money. When people gave her more money, she'd give that away too. Like when rich kids on their gap years insist on catching the Zika virus in order to give themselves a better story.

Church authorities began to get quite worried about Margery, who was prancing around the world wailing her little heart out, and decided to put her on trial in Leicester for something called Lollardism[3]. This was a sect begun by a fellow named John Wycliffe, who had been kicked out of Oxford for his criticisms of the Roman Catholic Church. He believed that everything they said and did was idolatry and therefore Bad. He was concerned with clerical power and corruption, and believed lay people could and should be able to read the scriptures and preach. Needless to say, the Catholic Church wasn't having it, from John, from Margery, or from anyone. The idea of female mystics or lay women being spiritual authorities made them feel itchy all over. Beyond suspecting Margery's religious ideas and her brazen lady-preaching, the authorities also weren't keen on the idea that somebody's wife could just stop having sex with her husband and travel the world weeping.

3. Lol.

What if other people's wives got the same idea? It'd be chaos. Thankfully for fans of weeping, Margery convinced them she wasn't as naughty as they thought, denied their accusations, and escaped burning at the stake. Hurrah!

Margery passed the rest of her days making money by praying for people, pilgrimming around, becoming gal pals with a fellow lady mystic, Julian of Norwich, and, of course, continuing to refine her weeping technique. In her last years, she hired a priest to record her memoirs into a book that may be the first autobiography in the English language, *The Book of Margery Kempe*. The priest was sceptical of her visions at first, until he apparently also started weeping whenever he read the Bible. Weeping can be contagious.

We wouldn't know a thing about Margery today, however, if it weren't for the poshest thing that has ever happened. In the 1930s, some English merrymakers went looking for a spare ping-pong ball in the back of a cupboard in their lovely country home, and there they discovered the one and only *Book of Margery Kempe*. We don't know, however, if they found a spare ping-pong ball. In any case, rich people should tidy out their cupboards more often.

*The Book of Margery Kempe* is likely not 100% accurate, but rather, a portrait of a late medieval life with a nice Valencia filter on it. Which is fair enough on Margery's part. Though she was never sainted, her book ensured her story would live on, even if she had to spend a couple of centuries gathering dust in the back of a posh person's cupboard first.

# Women with impressive kill counts

# 9

# Artemisia I of Caria

5th century BC

*Y*ou may remember Artemisia of Caria from the movie *300: Rise of an Empire*, the sequel to that all-time greatest hypermasculine wankfest of a film, *300*. If you haven't seen *300*, the plot consists of 300 men in the ancient Greek city-state of Sparta pointing their rock-hard pecs at each other and making poor military decisions. In the sequel, *Rise of an Empire*, we enjoy slightly less ab-tastic Greek forces locked in naval battle ten years after the Spartan heroes met their idiotic deaths. Their foe, this time, is Artemisia. You can tell she's a baddie right away, because she wears lots of eyeliner and her hair is a darker shade of brown than the Spartan women, and you can tell she is meant to be respected as 'one of the boys' and a soldier in her own right, because there's a whole introductory montage to show how bloodthirsty she is.

Artemisia lived in the 5th century BC in the Kingdom of Caria, in what is now the western bit of Turkey. She took over as ruler of Caria after her husband died, as so many of the husbands do in this book (RIP to all the husbands out there). Despite her Greek origin, Artemisia was an ally of Xerxes and the Persian Empire. You'll remember Xerxes from *300* for his facial jewellery, weird voice, and great eyebrows.

Artemisia was a skilled military tactician, unlike those fuckers in the first *300*, and the only female commander in the Greco-Persian wars. She apparently would swap her ships' Persian flags for Greek ones in the interests of sneakiness. The Greeks were so keen to capture her that they put a 10,000 drachma reward on her head, which is worth at least a fiver in today's money.

In the film the scaredy Greek soldiers whisper that Artemisia 'has sold her soul to Death itself', which cannot be historically confirmed or denied. It is also unclear whether or not she invited the leader of the Greek fleet, Theoblahblahblah, to try and convince him to join forces with her through the power of her seduction and her sexy, swinging breasts, an invitation he refused after a quickie, leading her to swear bloody vengeance. Which, I'm just gonna guess, didn't happen IRL, but who knows? People in Ancient Greece must have had sex, so why not on ships in the middle of negotiations?

The biggest battle Artemisia fought was in 480 BC, the Battle of Salamis, in which the Greeks and Persians fought over a delicious platter of salami[4]. Artemisia had advised Xerxes against the battle, and was proved right when the Persians were tricked into entering the straits of Salamis and routed by the Greeks' smaller, more agile ships. Nevertheless, she escaped unscathed, possibly by ramming into a fellow Persian ship so that the Greeks would think she was on their side, or so says the Greek historian Herodotus, a known messy bitch who lived for drama. Whatever happened, Xerxes was pleased with her work, and said, 'My men have turned into women and my women into men!' Good one, Xerxes.

So that's Artemisia. She got the job done with her smokey eyeliner and her naval battling gumpshun and her possible sexploits, as we all must in this life.

---

4. If you must insist on learning things, Salamis is actually the name of a Greek island, and the battle took place in the straits between Salamis and the Greek mainland. It was the first time that humans discovered the joys of ramming into each other with ships on a mass scale, and so is remembered as the first recorded giant naval battle in history.

# 10

# Æthelflæd

c. AD 870–918

*A* list of nasty women would be incomplete without talking about England's medieval queen who practically invented being a nasty woman: Æthelflæd, Lady of the Mercians.

No, I haven't just smashed my big sausage fingers on the keyboard – her name is spelled like that, with joined up As and Es, because medieval English people had NO space to spare in their illuminated manuscripts. To understand how it's pronounced, imagine the sound you make when you're about to take a shower but right before you get in you notice there's a spider by the drain. That's 'æ'.

Æthelflæd was born in 870 something, and was the eldest child of King Alfred the Great, who is remembered in history for being just great. One of the great things about dear Alfred was that he taught his daughter all the kinds of things you have to know to rule a medieval kingdom: military strategy, economic stuff, legal stuff, how to collect taxes and chill with monks, and most importantly, how to kill a Viking with a massive pointy sword.

This last skill would frequently come in handy over the course of Æthelflæd's life, including when she and her bridal party were attacked by Vikings and she had to fight them off until only she, a bodyguard, and a maidservant were left alive. Thankfully, though, Æthelflæd understood that it's important to keep a positive attitude in life, and didn't let a bloody massacre get in between her and her new boo. Her marriage to Æthelred, Lord of the Mercians, would consolidate the kingdoms of Wessex and Mercia, bringing the many kingdoms of Anglo-Saxon England one step closer to a consolidated kingdom – something the Vikings were probably keen to prevent. This is why nobody likes Vikings.

If you've watched *Game of Thrones*, you're probably aware of what a faff it is to try and unite lots of warring kingdoms, especially if you haven't got any dragons to spare and you keep getting distracted by tits. Though she didn't have any dragons, *that we know of*, Æthelflæd wielded significant political and military power in an age when women were not usually allowed to assume such roles.

When her Great father died, and her OK husband got sick, Æthelflæd took on more and more of the work of ruling, including leading and fighting in important battles. When some more goddamn Vikings attacked Chester in 905, she fought alongside her men, luring the enemy inside the city walls by feigning a retreat before slamming the gates shut, trapping them inside and surprising them with a vicious attack. Æthelflæd, a practised Viking-killer, then got in on the action with her trusty sword. Imagine caring that much about Chester.

In 911, Æthelflæd's husband died (RIP). Unusually, she was so respected by the aristocracy for her military and political skill, that she was able to stay on as the sole ruler with the title Lady of the Mercians, the girl version of her late husband's title, Lord of the Mercians. After all, they knew she'd been the one running the show for the previous decade or so anyway.

During her solo rule, Æthelflæd continued to win important battles and work toward the consolidation of the kingdoms of England with her little bro, Edward. She fought yet more Vikings to get them out of Wales in 915, then invaded Wales in 916 because the Welsh had murdered some English abbot and she was pissed off. In 917 she recaptured Derby from the Danes, and that's why we get to enjoy Derby today. The kingdoms of Leicester and York submitted to her rule outright. She rebuilt Roman roads and built the cathedral in Gloucester that still stands.

Æthelflæd was making great progress against the Vikings when, alas, she died in 918. Remarkably, her rule passed on to her daughter, Ælfwynn, who had been co-ruling with her mother, as any good daughter would. It would be the first woman-to-woman succession in all of Europe, not to be repeated for another 600 years with the succession of Lady Jane Grey to Mary to Elizabeth I.

However, Æthelflæd's brother Edward ended up coming along to unseat Ælfwynn. It would be his son, Æthelstan, who had been educated in the court of Æthelflæd, who, in 927, would finally succeed in unifying the Anglo-Saxon kingdoms.

And that, friends, is (kind of) where England comes from.

# 11

# Ælfthryth

c. AD 945–c. 1000

L et us turn to Ælfthryth. That's right, you're getting two Anglo-Saxon queens for the price of one. This book is excellent value. But just because they're both medieval English queens with similar funny næmes, it doesn't mean they're very much alike. For one thing, they lived about a century apart, and imagine if a thousand years from now someone assumed that people born in 1890 were pretty much the same as people born in 1990. That is, if there are still books and history and a world 1,000 years from now.

Anyway, Ælfthryth was born in 945ish in the kingdom of Wessex, which nowadays is basically a southern bit of England. She became the wife of King Edgar the Peaceable, who was known to be a peaceable kind of guy. But Ælfthryth wasn't just *any* queen. She was a *working* queen. A career gal. A woman who proved that you really *can* have it all. You *can* be a wife and a mother, you *can* make it as a lawyer in a man's world, AND you *can* install your son as king by murdering the rival heir to the throne! Lean in, ladies!

We'll start with her lawyering. Lawyers didn't exist in England in the 10th century as we understand them today, that is, as Alicia Florrick on *The Good Wife*. But there was such a thing as a *forespeca*, which is not a foreskin that wears spectacles, but rather a semi-official advocate and intermediary for individuals involved in disputes. This is what Ælfthryth did, mostly representing widows and unmarried women in their various legal dramas.

Speaking of legal dramas, why has no one commissioned a TV courtroom drama about Ælfthryth's life? Here, TV execs, you can have a bit of the script for free:

'Listen up, Leofric,' Ælfthryth grunts, rolling up her sleeves and lighting another cigarette. She takes her time. Makes him wait. He's sweating.

'It's time to cut the bullshit,' she finally says, flicking ash in Leofric's face. 'You and I both know that the Bishop Æthelwold is a good friend of mine. So I can cut you a deal.'

'But—' Leofric stammers.

*Ælfthryth slams her big, hairy hands on the table.*

'Shut the hell up, Friccy boy. What we're gonna do is get that pretty little wife of yours, Wulfgyth, a lifetime tenancy of her shitty little farm—'

'But she wants it to—'

'*WHAT DID I TELL YOU ABOUT SHUTTING THE HELL UP,*' she growls. Her pointy hat slips to the side, sexily.[5]

'Now. What we're going to do, Leo old pal, is get your wife a lifetime tenancy of her lands, after which they're going straight back to Winchester, *capiche*?'

*Leo looks at his hands, and murmurs his assent.*

---

5. Pointy hats were more of a Victorian interpretation of medieval fashion than actual medieval fashion, but it's a good image, so we'll let it stand.

*Ælfthryth leaves the room, returns to her queenly chambers, takes a hot bath, and makes love to the court jester.*

There you have it. Yes, Ælfthryth was much more than your average Anglo-Saxon queen. She could have kicked back and chilled. She could have passed her days looking out of tower windows, sighing, worrying about fairies in the nearby woods, drinking dodgy wine, and having an affair with the court jester.[6] Instead, she redefined what it meant to be queen, and also made herself some extra cash through her *forespeca* work. She was also a nuns' rights advocate, which is like a gun rights advocate, but with nuns instead of guns.

Ælfthryth was the first queen to be formally crowned, and saw her queenship as a job with the rights and responsibilities of someone holding a royal office. When her husband died, she continued to refer to herself as 'regina', the regnant queen. If there's anything medieval chroniclers hated, it was a politically powerful queen, and so Ælfthryth is accused in various histories of:

- Murdering her first husband.
- Witchcraft.
- Adultery.
- Murdering an abbot of Ely (using witchcraft, naturally).
- Masterminding the assassination of her stepson in order to establish her son, Æthelred the Unready, who was just never ready, as the heir to the throne.
- Being a meanie.

---

6. I am told by someone who knows better that the idea of an affair with a court jester is an anachronistic one. I'm pretty sure he's just jealous though, so again, we'll let it stand.

Of these accusations, the assassination of her stepson is probably the *most* true. But look, nobody's perfect. Who cares if a few nephews and maybe a bishop have to snuff it along the way to consolidate your power? They had it coming.

# 12

# Zenobia

c. AD 240–274

The key to a happy marriage is mutual respect and an equitable division of responsibilities, or so my grandmother, who was married for more than 60 years, told me one day while pouring herself her midday whisky lemonade. (Drinking whisky lemonades at noon may also help toward a happy marriage.) In any case, this was the strategy of the happy couple of King Odainat and Queen Zenobia of Palmyra, Syria, in the 3rd century AD. Odainat took out the bins and triumphed over the Persian Empire to the East, and Zenobia did the washing up and conquered the Eastern Roman Empire to the West.

The Queen of Palmyra had many names. To the Greeks, she was Zenobia. To the Arabs, she was al-Zabba'. To the Romans she was Augusta. To her enemies, she was 'Oh Shit Here She Comes We're All Gonna Die!' And to her mates, she was Z-licious. Zenobia was a 'Hellenised' (of Greek culture) Arab, and probably went by her Greek name, so we'll stick with that.

Zenobia was born in the year 240, and married Odainat in 255. She was said to be a mega babe, with big, dark eyes, and teeth so white they looked like pearls. But more importantly, she was a boss bitch, who would go hunting and riding and battling with Odainat, and later led the charge as a general from the front of an army on her own military expeditions.

In 267, Odainat was betrayed and killed by the Romans for gaining too much power of his own, and Zenobia was like, 'Well, fuck you guys.' She conquered Egypt, as you do, spreading propaganda that she was descended from Cleopatra to make her conquest of Alexandria with 70,000 troops a breeze. She controlled trade routes to India down the Nile, as well as other Eastern-Western routes. Odainat had already conquered Arabia, Syria, Mesopotamia and more for Palmyra, and Zenobia added Egypt and Asia Minor, a classic power couple move.

Zenobia came to something of an agreement with the Roman emperor Claudius, who was busy fighting in the Western bits of the empire, and so just ignored her, saying, 'Fine, have Egypt, ugh,' but in Latin. And so for a few sweet years, Zenobia was queen of half the world, ruling across a vast empire and enjoying the riches produced by the caravan trade. She filled her court with scholars and intellectuals to hold great debates about philosophy and science and the issues of their time, like ancient Roman podcasts, sponsored by ancient Roman Squarespace.[7]

But soon, a new emperor took power in Rome: Aurelian. He wasn't keen on having some girl from the desert rule half of his empire. And Zenobia was ambitious. She wanted her empire to rival Persia and Rome. She wanted to rule over a vast utopia. In

7. For those not familiar with Squarespace, it's what ancient Romans used to build beautiful, custom websites.

fact, she didn't just want to rule the Eastern Roman empire – she wanted to conquer Rome itself. Get it, Zenobia! You are strong and beautiful and you can do anything! She even designed the chariot she would use to someday enter Rome, like deciding what to wear to the Oscars before you've taken your first acting class.

Now, if you want to piss off a Roman emperor, (and let's face it, you do), the best thing you can do is put him on the *back* of a coin, instead of the front. If you want to piss him off even more, take him off altogether, put your son on the front and put *yourself* on the back of the coin instead. How are you supposed to tell which is the front and which is the back of an ancient Roman coin? I don't know, you'll have to ask an ancient Roman. But this is what Zenobia did. She put her son Wahaballat on the front of the coin, and Aurelian on the back, and then just took that fuckboy off altogether, and added herself instead. She depicted herself as Selene, the moon goddess, in order to get that witchy look. Anyway, Aurelian was deeply offended. Who did this upstart think she was? But for a time he was still busy with the empire's troubles in the West, fighting Goths and Vandals and other such troublesome teens.

Eventually, though, Aurelian returned to Rome, and persuaded the Senate to let him take back Egypt and the other lands under Zenobia's reign. Egypt was an important source of wheat for Rome, and Aurelian very much enjoyed running through fields of wheat. Unfortunately for Zenobia, she had stretched her forces thin, and the Arab tribes and Armenian allies that formed the backbone of her military might were not enough to save Palmyra. She had also ignored bad omens before throwing herself into battle, which is not a very moon goddess move tbh.

Aurelian fought Zenobia's forces out of Alexandria and Antioch and chased them back across towns and deserts until eventually they laid siege to the city of Palmyra itself and its 200,000 or so residents. Zenobia attempted to sneak out of the city to travel East and seek the help of the Persians, but she was captured by Aurelian.

After her capture, Aurelian wanted to bring Zenobia back to Rome to participate in his triumphal procession. He wanted to stick it to the senators who had made fun of him for getting beat by a girl, and to humiliate her before the plebs in order to make his willy feel big and strong. It didn't even make *sense* to be having a 'Triumph', which was meant to celebrate victories against foreign powers, because technically Palmyra was *part* of the Roman Empire. Or at least, that's what Rome thought.

What happened next is unclear, but it's likely that Zenobia preferred to take her own life than be carted back to Rome to be shown off to the plebs in a triumphal procession. Aurelian sacked the city, and six centuries of Arab empire in Syria came to an end (until the Islamic conquests four centuries later). In the centuries that followed, Palmyra would be destroyed and rebuilt many times, though it never returned to the cultural and economic pinnacle it had achieved in the days of Zenobia. Today, in what is left of Syria, Zenobia appears on the 500-pound-note, and Palmyra's spectacular ruins, once a popular spot for tourists, were largely destroyed when ISIS took the city and blew up the parts of the ruins it thought were too idolatrous. Way to go, ISIS! That'll show those 2,000-year-old gods . . .

# 13

# Tomoe Gozen

## c. 1157–1247

Not much is known about the life of the 12th-century Japanese warrior Tomoe Gozen. An account written in the 14th century says she was 'especially beautiful', but these histories of fearsome female warriors always seem to say exactly that. Maybe there's something about a woman who can twist a man's head off in the heat of battle that inspires everyone to remark loudly and frequently about her beauty and grace.

Although we don't know much about this legendary figure's personal life, she boasted an impressive and well-documented CV of her military career. According to the same chronicler who said she was a babe, Tomoe 'was prepared to confront both demons and gods,' and was 'a warrior equal to a thousand men,' as all women are. She was exceptionally strong, a skilled rider, and an unparalleled archer who rode into battle with a bigass sword and a bigass bow. Her hobbies included riding untamed horses at breakneck speed, and leading large armies into battle.

Tomoe fought in the Genpei Wars, a battle between two Japanese clans that lasted from 1180 till 1185. At her first battle, Tomoe personally defeated seven mounted warriors, no biggie. At another battle in 1183, she commanded 100,000 cavalry, adding more *leadership experience* to her résumé.

At her last fight in 1184 before retiring to, I dunno, take up knitting and gardening, Tomoe charged straight up to the feared, giant, muscled warrior Onda no Hachiro, who was flanked by 30 mounted fighters, and casually grabbed him, pulled him off his horse, pinned him against her saddle, the better to get the leverage she needed to *twist his head right off his fucken body*, and toss it casually aside like a cherry pit. It was a move that came to be known as Your New Recurring Nightmare!

I wonder if the last words Onda no Hachiro spoke were, 'Wow she's really stunningly beautiful but she would be even prettier if she smi—'

*Riiiiip.*

# 14

# Sorghaghtani Beki

?–1252

Sorghaghtani Beki became the leader of the Toluid line of the Mongolian imperial family when her husband, Tolui, died in 1232, something I know we're all still upset about. (RIP Tolui, we will never forget you, may angels lead you in.)

Sorghaghtani was a conniving political schemer with an insatiable thirst for power who would do whatever it took to install her son Mongke on the throne. Sounds like my ex-wife! Sorghaghtani successfully held her family apart from the various squabbles between different royal families in the 1230s and 1240s, like when your parents and siblings are all arguing and you politely refuse to take sides to remain the hero of the family and the sole inheritor of your great-uncle's fortunes. She also positioned her family to be at the service of whoever happened to be ruling at any given moment, providing armies to support their campaigns, and presumably sending nice gift baskets with fancy cheese and fruit and jam.

Sorghaghtani was admired across the world for her intelligence and political skill. The Persian historian Rashid al-Din praised her 'great ability, perfect wisdom and shrewdness', and a Syrian scholar Bar Habreus quoted a bit of poetry in describing her: 'If I were to see among the race of women another woman like this, I should say that the race of women was far superior to men.' Which is basically the 13th-century equivalent of a guy saying, 'You're not like other girls . . .'

Anyway, by playing enemies against each other while being

everybody's best friend, Sorghaghtani managed to manoeuvre her family into graciously accepting power for itself. 'Oh, I guess we'll step in and help out running things if you guys can't figure it out!' The competing branches of the royal family came together and elevated Mongke to be the new *khaghan*, the emperor. There were still two dissenting princes who wanted the throne for themselves, however, and planned to assassinate Mongke at his coronation. They would have got away with it too, if it weren't for a meddling falconer who, while out searching for a lost animal of some kind (I'm gonna say it was a falcon), came across an abandoned wagon belonging to the plotters that was absolutely stuffed with weapons. The princes were revealed, and paid the price. RIP princes.

Mongke decided the only thing he could do was have a purge, and swept all of Mongolia in search of plotters and conspirators. Sorghaghtani even found the mother of the princes guilty of treason, and accused them of black magic to add a little extra oomph to the charges, and so they too met their sorry end. Sorghaghtani had succeeded in making her son the *khaghan*, and wasn't about to let anyone threaten her family again. Not after spending so much money on lovely fruit baskets.

And that, kids, is why you don't plot to assassinate the *khaghan*. Just say no!

# 15

# Wǔ Méi

16th/17th century AD

The Five Elders of Shaolin may or may not have existed, but if they did, they may or may not have lived at the Shaolin Temple, which may or may not have been destroyed by the Qing dynasty of China in either 1647, 1674, or 1732. If these events did happen, then one of the Five Elders may or may not have been Wǔ Méi, also known as Ng Mui, and if she was, then she is the inventor of several powerful and deadly martial arts forms.

For the sake of argument let's just say all of the following is true.

Once upon a time a young woman named Yim Wing-chun said she'd only marry some crappy local warlord whose proposal she had rejected if he could beat her in a fight. She wasn't into him at all, so she went to our girl Wǔ Méi to learn how to fly-kick a man in the face which, as everyone knows, is the best reason to undertake any type of exercise. Wǔ Méi said that her system was inspired by a fight between a snake and a crane. It was such a deadly method that she generally kept it to herself, but she went ahead and taught it to Yim Wing-chun, according to the doctrine of sisters before misters.

And so young Wing-chun kicked that warlord's ass, and the martial art style came to be known as Wing Chun. It's a system in which your attack and your defence are wrapped up in a single move, like when you're at a club and avoid the advances of a creepy rando by making out with some other OK-seeming dude.

If our girl Wǔ Méi did exist, she also may or may not have chopped off the head of a tyrannical emperor, before retiring to become a Buddhist nun – a nun who fought for justice with the power of fly-kicking men in the face. And she may have once kicked a kung fu master in the neck in defence of a 14-year-old boy. Or she may not have. Who's to say?

That's about all we know about Wǔ Méi, but honestly it's more than we deserve.

# 16

# Kosem Sultan

c. 1589–1651

osem Sultan was one of the most powerful women in the 600-year history of the Ottoman Empire – having started her life in slavery. Born in 1590ish on a Greek island, Kosem was sold as a slave to an Ottoman official in what is now Bosnia, who then sent her to the imperial harem in Istanbul's Topkapi Palace.

As we saw with Khayzuran, male European travellers to the Ottoman Empire, frustrated that they were not allowed inside, depicted the harem as a place of 'exotic' women in a constant state of naked languishing. But let's forget what those horny white boys thought was going on, because the imperial harem was so much more than that. In this private women's sphere of the palace, spanning 400 rooms and inhabited by the Sultan's relatives, concubines, wives, and servants, Kosem was educated in theology, maths, music, and literature. The harem was a centre of significant political power in the imperial administration, and none of its inhabitants was more powerful than the mother of the reigning sultan, the *valide* sultan. Kosem would work her way up the ranks of the harem, becoming the legal wife of Sultan Ahmed I, and later the *valide* sultan, the queen mother and ultimate matriarch of imperial life.

Kosem Sultan would rule, directly and indirectly, for nearly five decades, during a period of Ottoman history known as the 'Sultanate of Women'. This was a 130-year period in which lots of powerful wives and mothers of the imperial harem de facto ruled the empire via their weak husbands and their garbage sons. Kosem asserted her influence through her husband Ahmed, her two sons Murad and Ibrahim, and finally her grandson Mehmet, deploying a combination of milk and poison. The five-year period in which she ruled while Murad was underage was the first time in history that a *valide* sultan was official regent and therefore directly governing the empire.

Kosem's life story – which is now the subject of a popular Turkish soap opera which I would very much like to binge-watch if I weren't so busy writing an excellent book – shows two very different sides to her personality. As she explained it: 'I have chosen to let my poison out into the palace and give my milk to the people.'

Kosem gave her milk to the people by way of giving her wealth to charity, helping orphans and particularly orphan girls to find husbands and receive an education, and by founding shelters and soup kitchens across the empire. She founded a beautiful mosque that still stands in Istanbul today, and she was known to be magnanimous and generous to the people.

But it's no small feat to maintain political power, even unofficial political power, for as long as she did. Her manoeuvring involved a lot of intrigue, and, well, a bit of murder on the side.

While ruling with her son Murad, the two would take part in such mother–son bonding activities as executing the chief legal jurist of the empire, reconquering Baghdad in 1638, and putting down various rebellions. Much as mothers and sons enjoy doing today.

The way that succession worked in the Ottoman Empire before Sultan Ahmed I meant that any son, no matter if he wasn't the firstborn, could become the next sultan if he could gain the necessary support for his rule. This made having brothers a risky business – and so many sultans would have their brothers killed.

This was, understandably, not a very popular practice among the general public, and so Sultan Ahmet instituted a new policy of putting brothers of the annointed successor in a 'golden cage' – keeping them secluded in a part of the palace and so unable to curry the support to threaten the next sultan.

For the sons of Ahmed I and Kosem, this meant that while Murad was sultan, his younger brother Ibrahim would be isolated from the world. This would seriously damage his health, and later earn him the nickname 'Ibrahim the Mad'.

Ibrahim was in fact so unfit to rule that it was his older brother's dying wish to have Ibrahim killed rather than allow him to rule and therefore carry on the dynasty, but Kosem did not allow it, instead seeing the opportunity to continue her indirect rule via her most incompetent son.

During Ibrahim's rule, Kosem had to contend with a harem full of power-hungry wives and concubines, foremost among them Sechir Para, 'Sugar Cube', an Armenian woman who had been recruited in order to fulfil Ibrahim's orders to his advisers to find 'the largest woman in the empire'. She was his absolute favourite, and convinced him to kill his other concubines.

As things got out of control, Kosem plotted to depose and execute Ibrahim and replace him with her seven-year-old grandson, Mehmet. Her plot failed, but eventually a revolt would depose Ibrahim, who was then summarily strangled. Once Mehmet was in power, however, Kosem met a rival nearly as ambitious as she: Turhan Hatice, Mehmet's mother and her daughter-in-law. Kosem next plotted to kill Mehmet in order to install her other grandson, Suleyman, whose mother was less ambitious and just happy to be there tbh. But Turhan got there first, and had Kosem strangled.

She died in 1651 at the age of 61 or 62, after an unprecedented length of time ruling the harem and so the empire.

So as we can see from this story, women are generally too meek and docile to make effective leaders, and that is why America can't have a female president.

# Empress Wu

AD 624–705

When a man excels at politics, the navigation of relationships with rivals and allies, and ascends to the very pinnacle of power, he is held up as a Great Man of Politics and gets his own Netflix drama. When a woman has these skills, and puts them to use, she's a power-hungry schemer, a manipulator, a tyrant, and likely also a witch. This is the legacy of Empress Wu, the only female sovereign in China's long history to rule in her own right, under her own name, rather than as the regent for some shitty baby or as the 'real power' behind her crap husband. To be clear, she absolutely was a tyrant. She has a *very* impressive kill count. I'm just saying that women won't know true equality until we can murder freely and keep a harem of men, as Wu did, but also be remembered fondly for it.

So what exactly did Wu get up to in the 7th century? She started from the bottom. Wu was among the lowliest-ranked of 122 wives in the palace of the Emperor Taizong, who had gained power in 626 AD after killing off his brothers. Boys will be boys! Wu's position in the concubine pecking order pretty much meant she was a glorified chambermaid. Nevertheless, she caught the eye of the emperor while helping tend to his stables, engaging him in his favourite topic of conversation, horses. It's like when men try to flirt with you by talking about feminism. It didn't hurt that she was a looker, like when you don't mind a man explaining feminism to you if he's also quite hot.[8]

In Tang China, the great historical roulette of arbitrary beauty standards had spun and landed on 'stout', and Wu was considered one of the most beautiful women in the land. She rose to the top of Taizong's favourites, but Wu's position became precarious when Taizong died. Men ruin everything! Luckily, though, Wu had also caught the eye of one of the emperor's sons, Gaozong, while helping to nurse the ill Taizong. Crucially, Gaozong was not one of Taizong's many garbage sons, as before Taizong died he had had to *eliminate* four of his crap princelings for their various treacheries, and their women along with them. No, Gaozong was just fine, and easily manipulated, to the delight of court advisers, and of Wu, who had survived the purge of princes and concubines.

In the 7th-century Tang dynasty, the girls had gone wild. Inspired by their Turkic neighbours, women were brazenly riding horses, shortening their veils to sluttier and sluttier lengths, and committing that gravest crime any woman can sink to: trouser-wearing. The absolute slags. The timing was ripe for Wu to rise higher in

---

8. Hello, gentlemen readers! I'm so glad you could join us. Just wanted to let you know it's best not to test this theory, ever, with anyone. This is just an innocent joke, and not meant to be taken as a guide of any shape or form. Thank you, and enjoy!

power than any Chinese woman ever had, or ever would. It wasn't a simple matter of just marrying Gaozong, however. After the death of an emperor, his wives were meant to shave their heads and retire to a life of quiet reflection and prayer far from court. Wu, though, was a saucy minx, who encountered Gaozong while apparently mourning for his father, as a good and pious woman would. Gaozong was super into it, and Wu was allowed against all tradition to return to the palace and become the wife of her first husband's son, which is pretty gross tbh.

The other trouble was that Gaozong already had a chief wife, the Empress Weng, who Wu served as a lady-in-waiting. Wu had a plan to replace her, however, and ho-ho-holy shit was it dark. Wu had already borne several children for Gaozong, while Weng hadn't yet given him an official heir. The Empress Weng's fate was sealed, however, when one day she came to visit a baby girl that Wu had recently birthed. She found herself alone with the baby, presumably just said, 'What's up,' to it (or whatever it is people say to babies) and left, but when Wu returned, she cried out that her baby was DEAD. She demanded to know who had been the last person alone with the baby, and oh look at that, it was Empress Weng, who then appeared to be a baby-murderer in the eyes of everyone in the palace. In the ensuing fallout, Empress Weng made things even worse for herself by trying to exact revenge on Wu with a bit of witchcraft, which was truly a no-no. After some careful lobbying on the part of Wu and Gaozong around the palace advisers, Empress Weng was demoted, and in 655 Wu was made the new chief wife and Empress.

How the fuck did that baby die? I don't want to know because oh lordy it's all bad. Even if it was a natural cot death, Wu absolutely used her baby's death to political ends. Yikes, Wu!

Anyway Wu took it upon herself to put Empress Weng and

another concubine who'd helped with the witchy stuff under house arrest, and eventually had them brutally killed, subjecting them to torture and leaving their still-alive bodies to stew in vats of wine for days until they died. Sounds like my plans for Friday night, amirite?!

And so Empress Wu gained the nickname 'Treacherous Fox', and lived a number of happy years as Gaozong's chief wife. They passed their days scheming, meting out punishments to traitorous family members, and enjoying a spot of weird sex stuff. One of the reasons Wu had risen to be Gaozong's favourite, apparently, was because she was the only one willing to do ~some unknown sex thing~ that remains a mystery but has probably since been inadvertently described in the pages of *Cosmo*. Whatever it was, they supposedly enjoyed doing it in a bed surrounded by mirrors, the better to check out their hot, stout bodies. Courtly advisers grew concerned that the pair was in fact *too* monogamous, which was seen as dangerous to a man's health; wasting all his semen and energy on a single succubus such as Wu rather than drawing from the life force of dozens of young ladies, as "natural".[9]

Wu had climbed to great heights, both politically and sexually speaking, but would rise even higher – on both fronts. In the year 660, Gaozong had a stroke, and entrusted Wu to manage more affairs of state. Everything was going according to plan: Empress Wu saw herself as being the one true emperor after her husband's death. It would take a couple more sly poisonings and a banishment or two, some decrees to placate the people, and a handful of auspicious omens and before long Wu was well on her way along the

---

9. Hi again, gents! Just another friendly piece of advice while I have you: This is ALSO not a great argument to make in the modern world, at any time, to anyone, ever! Don't try it! Trust me! OK carry on.

path to power. Her only trouble was a deep fear of being haunted by the ghosts of her tortured and murdered enemies, because you fucking would be terrified of that after the wine thing, wouldn't you?

Wu had two sons left standing by the time Gaozong died in 683. One of them, Zhongzong, she kinda hated, but as the elder he was installed as the next emperor. The other, Ruizong, was mummy's little princeling, and another easily manipulated man for Wu to rule through. What mummy wants, mummy gets, and Zhongzong managed only six weeks in power before Wu declared him a traitor and had him deposed. Once Ruizong was in power, Wu told everyone he had a speech impediment, and that she would do all the talking for him, naturally. After six years of Ruizong's powerful, impressive, not-at-all-secondary-to-his-mother's rule, he finally said, totally of his own accord, that wouldn't it be nice if he just abdicated and Wu took over instead.

And so Wu came to power in 690. She wasn't just the empress, she was the emperor, the sovereign, the ~Sage Mother of Mankind~ and a living god. She ruled for 15 years this way, which were actually quite uneventful, apart from the continued weird sex stuff. In 699, Wu created something called the Office of the Crane, which was tasked with coming up with potions and elixirs to help her elude death. It was also staffed by hot young men who chilled in silky robes and wore make-up to enhance their beauty. After all, if sex with young women was meant to prolong the life of an emperor, why shouldn't Wu enjoy the same health benefits? Her two faves among her toy boys were the Zhang brothers who, when she fell ill in her old age, were the only ones allowed near her. Even into her 80s, Wu was getting it on, the saucy minx.

Eventually, though, Wu would get a taste of her own medicine. Fed up with the sexy weird court his mother presided over,

Zhongzong, Wu's ousted son, arrived with conspirators one night to behead the hated Zhang brothers (RIP) and carry out a coup. Wu left the palace a few days later, after five decades of running China in one way or another. Say what you will about her murdering ways, but Wu had a good run.

Wu's legacy has mixed reviews. She was the subject of a 16th-century porno novel entitled *The Lord of Perfect Satisfaction* which involved an older Wu getting it off with a handsome, bedicked youth, who she would call 'Daddy' in the novel. Centuries later, she has featured in less X-rated novels and biographies as well as films. A Chinese-language biography of Hillary Clinton from 1996 had the subtitle *Empress Wu in the White House*, which is pretty lol considering all of the above.

Was Wu an extra bad baddie, for all her court machinations? Or was she actually just par for the course as far as imperial scheming goes? But also, wow did she murder people! She suuuure did.

If nothing else, we can all agree that the Empress Wu deserves an Oscar-winning biopic. Maybe Scarlett Johansson can play the lead? Or whoever the latest white lady is who gets to play Asian roles – unless of course Hollywood someday decides to change its lily-white ways.

# 18

# Laskarina Bouboulina

## 1771–1825

Laskarina Bouboulina proved that you're never too old to get started as a naval commander. She was 40 years old, twice widowed, the mother of seven children, single, and ready to mingle by the time she set about building up her shipping empire.

Laskarina was born in 1771 inside a prison in Istanbul where her mother was visiting her father, who had been jailed for his participation in a 1770 independence uprising against the Ottoman Empire. The family hailed from the Greek island of Hydra and like most Greeks in maritime communities they were skilled sailors. Laskarina was a hard drinker and, as the story goes, so ugly the only way she could get laid was to point a pistol at a man and threaten him. What is the truth of it and what is the locker room talk of sexually rejected men, we will never know.

Laskarina's second husband, Dimitri Bouboulis, from whom she got the name Bouboulina, died in 1811 in battle with pirates, a leading cause of death in the day. He had four ships to his name, which she took over and began to build up into a formidable fleet, crowned by the massive warship Agamemnon, evoking the Trojan War. Laskarina and her fellow Greeks had been preparing for another independence uprising for years as part of the innocently named underground organisation 'The Friendly Society'. She recruited a private army of men from the island of Spetses, and spent the fortune she had inherited from her husbands on feeding and paying her men. Laskarina had also been secretly amassing arms and keeping them in her house. Imagine an Ottoman official coming to inspect this middle-aged Greek mother's home and finding the building blocks for a private army. 'Oh, these? Oh no, just a hobby, don't mind silly old me!'

When the Greeks rose up in their bloody bid for independence, Laskarina commanded her ships all round the Greek islands, fighting in key blockades and battles and sieges of Turkish forts, and assisting Greek forces wherever they were. Though outnumbered, the Greeks were better sailors and a mighty match for the Ottomans. When sea battles weren't enough for her, Laskarina came ashore to fight the revolution on horseback.

When the Greeks captured the town of Tripolis, Laskarina negotiated a prisoner swap with the defeated Turkish commander in order to save the lives of the Turkish women and children of the harem of the Ottoman governor Hourshid Pasha. She had made a promise years earlier to the mother of the Sultan that she would protect Turkish women in need, in exchange for returning her confiscated fortune. And so in the midst of a war marked by brutal massacres of civilians, she commanded her soldiers not to harm these women and children, warning them that, 'Whoever attempts to do so will have first to pass over my dead body.' The women and children were safely evacuated.

The Greek War of Independence lasted from 1821 until 1832 and resulted in an independent Greek state, but Laskarina wouldn't survive to see it. After all her daring feats at sea and on the battlefield, Laskarina was killed in 1825 in a family dispute, when her son ran off with the daughter of another family and someone shot her. It just goes to show that no amount of revolutionary spirit and battle experience can save a person from their family drama.

# 19

# Ching Shih

## 1775–1844

*L*isten. The most important thing you need to know about Ching Shih, or Zheng Shi, is that not only was she a pirate who fucked up vast stretches of sea in the 19th century but *she was the most successful pirate in fucking history*. She fucked up that glass ceiling that's been holding lady pirates back too long. She commanded a goddamn fleet of motherfucking tens of thousands of pirate underlings.

She fucked up the British. She fucked up the Portuguese. And the British and the Portuguese were some of the worst mother-fuckers on the sea! She saw the Qing dynasty, she thought, 'Why hello there', and fucked it up too.

Ching Shih was born in 1775 in Guangdong, China, and started out as a sex-worker in a brothel. Does this matter? Fuck no. It doesn't matter who you are or where you start from so long as you work hard and become the most fearsome pirate of all time.

She started her proper pirating after marrying her pirate boo, and together they joined in pirate activities. At some point, he fucking died. Men always let you down.

Ching Shih carried on commanding their fleet of ships and turned it into an even bigger one. Her fleet had it all. It had loot. It had men. It had bigass ships. It menaced the goddamn *ocean*. It was so rich and so successful that it ended up a fully fledged business empire, thriving off taxes from captured coastal towns. She taxed her pirate underlings on their booty (lol) and got really fucking rich. Ching Shih's pirate empire had fucking *laws*. If you broke the laws, RIP you. If you captured a wife but weren't faithful to her, RIP you. If you raped someone, you were dead. It was a very well-oiled machine, and they called her 'The Terror of South China', which is pretty metal.

The Chinese government was so sick of her shit that they offered her and all her pirates amnesty if she would just stop fucking them all up for a second. They even let her keep her loot. She was such a fucking good pirate that she lived long enough to *retire* from piracy, and take up bingo or some shit instead. (She actually got married, had a kid, and opened a gambling house.)

Where are the lady pirates in our children's stories? Where are the strong, empowered lady pirates who don't need no man pirates?

We need more lady pirates.

We need to take to the seas.

GIRLS, STUDY YOUR NAVIGATION, IT IS TIME TO TAKE TO THE SEAS.

Why don't we know that the most successful pirate in history was a woman? Why when we think of pirates do we dress up as goddamn Johnny ass Depp instead of ass-kicking, cool-ass bitch Ching Shih? I'm livid. These are questions someone must answer post-haste.

That's what you need to know about Ching Shih.

Women who were geniuses
despite the fact that
they were girls

(everyone knows that
girls can't be geniuses)

# 20

# Hypatia

c. AD 355–415

ypatia lived thousands of years before Internet trolls existed, so sadly nobody ever informed her that actually girls are really bad at maths because their brains are too frilly and emotional, and also that she was an ugly slut. And so, without this crucial warning, she became the greatest mathematician and astronomer of her time.

Hypatia was born in 355 AD in Alexandria, Egypt. She wrote on geometry and number theory, which I know nothing about because alas, I have been told my brain is too frilly and soft and strawberry-flavoured to ever understand such matters. Hypatia's father was also a mathematician and astronomer, and the last known member of the Alexandrian Museum, that great institute of learning and scholars and pretty walkways that contained, once upon a time, the Library of Alexandria. Together, Hypatia and her father strived to preserve the work of ancient Greek nerds in these troubled times in Alexandria, as Christians, Jews and pagans battled over who God(s) liked best.

Listen, we're all mad about the Library of Alexandria burning down. How dare they! Those were good books. Someone should have at least thought to do a backup on the Kindle of Alexandria.[10] Ancient people were so dumb!

---

10. Hello Amazon, in exchange for this joke can I please have an unlimited supply of Kindle chargers, I keep losing mine, thx.

The library had been founded in 295 BC with the aim of collecting all the books in the world, just for the bants. While the main library with its hundreds of thousands of books was destroyed as a result of some Caesar fuckery in 48 BC, the library's 'overflow' section with tens of thousands more was housed at the Serapeum temple until Hypatia's time when some further fuckery abounded.

In 385 AD Saint Theophilus was made bishop of Alexandria. He had apparently been a gifted student and scholar himself, but unfortunately he was also a bit of a silly twat. He was violently opposed to anybody not a Christian, and set about destroying all the non-Christian shrines of North Africa, with the blessing of the Roman emperor Theodosius II. To this end Theophilus razed the Serapeum in 391, a temple dedicated to the Greco-Egyptian god Serapis, i.e. the wrong god, taking with it perhaps the last of the books that had been part of the legendary Library of Alexandria. Jesus would have been thrilled. He would have been like, 'Yes, this is exactly what I was after, thanks man, here, be a saint.'

Anyway that's where all the books went. RIP centuries of human knowledge. If it weren't for all the fuckery, we'd have teleportation by now, and you'd never have to pee in a plane toilet again, and worry when you flush it that you'll get sucked out of the plane and tossed into the air at 30,000 feet with your pants round your ankles.

If your job is to be a famous intellectual, it's a pretty bad sign when the society you're living in destroys all its books. But since Hypatia was so popular among her students, one of whom was mates with Theophilus 'the dickhead' himself, she was left alone for a while despite her pagan-ness and her uncouth interest in science. So she continued with her witchy, mathsy studies, her teaching, her philosophising, her flouncing about Alexandria being smarter than everyone, and, of course, Pilates twice a week. In the end, though, Christian zealots gonna Christian zealot, and Hypatia was brutally murdered by a Goddy gang under the reign of a new bishop, Cyril, who was an ignorant fuck.

Jesus would have absolutely been on board with murdering a mathematician, the bloodthirsty guy. 'Exactly what I meant!' he would have said to the gang of Christian zealots. 'Keep up the good work, see you boys in heaven!'

# 21

# Fatima al-Fihri

c. AD 800–880

*I*f you're a fan of knowledge, medicine, numbers, education, or human progress, you should give thanks to a woman. (Surprise! Bet you didn't see that coming.)

Fatima al-Fihri lived in the 9th century. Her family moved from present-day Tunisia to Fez, in Morocco, a city of growing population, wealth and importance in the medieval Muslim world. Her father was a wealthy merchant, and when he died he left Fatima and her sister Mariam a large fortune. It is a truth universally acknowledged that a woman in possession of a good fortune must be in want of a massive infrastructure project, and so the girls took it upon themselves to build up their city. Girls and their daddy's money, amirite?

Mariam commissioned the al-Andalus mosque, which still stands today in modern Fez. As one Tripadvisor reviewer DaveRuss said of this beautiful, ancient, still-operational mosque: 'Don't bother!' Fatima, meanwhile, took it upon herself to found what is considered the oldest continuously operating university in the world, al-Qarawiyine, in 859.

Now, there's really not much more known about Fatima or her family. The details have been lost in the sands of time, like the details of so many women's lives. But that doesn't mean she shouldn't get to take up space in a history book. Here, Fatima, have some space:

[THIS SPACE INTENTIONALLY LEFT BLANK IN HONOUR OF ANCIENT WOMEN WE DON'T KNOW MUCH ABOUT BUT WHO WERE DEFINITELY THERE AND DID COOL THINGS]

While we don't know enough about Fatima, we do know a lot about her university's legacy. Al-Qarawiyine put Fez on the cultural map; it served to unify the knowledge of the Islamic world, and facilitated the exchange of knowledge between Europe, Africa, and Asia. In the centuries after its founding, poets, mathematicians, jurists, and all manner of nerds came from around the world to think scholarly thoughts at al-Qarawiyine.

It was after studying at al-Qarawiyine that Pope Sylvester II brought Arabic numerals to Europe. What are Arabic numerals, you ask? They're these bad boys: 0 1 2 3 4 5 6 7 8 9, i.e., numbers. It's thanks to this transfer of knowledge that we're not all sitting round trying to work out what MCMLVII means. Other Europeans not busy murdering each other in fields, a favourite medieval European pastime, travelled to al-Qarawiyine and brought back knowledge of astronomy and logic and medicine and translated them into Latin and other European languages. While Europeans forgot about science and focused their energies on drinking mead and shitting where they ate, centuries of learning were preserved and developed and disseminated from within the walls of al-Qarawiyine.

And so pals, if you like stars and reason and living past the age of 30, this is why you should thank Fatima al-Fihri. Women invented knowledge. Women invented the entire world. If you disagree, please write down your complaint on a piece of paper, dip it in your tea and eat it.

# 22

# Wáng Zhēnyí
1768–1797

Wáng Zhēnyí was the kind of girl who could make anybody feel like trash. It wasn't her fault, she just lived a life devoted to learning and produced a nearly inconceivable amount of work from a very young age. It's not her fault we're all trash. Why can't we just sit down and learn things and work hard? Why must we faff about and stare at our phones as the hours pass away and we drift ever closer to our deaths?

But as I say, this is not Wang's fault. She was born in 1768 and became one of the most famous scientists of the Qing dynasty of China. Her grandfather was an avid book collector, said to have 75 bookcases' worth in his home, in what must have been a huge windfall for whatever the 18th-century Chinese version of IKEA was. When Wang's grandfather died, her family went to his funeral and stuck around at his place for five years, giving Wang enough time to read as much of his library as she could. She learned horse riding and archery, and confessed she liked to 'practise martial arts while galloping on horseback,' which to this day remains the best way to arrive at your office on a Monday morning.

It wasn't long before Wang had made a name for herself as a top-notch scientist. She focused on natural science and astronomy, coming up with important explanations of lunar and solar eclipses, as well as equinoxes and the number of stars in the sky. (It's loads.) She conducted experiments in her home proving that the Earth was round and recreated the movement of the planets and the sun, by using a lamp as the Sun, a table as the globe, and a mirror as the moon in order to observe their relative motion and relationship to each other. She advocated for the adoption of the Western calendar, which she liked for its centring of the Sun, or rather her lamp.

In her free time she also wrote dozens of books, including 13 volumes of poetry and a series of mathematical textbooks whose aim was to make the basics available to a wider audience. Sometimes the simplest concepts can be the hardest to explain well, as I discovered when a kid once asked me to explain what numbers were. I couldn't do it, so somewhere out there is a teenager who still doesn't know what numbers are. Sorry!

Wang was also fiercely opposed to traditional values that prevented women from receiving an education. She said that men and women 'are all people, who have the same reason for studying,' which of course we all know is putting off finding a real job, getting discounts on rail fares, and being able to sleep in most days. Why shouldn't women get to be students, too?

In one of her many poems of the classic 'ci' style, which adhere to strict patterns of meter and rhythm and numbers of characters, Wang asked the question:

> *It's made to believe*
> *Women are same as Men;*
> *Are you not convinced*
> *Daughters can also be heroic?*

Wang was only 29 when she died, having produced a mind-boggling amount of work. Most people haven't even gotten out of *bed* by age 29. Shout-out to you, Wang, and thanks for making us all feel terrible.

# 23

# Jang-geum

15th–16th centuries AD

Jang-geum was the first known woman doctor in Korean history, who lived in the early 16th century, a time when a woman studying medicine was totally unheard of, let alone a woman treating the king. I suppose if you're the only one who can cure a man, they bend the rules. 'Hmm, on the one hand I'm very ill and only you can save me. On the other, you seem to have a vagina. Whatever shall I do?' Such a dilemma honestly.

In her position as royal doctor, Jang-geum was apparently so important to the king that she rose to become the third-highest-ranking member of the Court. As with any cool woman in history, some cheeto dust-covered haters contend she didn't exist, but non-cheeto dust-covered scholars point to multiple references to a 'female doctor' in the *Annals of the Joseon Dynasty*, a great beach read written in the 16th century if anybody's looking for one. In one such shout-out, the king Jung-jong, who ruled from 1506 to 1544, says that, 'No one knows my illnesses as well as Jang-geum.'

Thankfully, though, it only took this one line of reference to the doctor to inspire a top-rated Korean TV drama in 2003. The show *Daejanggeum* or *Jewel in the Palace*, which funnily enough was my nickname growing up, depicts the rise of Jang-geum from a lowly commoner to the person with the most intimate knowledge of the king and all his gross bodily ailments. The TV drama has brought Jang-geum back to life and transformed her into a household name in Korea.

So girls, if you want to be remembered beyond your lifetime, learn the grossest secrets of someone in power, and make sure you get a mention in the *Annals of the Joseon Dynasty*.

# 24

# Artemisia Gentileschi

### 1593–c. 1653

An extremely glamorous woman once remarked to me that wasn't it a shame that whenever we talk about female artists, we only ever talk about Artemisia Gentileschi, and not all the other Baroque Italian female painters. Oh yes, I nodded in the manner of someone who could rattle off a Baroque Italian female painter for every letter of the alphabet. Yes, what a shame it is! Yet here we are, about to talk about her again. My apologies to all extremely glamorous women out there, but Artemisia is just so, so good. And I couldn't be bothered to look up the others. But it's nice to know there were loads of other Baroquettes, as they are known to no one.

When Artemisia does get talked about, though, she is often described first and foremost as a victim of rape whose art apparently reflects a kind of fiery vengeance she held against men. When she was 17, Artemisia was raped by one of her father's associates, who then tried to argue in a much-publicised trial that she had not been a virgin. He did this in order to damage her reputation, much in the same way that nothing can damage a person's reputation like being stolen from or murdered. (How can we be so sure a murder victim hasn't been murdered before?) Artemisia then went on to paint one of her most famous works, *Judith Slaying Holofernes*, which depicts a woman sawing off a man's head. We shouldn't assume this was a direct response to what had happened to her, however, because it would be ridiculous to assume that being raped is the only reason a woman would want to paint a man having his head thwacked off, or give special care to the blood splatters, as she did.

The painting depicts a story from the sort-of-biblical *Book of Judith* in which old Judy herself murders an Assyrian general, who was about to destroy her hometown, after getting him drunk, which truly raises the question, how can we be sure that Holofernes didn't *want* to be murdered? If he didn't want to be murdered maybe he shouldn't have drunk so much. Anyway if you compare Artemisia's painting to the same scene painted by Caravaggio, he shows a very reluctant Judith who's quite creeped out by the whole ordeal, which is exactly what a man would think – that Judith didn't *relish* the splatters of blood. In Artemisia's version, though, she's just loving every minute of it. She's getting the job done 'cause she's a cool, calm professional lady with a task to complete, and nothing's gonna get in her way, certainly not a river of hot, bubbling blood. In an age before action films could sate the bloodthirsty masses' need for a bit of gore, Artemisia was merely giving the people what they wanted. And she was incredibly good at it.

Artemisia was such a successful painter that she was able to live off the proceeds of her painting, every art student's thwarted dream. And unlike the male painters of the day, who apparently never got to see boobs IRL, Artemisia painted real boobs in all their glory, swinging in the wind, not looking like small, hard bowls placed upside down on a table.

Rather than thinking of Artemisia as a victim, we should think of her as a boss bitch who was one of the finest painters in Italy, man or woman. Even if she did want revenge, everyone knows that the best way to get it is to become rich and famous for your unrivalled talents, which she certainly did.

# 25

# Raden Ajeng Kartini

1879–1904

aden Ajeng Kartini was born on 21 April 1879 in Mayong, on the island of Java in Indonesia. Today, April 21st is celebrated in Indonesia as Kartini Day, which is your first hint that she's kind of a big deal to Indonesians. Her family was aristocratic – 'Raden Ajeng Kartini' is like 'Lady Kartini' – and her father worked with the Dutch colonial government. However, Kartini utterly rejected the concept and practices of the Javanese aristocracy.

'I think nothing is so ridiculous, nothing more silly than people who allow themselves to be honoured on the basis of their so-called "high birth",' she wrote to her pen pal, the Dutch feminist Stella Zeehandelaar. 'What value is attached to being a count or a baron? I cannot with my simple mind comprehend it.' (Girls: let's incorporate 'I cannot with my simple mind comprehend it' into our day-to-day sarcasm.)

From the age of 12, Kartini was kept inside her family compound for a full four years, as was demanded of a girl of her status upon reaching puberty. She was totally miserable, but spent the time reading and educating herself. From her childhood, Kartini was already shaking off expectations of high-born girls, especially as she saw that certain traditions of the Javanese aristocracy such as polygamy and arranged marriage could be harmful to women. She wrote to Stella: 'I was a "kuda kore", a wild horse, because I rarely walked but constantly jumped and skipped about. And why else did they scold me? Because I often laughed out loud and unashamedly (!!!) bared my teeth.' The exclamation marks are all hers: Kartini was simply not having it.

But Kartini didn't save all her scorn for her traditional upbringing. She also rejected Dutch colonialism and the racism upon which it was founded – though more so in her private letters than her public articles and statements: 'Why is it that so many Hollanders find it unpleasant to converse with us in their own language?' she asked Stella. 'Oh, now I know, Dutch is too beautiful to be uttered by a brown mouth.'

Kartini also believed that the way forward for Indonesians of all classes was progressive education. In 1903, Kartini wrote a memorandum to the Dutch colonial government titled 'Educate the Javanese!' advocating mass education and the education of women. She was a proper intellectual, and someone who didn't let the confining circumstances of class and gender prevent her from lobbying the powers that be.

Kartini did a lot in her life, as she acknowledged to Stella: 'Sometimes I wish I had two sets of hands to be able to do everything I wish to do.' One of the things Kartini advocated for was better medical care and midwifery – but she herself would die in childbirth in 1904, at the age of 25. Kartini's writings, however, live far beyond her short life. Her ideas formed parts of platforms of future

Indonesian nationalist movements, and her thinking on gender was far ahead of her time. She saw that the turn to nationalism would be accompanied by an uprising of women to demand their rights, much to the bother of men: 'When the battle of emancipation of our men is in full flight,' she wrote, 'then the women will rise up. Poor men, what a lot you will have to put up with.' Poor men indeed.

But Kartini's greatest passion was education, and her dream of dreams – a school for native Javanese girls that did not discriminate according to class – would not die with her. In the years after her death, such schools were founded and named for her: Kartini Schools. In 1901, Kartini wrote to Stella about her great desire that such schools would someday exist: 'What an ideal institution that boarding school for native young ladies would be: the arts, academic subjects, cooking, domestic economy, needlework, hygiene and vocational training will and must be there. Dream on, dream on, if it makes one happy, why not?'

26

# Emmy Noether
1882–1935

*I*f you can name a prominent woman in the history of mathematics, it's probably Ada Lovelace. So this chapter is not about Ada Lovelace. Shout-out to Ada, you mad queen of algorithms, may your memory live on, except for right now.

No, this chapter is for another woman mathematician, a certified genius whose work contributed to the understanding of the entire universe, who you may never have heard of, because History Is Bad. Her name was Emmy Noether.

Emmy Noether was born in 1882 in Bavaria to a mathematician father. She wasn't a spectacular student, but she once solved a complicated logic problem at a children's party. Because apparently setting complicated logic problems for children was the done thing at kids' parties in 1890s Bavaria.

Emmy qualified as an instructor in English and French, but decided she wanted to go to university to study maths instead. It's what her dad did, so why not her? And it all worked out perfectly well! She was accepted into the university as an equal to her male peers, and went on to enjoy a successful and richly rewarded career as an academic.

Ha ha, just kidding. It wasn't that easy, because, SURPRISE, men are bad, and she wasn't allowed to properly enrol in the University of Erlangen. This was on account of her having lady bits. According to the opinion of the day, only people with willies could do maths, because willy-having and mathematical ability were directly related. Strangely enough, some very lonely people still believe this today.

Told she couldn't enrol as a proper student, Emmy could only audit classes with special permission granted by each professor. So that sucked. Eventually Emmy took an examination to let her officially pursue a doctorate, and destroyed it with her big, mathsy brain. At this point the university was like, 'Fine'. She went on to get a PhD writing a dissertation which she later actually described as 'total crap'.

Crap or not, she stayed at Erlangen to teach for the next seven years, for which she was well respected and even better paid.

Ha ha, just kidding. Gotcha again! You forgot that the world is bad and always has been. The university let her teach, but only on the small condition that she wouldn't be paid. At all. For seven years. Yes, a century before *Lean In*, there was the much less inspiring *Teach for Seven Years Without a Salary for Love of Your Work and Out of Gratitude for Being Allowed To Work At All*.

The mathematician David Hilbert then invited her to come and work with him at the University of Gottingen, but, SURPRISE, the university wasn't having it, on account of her having a big ol' vagina. While the lovely nerds over in the mathematics department were happy for her to join them, knowing her to be just as mathsy as they were, the other departments were firmly opposed to the idea of a woman faculty member.

One professor, whose name literally doesn't matter, apparently asked Hilbert, 'What will our soldiers think, when they return to the university and find that they are required to learn at the feet of a woman?'

Oh yes, professor. What a very good point that is. What could be worse than returning from the hell of trench warfare to find that your maths professor has BREASTS? What could be worse than surviving the unimaginable horrors of the First World War only to have to lie down at the feet of a lady person to learn! (Also, didn't these people have desks?)

Hilbert replied to the professor that Gottingen was a university, not a bathhouse, so it really shouldn't make a difference if Emmy were a man or a woman.

Again, the university was like, 'Fine', and let her teach. Kind of. She had to teach her courses listed under Hilbert's name, to create the appearance of it being a man's lecture.

And she still would not be paid a salary. Is that not the most being-a-woman thing you've ever heard?

Emmy was at least privileged enough to carry on in this way, with slightly mysterious sources of funding, and so she did. She also kept up her jovial nature in the face of the ridiculous hoops she had to jump through in order to do the thing she was good at. It's a skill shared by so many of the women in these pages: the ability to leap through great flaming hoops of bullshit while keeping a smile on their faces.

At Gottingen, Emmy would take long walks with her students to talk about mathematics and develop an all-encompassing theory of the universe while also getting a bit of invigorating exercise. (I apologise to any reader who happens to be lazily lying in bed while reading that sentence.) Her students came to be known as 'Noether's Boys' – which would incidentally be a great name for a punk band.

In 1918, Emmy published Noether's theorem. What is Noether's theorem? I don't know, I'm not Emmy Noether, am I? Thankfully, though, I have made my pal Kelly, the queen of science, explain: 'It's the idea that if an object obeys a certain law of symmetry it will also follow a corresponding law of conservation. For example, if a process happens in the same way regardless of when you do it, so it has a sort of symmetry in time, you know energy will be conserved, meaning it can't be created or destroyed, within that process too.'

Emmy's work proved foundational to theoretical physics, supplemented Einstein's theory of relativity, and also, on the side, she invented something terrifying called 'abstract algebra'.

So after publishing one of the greatest mathematical theories of all time, and with the support of woke baes Hilbert and Albert Actual Einstein arguing on her behalf, the university was finally like, 'Fine', and in 1919 allowed Emmy to lecture under her own name at last. Finally, in 1922, the university granted her a small salary for the first time, as well as a title approximately equivalent to 'Associate Professor Without Tenure'. They may as well have given her the title, 'Eeeeew, A Girl Professor! Gross! Don't Let Her Touch You Or You'll Get Girl Germs!'

Luckily, Emmy Noether really loved maths, and focused on her work instead of the cascade of bullshittery being constantly flung at her by the world.

But imagine what she could have done if men were less terrible, you know? Imagine having to try and convince men that having lady bits instead of a willy has nothing to do with mathematical ability? Imagine watching your less-spectacular male colleagues surpass you in position and pay at the university, when all you really want to be doing is uncovering the mathematical mysteries of the universe in peace?

That's a lot of wasted energy.

Then again, Noether knew a lot about the fact that energy can be neither created nor destroyed. I'm sure there's a great metaphor in there somewhere – please consult your local theoretical physicist, or my pal Kelly, to explain it properly.

Emmy's story ends, as too many have, with the fucking Nazis. Actual old-timey Nazis, not Twitter Nazis, or virgin-basement Nazis, or jizz-stained sweatpant-wearing Nazis, or senior adviser to the President of the United States Nazis.

Nope, these were actual 1930s Nazis, who dismissed all women and Jews from academic jobs – so that was Emmy doubly out, as a Jewish woman. Used to working without pay, she carried on doing some teaching in secret. Once, a student turned up in a Nazi uniform. She carried on teaching, and apparently laughed about it later. Because, well, how ridiculous of him, to be a Nazi.

Emmy then moved to the US in 1933, taking up a position at Bryn Mawr where she resumed her mathematical walks with a group of 'Noether Girls' – which would incidentally *also* be a great name for a punk band.

She died only two years later in 1935 after complications from surgery for an ovarian cyst. So, Nazis and poor women's health care took her in the end. In a letter to *The New York Times* shortly after her death, Einstein called her a genius, and the best-yet example of what could become of the education of women.

How many more Emmy Noethers could there have been in the world? How many with the ability to shape the course of human knowledge, but who couldn't afford to work for free – or were stopped before they even began, by people who fervently believed that having a willy counted for anything? You'd need a great mathematician to work out the number.

# 27

# Nana Asma'u

## 1793–1864

Nana Asma'u was born in 1793, one of the many children of Usman dan Fodio, the founder of the Sokoto Caliphate in what is now northern Nigeria. He was a great proponent of the education of women in Islam, and Nana benefitted from the tutelage of her father, her siblings, and her stepmother. She spoke four languages perfectly and was one of those prodigy children everybody dreads hearing about in other people's Christmas round robins.

By age 14, Nana was a teacher herself, first lecturing the women and children in her own household, and then expanding her educational ambitions to the women of surrounding villages. Nana was such a keen bean, in fact, that she set up an entire network of women educators who fanned out into remote and rural corners of Sokoto to lecture and teach. Children, young women, and women in middle age benefitted from Nana's organisational zeal, and a system which enabled women to take lessons while still looking after their families and their homes.

As anyone who has one in their family will know, teachers always get a ton of presents, and women sent honey, grain, butter, cloth, and other such gifts to Nana, the head teacher of the whole region. Since she was, well, rich, and also a keen bean, as we have discussed, she donated these goods to the disabled, sick, and needy. Yes, she would be a terrible person to have known on Facebook in moments of low self-esteem.

Nana didn't spend all her energy on educational reform, however.

She also liked to kick back, relax, and write intensely complex poetry in one of the languages in which she was fluent. Nana adapted classical Arabic poetic forms to the languages of Sokoto like Hausa and Fula, and as she got older was so respected for her fine, ridiculous mind that she was called upon to advise emirs and caliphs.

Today, she is still remembered in Nigeria for being a keen bean, a woman who probably everybody should try to be more like, and an early example of someone who lobbied for the rights and education of women. Basically, she was a 10/10 good egg, and while she faced some conservative haters who disagreed with the idea that women should be educated at all, she was incredibly good at explaining to them, in four languages, why they were actually idiots. This is a skill we must all practise and develop.

# 28

# Jean Macnamara

1899–1968

*I*n order to be a good sexist, you need to be able to do some impressive mental gymnastics to find reasons why women cannot and should not do things. One great example of this in history was the excuse used for years as to why women couldn't be doctors in Melbourne at the start of the 20th century. Was it that they might swoon at the sight of blood? Was it that their periods would get all over the hospital floors and make everything horribly slippy? No, the reason given to Jean Macnamara in 1923 at Melbourne's Royal Children's Hospital as to why they couldn't possibly employ her, a woman, was this: 'Soz, babe, there aren't any girls' toilets.' Well, not in that language exactly. Or, maybe in that language exactly – after all, we are talking about idiots.

Anyway, they did end up letting her work there, and it's a good thing too, because she only went ahead and helped cure polio. She also must have figured out how to hold her wee for a full working day.

A polio epidemic in 1925 led to Jean's research which discovered that there was more than one strain of the polio virus. It was a vital step toward the eventual vaccination created by Jonas Salk in 1955, thanks to which you and I in 2017 don't even have to know what polio *is*. Some of Jean's other theories about the treatment of polio would later be questioned, but if you would like to criticise her for that, please revolutionise some aspect of medical science and then go right ahead.

Jean was born in 1899 in Beechworth, Victoria, and was witty and blunt, both in her manner and in being five feet tall. She worked non-stop and was so trusted as a doctor – especially by children – that families would wait as long as it took to be seen by her. Her specialism in orthopaedics led her to devise new ways to splint different parts of the body, and she advocated new methods for the care of disabled people, particularly children. She was invited to the White House to meet President Franklin D. Roosevelt, who had been paralysed by polio himself.

The other bit of Jean Macnamara's legacy is kind of grim if you're into rabbits. See, in the 1880s, some English hunter types introduced rabbits to Australia, which would have been fine if they'd shot them then and there. But nope, those rabbits got loose and did what rabbits do best – rabbit fuckin' – and by 1950 there were a full-on billion rabbits wreaking havoc on Australian agriculture, doing all kinds of bad rabbit shit like eating sheep food and pooping everywhere and rabbiting around getting up to all kinds of naughty, rabbity japes.

Jean encouraged the government to make use of the rabbit-murdering myxoma virus to reduce the population. When at first it didn't work, she pushed them not to give up on the experimental method. When myxomatosis at last began to be spread by mosquitos and to truly go viral, as the kids say, she was proven right. The rabbit population was fucked up, and the headline of the *Lyndhurst Shire Chronicle* in 1952 read:

## GRAZIERS THANK WOMAN SCIENTIST

The sheep farmers – who had been saved about £30 million thanks to the end of the rabbit menace – gave her an £800 wool coat and a nice clock as a thank you.

Next time you are menaced by a rabbit, or feel grateful to have not died in childhood of polio, don't forget to remember Jean, and, like the graziers,

## THANK WOMAN SCIENTIST

# 29

# Annie Jump Cannon

## 1863–1941

While researching the life and work of the astronomer Annie Jump Cannon, I quickly realised that I couldn't properly tell the story of the women astronomers at the Harvard Observatory at the turn of the 20th century without also talking about Cecilia Payne-Gaposchkin, who followed in Annie's footsteps and went above and beyond in her scientific achievements. So, lucky you, we will be hanging out with the ladies of Observatory Hill in Cambridge, Massachusetts, for two whole chapters.

If I know anything about space, and I don't, it's that there's quite a lot of it. If you asked me how many stars there were in the universe, I would say, 'loads'. If you asked me to categorise all the stars in the night sky, I would say, 'No thank you, I would rather spend the time in bed watching *The Bachelorette*.'

When Annie Jump Cannon came to work at the Harvard Observatory in 1894, however, *The Bachelorette* didn't exist yet, so instead she spent her time inventing a stellar classification system which was SO stellar that it's still used today – and used it to record and catalogue 400,000 stars. Which, if you're unfamiliar with the subject, is loads of stars.

Annie had been interested in the stars since her childhood in Delaware, where she and her mother would observe the night sky from their DIY observatory in the attic. Her supportive parents sent her to study physics at Wellesley, a women's liberal arts college, after which she spent a decade wandering about and dabbling in photography and music, as 20-somethings of any era are prone to doing.

When she joined Edward Pickering's team at Harvard[11], she was just one of many women he employed as computers in the Observatory. In those days, a computer was a person, rather than something you use to watch *The Bachelorette* in bed. Pickering employed women because you didn't have to pay them as much as men, a ridiculous idea that has thankfully died out with the passage of time and has never affected me personally, or any women I have ever known. Together, the women were known at the time quite creepily as 'Pickering's Harem'.

So what was Cannon's and the other women's task, for which they were paid little more than unskilled labourers, and a whole lot less than a male scientist? At the turn of the century, there were about 20 different systems proposed for the classification of stars, and no one could work out the best way to do it. Annie came up with a system of letters and numbers by looking at their spectra – basically, if you put a certain star's light through a prism, what

11. JUST A QUICK FOOTNOTE TO SAY THAT HARVARD DIDN'T GRANT DEGREES TO FEMALE STUDENTS UNTIL THE 1960s, AND DID NOT REACH A PARITY OF MALE AND FEMALE STUDENTS UNTIL TWO THOUSAND AND FUCKING SEVEN, JESUS CHRIST.

kind of rainbow would you see? The pictures of the spectra for each star were not however nice Instagram photos of rainbows, but rather, glass plates with smudges and dots and blurry bits.

Annie, who was deaf for her entire career and relied on lip-reading, would remove her hearing aids while she worked in order to have absolute focus. She could read out what kind of star each of the spectra indicated by merely glancing at the plates. 'She did not think about the spectra as she classified them,' one of her colleagues explained. 'She simply recognised them.' She did this for more than 200,000 stars visible from Earth down to the ninth magnitude, which are incredibly dim (no offence to ninth-magnitude stars). Later, she expanded the work to go all the way to the 11th magnitude, which are the most idiot stars of all. Our sun, the most popular star among Earthlings, is a G2. This means it's one of the second hottest types of yellow stars. (But don't worry, Sun, you have a way better personality than the first-hottest stars.)

Her work was published in nine volumes between 1918 and 1924. Was her system called the Cannon method? The Annie J method? The Annie Can(non) Jump method? Nope, it was called the Harvard System. Which is, as Alanis Morissette would say, a little bit ironic, given that Annie was not made (or paid as) a member of the Harvard Faculty until she was in her 70s in 1938, just three years before she died.

For years, Annie hadn't even been allowed to use a telescope alone, as it was seen as dangerous for a woman to do so. Which makes absolute sense. What if she saw something in the heavens that made her swoon or hurt herself or win a Nobel Prize? And, of course, a man and a woman using a telescope together, at night, when the stars were out, was an impossibly scandalous prospect. Women weren't allowed to use the best telescope in the world, at the Palomar Observatory in southern California, until the 1960s.

And no female astronomers – despite the fact that from the 19th century about a third of all those who worked in the field were women – would be elected to the National Academy of Sciences until 1978. (One Professor Johns Hopkins would vote against Annie's election to the academy because . . . she was deaf. I can't even understand the logic of this enough to make a joke about it. Just, what the fuck?)

As some fucking guy said to another female astronomer, Sarah Whiting, at the end of the 19th century: 'If all the ladies should know so much about spectroscopes and cathode rays, who will attend to the buttons and the breakfasts?' This guy, a senior European astronomer who considered himself very clever yet didn't know how to make his own toast, sadly died shortly after making this statement by tripping over a box of buttons and landing face-first in a frying pan.[12]

The thing about Annie Cannon's work, and the work of all the underpaid computers and astronomers in the Harvard Observatory and elsewhere, was that it was seen as a fundamentally female job. Even if women wanted to put forward their own theories, and do the fun, experimental bits of science, a huge amount of their time was taken up with rote labour and the collection and classification of data – which men would then use to publish papers under their own names, of course. Women like Annie were tasked with things like planning social events and fundraisers, and generally mothering everybody, much like things turn out in every office on the Planet Earth as we all hurtle together round and round our pleasant G2 sun.

A reporter for the *Camden Daily Courier* in 1931 wrote this when

12. I didn't bother looking up how he actually died, so who's to say it *wasn't* by tripping over a box of buttons?

Annie Cannon won an important award for her work: 'Housewives may be a little weak on astronomical physics. But they will understand just how Miss Cannon felt. Those heavens simply HAD to be tidied up.' Shortly after publishing his report, that journalist sadly died by tripping over a large pile of laundry his wife had left untidied.[13]

Annie never had a family of her own, and lived, worked, and breathed the observatory. She was beloved by female and male astronomers alike – the men saw her as unthreatening to their greater man's work. She was indeed a motherly figure, and received many awards in her lifetime for her classification work. She was the first woman to receive an honorary doctorate from Oxford University, which, if you haven't heard of it, is a university that people go to in order to learn how to become insufferable for the rest of their lives.

While Annie broke down barriers and supported other women in science for her entire life, in addition to her work toward women's suffrage in the US, she was still quite a traditional person who believed that yes, certain types of science were more suited to women than others.

But other women in the lab were more radical than her, fighting against their poor working conditions. Williamina Fleming, who had taught Annie Cannon, pushed back against the fact that she was paid a thousand dollars less than her male counterparts yearly – a lot of money in those days. And, hell, a lot of money now. Fleming wrote that Pickering 'seems to think that no work is too much or too hard for me no matter what the responsibility or how long the hours. But let me raise the question of salary and I am immediately told that I receive an excellent salary as women's

---

13. Presumably.

salaries stand.' Beware bosses who say you should simply be grateful to be there.

Another woman working in the observatory, Antonia Maury, wanted recognition for her work. She wanted credit, and she did eventually manage to scrape some for herself. And another, Henrietta Leavitt, worked herself to death for Pickering, who published the results of her work under his name in 1912. Leavitt's observation of something called the period-luminosity relationship meant that for the first time ever, scientists could work out the distance of stars, and indeed, the size of the entire universe.

But none would fight harder, or achieve more, than Cecilia Payne-Gaposchkin, the subject of the next chapter, who said that Pickering's employment of Leavitt to 'work, not think' would 'set back the study of variable stars for several decades'. Now let's hear more about Cecilia.

# 30

# Cecilia Payne–Gaposchkin

1900–1979

*Y*ou'll already be familiar with the conditions under which Cecilia Payne-Gaposchkin carried out her work as a female astronomer at the Harvard Observatory, because you've just read the last chapter. I know you have just read the last chapter, because you're not the kind of person who sits on the toilet and randomly turns to any page where your curiosity might lead you, like a monster.

Because you are not reading this carelessly on the toilet, but in a handsome leather armchair beside a roaring fire, you will remember quite clearly from the previous pages that Cecilia Payne-Gaposchkin was one of the many women who worked in the Harvard Observatory in the early 1900s.

Cecilia kicked off her academic career in brilliant style, proposing in her PhD thesis – which is still today considered one of the most brilliant astronomy PhD theses of all time – that the stars were not made up of the same elements as Earth or other planets, but rather were mostly hydrogen, with just a splash of helium. She showed this by building on the work of an Indian scientist named Meghnad Saha to prove that the different spectra classified in earlier years by Annie Jump Cannon & Co. were actually related to the relative temperatures of stars, that is, how smokin' hot they were.

Now, science isn't about being right all the time. Before you can advance the great spectrum of human knowledge, you're probably going to be wrong a lot of the time. And yet, friends, here we have a young Cecilia being exactly spot on right out of the gates. Her thesis wasn't just the best, but was actually the first astronomy PhD at Harvard by anyone – she hadn't been allowed to get a PhD in Physics, and so cobbled together a committee to create an astronomy PhD programme for herself instead. And, well, technically she received it from Radcliffe College, the bit of Harvard that could give PhDs to women, because Harvard itself certainly wouldn't. Harvard has since gotten over itself, in this regard at least.

Speaking of the committee, Cecilia received pushback from two supervisors, Arthur Eddington and Henry Norris Russell, who read her idea that stars were made of mostly hydrogen and just weren't having it. They encouraged her to play down this aspect of her thesis, and she did. Russell would, however, a few years later come to the same conclusion on his own, and decide she was right after all. He, being a man, got to share the credit for the discovery, but Cecilia did shoot to international fame. She was the youngest astronomer to ever be featured in a publication called *American Men of Science*, which was ironic, because she was actually originally English.

After getting her PhD, Cecilia started lecturing at Harvard – but her classes would not be listed in the course catalogue for a full 20 years. The president of the university, A.L. Lowell, a man with many buildings and streets and libraries named after him, told her he would never in his lifetime give a faculty position to a woman. Sadly, after making this statement, he died by being crushed by a course catalogue falling from a great height.[14] Cecilia wouldn't become a full professor until 1958, when she was in her 50s – the first woman to be tenured from within Harvard. In the meantime, she was paid terribly, and struggled to make ends meet for most of her career, having to pawn her jewellery to get by.

While Pickering headed up the observatory in Annie Jump Cannon's day, Cecilia worked under Harlow Shapley. This was a man who she once shocked by giving a talk at Brown University while pregnant, which is fair enough, because everyone knows that pregnant women are rendered incapable of speech.

Cecilia had actually been denied a full professorship years earlier, in 1944, due to her 'domestic situation'. It was one thing to be a matronly woman without children like Annie Jump Cannon – it was another to try and be a wife and a mother and to carry on in her work. She managed to raise three children while maintaining her career – which was not the done thing in the day. She'd bring her kids to the observatory, where they would run around pissing people off while she worked. In her limited free time, Cecilia's hobbies included chain-smoking and punning in different languages.

Struggling under financial hardship, and being burdened with much of the social and busy work of observatory life because she was a woman, Cecilia nevertheless carved out a reputation for herself as a scientist of the highest order, and became the chair of her department.

14. This is not a true statement, but rather a joke carried on from the previous chapter, which you would have recognised if you were reading things in order like an adult.

The next time you look at the night sky, make sure to remind whoever is attempting to share a romantic moment with you that so much of what we know about the stars is down to a room full of underpaid and underappreciated women scientists. If they are not put off by this fact, you may kiss them.

# 31

# Hedy Lamarr
1914–2000

Girls can either be pretty, or they can be smart. Any overlap between the two traits would be far too confusing for society to accept. If a woman is both, how are you supposed to know whether to get a boner or just to get angry? Being beautiful as well as intelligent has therefore been rightfully banned. Hedy Lamarr, though, was a brazen rule-breaker who was *both* a glamorous movie star *and* an inventor, the dangerous harlot!

Hedy was born Hedwig Eva Maria Kiesler in 1914 in Vienna, Austria-Hungary. In the 1930s she was a stage actress in Vienna who came to be known as 'the most beautiful girl in the world', a title now held by my friend Gena. She starred in her first film in 1931, *Ecstasy*, which was as scandalous as its sounds, featuring naked running, naked swimming, and simulated sex. It was banned in Germany, not because it was too scandalous, but because its cast and crew included many Jewish people, including Hedy, though she was brought up Catholic. Even the Pope condemned the film for depicting a simulated female orgasm, which as we all know is an invention of the Devil.

Hedy's first marriage was to an abusive bastard, a wealthy weapons-mogul who sold arms to all the biggest bastards of the day. He loved fascism, for Europe as well as in his home, and cut off Hedy's finances and controlled her every move. She later described herself at 19 as living 'in a prison of gold'. When Hedy's scandalous film was submitted to US censors for a possible release there, he bought and burned all copies of the film he could get his hands on.

Hedy knew she had to escape if she wanted to survive and continue her acting career. 'I was like a doll,' she said. 'I was like a thing, some object of art which had to be guarded – and imprisoned – having no mind, no life of its own.' She made her escape, she said later, by disguising herself as a maid and fleeing to Paris, where her husband tried and failed to pursue her. She then went to London and managed to arrange a meeting with the president of MGM, Louis B. Mayer. He thought her work far too risqué for an American audience, though, telling her she would 'never get away with that stuff in Hollywood' and that 'a woman's ass is for her husband'. (Actually, Louis, a woman's ass is for sitting, pooping, shaking to Shakira songs, and marching women to courtrooms to divorce their rich husbands and milk them for all they're worth.) He did offer an entry-level contract for MGM if she paid her own route to get to Hollywood, but Hedy wanted much, much more for herself. So she snuck onto his ship, pretending to be the governess of a boy on board, to continue their negotiations on the way to America. By the time they arrived in the United States, she had a contract to be one of MGM's new stars, and the stage name Hedy Lamarr.

Hedy's breakout role was in the film *Algiers* in 1938, in which she played a mysterious hot woman, who didn't speak much, as Hedy was still working on her English and playing down her Austrian accent. The film was a huge hit, and Hedy a new star, as women sought to imitate her black wavy hair parted down the middle and her sensible skirt suits.

But Hedy didn't put much stock in her celebrity as a beautiful woman. 'Any girl can be glamorous,' she said. 'All she has to do is to stand still and look stupid.' They don't give you that advice in women's mags, do they? Hedy was also not one to go out and party with the Hollywood elite. Instead, she preferred to stay home and sketch out inventions at a drafting table.

Her most important invention was something called frequency-hopping. She had recalled from her days married to her first bastard weapons-mogul husband that a problem of torpedoes was that their radio guidance could be jammed and hijacked by enemies. And so Hedy and her friend George Anthiel developed frequency-hopping, a technology vital to wireless communications, which prevented this problem. The pair were granted a patent in 1942, but it would be a few more decades before the US military would begin to make use of it.

Today, this frequency-hopping technology is the basis of Wi-Fi and mobile phones, things that nowadays people literally die if they are left without for more than a couple of hours. Who knows how many teenagers have been saved by Hedy's invention?

Because Hollywood values its boners more than its people, as Hedy began to age, the roles began to dry up. In WWII, Hedy wanted to move to DC and join the Inventor's Council to help the war effort with her inventing skills, but she was told she'd be of more use as a movie star touring the country selling war bonds. She raised $25 million this way, and also worked entertaining soldiers. During the war, at the Hollywood Canteen, a club which saw off soldiers about to go overseas, Fridays were Hedy's night. She would try to dance with every single one of the thousands of soldiers who gained free entry with their uniforms.

She spent her later years enjoying those classic old people pastimes of shoplifting, suing people, and moving to Florida. In her life, she married and divorced six men. She was never one to stick around if something wasn't working. Once, unbothered about attending her own divorce hearing, Hedy sent her old Hollywood stand-in in her place.

Before she died in 2000, Hedy finally gained recognition for the many technologies spawned from her frequency-hopping patent, as well as residuals. Girls: make sure you get paid what you're worth, no matter who you have to sue. It's what Hedy would have wanted.

# 32

# Louisa Atkinson

## 1834–1872

Caroline Louisa Atkinson, known as Louisa to her buddies, was born in 1834 in New South Wales, Australia, and from a young age became interested in botany and zoology. Australia is a very good place for a person to be interested in the natural world, as it is famous for its ten-foot-tall spiders, talking kangaroos, insatiably horny rabbits, and murderous, rabid koala bears known to drop from trees and kill unsuspecting passers-by. Or at least this is what I have been led to believe about Australia.

Louisa was a frail child, as 100% of 19th-century children were, but enjoyed learning all she could from her mother Charlotte, a former teacher who home-schooled her. When Louisa's father died, she and her mother moved to Kurrajong Heights, west of Sydney, to live with her mother's new boo. There, she loved to explore the forests around her new home. She began writing articles and sketching the plants (and talking kangaroos) she saw on her excursions. Louisa sent specimens to the various rock star botanists of the day, and in this way got to put her name on a few new species she'd identified, such as the *Erechtites atkinsoniae* and *Epacris calvertiana* (for her married name, Calvert), which everybody knows and loves today, and are probably plants of some kind, or possibly varieties of talking kangaroos.

Louisa gained fame for her natural history and botany publications and her plant discoveries, but she also wrote popular novels and fictional serials for Sydney newspapers in the 1860s and 70s, because it's always good to have a side-hustle. Like so many aspiring scientists and adventurers of the 19th century though, Louisa created a stir by trading her unwieldy skirts for trousers, much more practical for trudging through forests. She was judged for this, by people who we can confidently assume never did anything interesting in their entire lives. You can find their biographies in my next work, *People Who Never Did Anything Interesting In Their Entire Lives*, coming soon to a bookshop near you.

# 33

# Laura Redden Searing

1839–1923

Laura Redden Searing was a journalist who reported on the US Civil War – that's right, lady journalists go *way* back, and not just covering fashion and cooking, despite what modern male editors may believe women are most suited to. In addition to her journalism career, Laura was also a poet, was deaf, and had the strange and awkward honour of being friends with both Abraham Lincoln and his future assassin, John Wilkes Booth, and also Ulysses S. Grant, because apparently there were only about five people who lived in Washington DC in the 1860s. I guess if you were friends with two people and then one shot the other, you'd quietly unfriend the murderer on Facebook and not bring it up at the funeral.

Laura graduated from secondary school at the Missouri School for the Deaf in 1858, and performed her poem 'A Farewell' in sign language at the ceremony. This was a time when there were debates about the education of deaf people, with some believing that teaching sign language rather than speech would prevent the mastery of English language and even of abstract thought. Laura's ability to write in rhyme and also speak poetry in sign language proved these assumptions about deaf people wrong.

Soon after graduating, Laura took a job at the *St Louis Republican*, which is not a man who lives in Missouri and supports limited government, but rather, a newspaper. The *Republican* sent her to DC to write on the Civil War and the politics and personalities of the day. She wrote under the pen name Howard Glyndon, perhaps to conceal her gender, perhaps to separate her reporting from past pro-Union editorials she had written in the name of reporting neutrality, or perhaps because Howard Glyndon is such a beautiful name.

In fact, when a rival, Southern-supporting newspaper reporter decided to 'out' Howard Glyndon as not a strong, strapping man, but a young deaf woman, people didn't really care. It just made her and Howard more famous. In fact, she became so famous that her poetry and reporting were read all over the country, and some guy in Minnesota founded the town of Glyndon in Howard's honour in 1872. It would be at the point of towns being named after you that you might start to regret going by a pen name. She would publish her later books under the byline HOWARD GLYNDON with (Laura C. Redden), her maiden name, underneath it in smaller, parenthetical text. It is unknown whether residents of Glyndon, Minnesota today refer to their town as Glyndon Parentheses Laura C. Redden, Minnesota.

At the time, there were no colleges for deaf women, so after the war Laura went to Europe and taught herself German, French, Spanish, and Italian, as you do. She got a job as the Europe correspondent for *The New York Times*, and later went on to other publications such as *Harper's* magazine. She published books on politics as well as her poetry collections, and received fan letters from all over the country. She ended up, as everyone should, retired in California, her incredible career behind her, presumably trying to forget she ever hung out with John Wilkes Booth.

# 34

# Gabriela Brimmer

1947–2000

Gabriela Brimmer, or Gaby for short, was born in 1947 in Mexico City, only a few years before my mother, who will take issue with the fact that someone born in 1947 could be in a history book. Sorry, Mum, that's just how time works!

Gaby's parents had come to Mexico from Austria as Jewish refugees in the 1930s. Gaby was born with severe cerebral palsy, which prevented her from being able to speak. The only part of her body she could really use was her left foot. But with the help of her lifelong caretaker, Florencia Sanchez Morales, she learned to communicate by using her toe to point to letters on an alphabet board at her feet, and type on a typewriter. Gaby not only learned to write, but learned to write better than, well, most people.

Gaby started her education at an elementary school for children with disabilities, but her mother Sari fought to convince the local public school that Gaby's disability had nothing to do with her intellectual abilities. Sari shared her daughter's poetry with the school officials, and after she passed the entry examinations, the school eventually had to accept Gaby. Doctors had told Sari that Gaby would not live past the age of ten, but not only did she outdo her able-bodied classmates in high school, but went on to attend the elite National Autonomous University in Mexico City to study Social and Political Sciences. After that, she became a journalist and a bestselling author, and launched a disability rights movement in Mexico. Wherever people doubted her intelligence due to her cerebral palsy, she would shut them down with a quick quip. In her 1980 autobiography, co-written with celebrated French-Mexican writer Elena Poniatowska, we get a bit of Gaby's take on her university days:

> Okay. I enrolled in the U.N.A.M. Fuckers! The teachers just as much as us, the students. So many courses that could have been useful but that weren't in the least because in some of them the teachers were afraid to engage in interesting political discussions, and in the others all anybody talked about was theory. Why the hell do we – the students – have a mouth or any thoughts?

Gaby wrote poetry her whole life – on her typewriter nicknamed 'Che' for Che Guevara – sometimes inspired, as so many of us are, by her angst about boys. Here she is in a poem complaining (lovingly) that one of her *gentlemen friends* was far too much of a whiner:

> *Beloved, hate me, respect me,*
> *but be yourself through and through.*
> *Accept for once*
> *that life is harsh but beautiful*
> *and that the sun is shining*
> *for you.*

Her autobiography was so successful that it launched her to stardom in Mexico, and was the subject of the 1987 film *Gaby – A True Story*, which details her rise to becoming a published writer, and all the flirty glances that happened along the way. The film centres on the relationship between Gaby and her lifelong caretaker Florencia, an indigenous Mexican woman who accompanied Gaby throughout all her schooling, carrying her up and down stairs at the university and interpreting her speech in lectures. When Gaby eventually adopted a daughter, Florencia looked after her as well. Florencia enabled Gaby to fulfil her dream of having a child to break the quiet monotony of adult life. 'Silence is what adults do, and we adults are boring,' she wrote in her autobiography.

Gaby became a celebrity in Mexico thanks to her writing and the film about her life, and today schools and streets are named after her in Mexico City. She founded the organisation Adepam, an acronym for *Asociación para los Derechos de Personas con Alteraciones Motoras*, or Association for the Rights of People with Motor Disabilities, in order to work towards the rights of disabled people in three main areas, as detailed in her autobiography:

1. We shouldn't be isolated or marginalized from the 'normal' world.
2. Sources of work should be opened up for us so we can be financially independent, at least partly.
3. The issue of cerebral palsy should be publicized, so we can demand our rights from the authorities, like any other citizen can.

Gaby died in 2000 at the age of 52, having achieved so many of the dreams she wrote about as a girl, including her wish to have 'a book come out about this cruddy life I've managed to lead,' as she put it in her autobiography. 'Then people will see what a human being whose body practically doesn't function at all can do, some-body who is left only with a brain and her left foot to more or less live or survive in this crazy society that marginalises anyone who can't "produce" scalable items for someone else to consume for no reason at all.'

Here are the finishing lines of one more poem of Gaby's to end on:

> *What do you know of yourself?*
> *I only know one thing*
> *but I know it well.*
> *What?*
> *I am alive.*

# Women who wrote dangerous things*

# 35

# Murasaki Shikibu

c. AD 978–1014

Murasaki Shikibu was born in Kyoto, Japan, in 978. She wrote *The Tale of Genji* at the start of the 11th century, which at over 1,000 pages in its English translation is considered the oldest full-length novel in the world. So let's start out by thanking Murasaki for inventing the novel, without which, we would have nothing to do at the beach but try and get the sand out of our ears. *The Tale of Genji* was popular at the time, but became even more widely read with the advent of woodblock printing in the 17th and 18th centuries. The story is filled with romance and intrigue, which has caused Murasaki to be the subject of much moral agonising over the years. Some in the 17th century thought she must have been a chaste and devout woman and that the book was a *criticism* of romance and intrigue, while others thought she was a harlot and would go to hell for writing it. Some people just need to chill and enjoy a bit of romance and intrigue.

Murasaki Shikibu wrote *The Tale of Genji* while a lady-in-waiting at the Japanese court. The story goes that the Emperor's daughter was bored of everything she had to read, and gave Murasaki a royal order to write something magnificent, and so she retired to the Ishiyama temple and did. She understood Chinese as well as Japanese, which was unusual for a woman, and she incorporates this knowledge throughout the 54 chapters of the book which follow the main character, Genji – a courtier, a lover, and an absolute lad – through his many romantic conquests.

It's possible that Murasaki joined the court when her husband died after just two years of marriage, having been presented with the option to either remarry or to join the women-only literary salon of the empress. What would you choose?

Here's how Murasaki was described by some clearly unloved man writing about her in 1658:

At the time of Emperor Ichijo there was an attendant lady to Jotomon'in named Murasaki Shikibu, who was an intelligent woman. Her figure was extraordinarily beautiful, like a willow swaying in the wind . . . Her lips like a lotus flower, her breasts were [as if] bejewelled. Her figure was as beautiful as the plum and cherry blossoms spilling over in the sunset.

Why are men like this? Why could he not just stop after 'an intelligent woman'? Alas.

# 36

# Ulayya bint al-Mahdi

## c. AD 777–825

Even when not a lot is known about a woman in history, we should still honour her as best we can, especially if she wrote torrid love poetry. There are too many Arab women love poets to include them all, but I want to give a special shout-out to one anonymous poet who wrote this instruction to straight men everywhere for all time:

> You don't satisfy a girl with presents and flirting, unless knees bang against knees and his locks into hers with a flushing thrust.

Oh my!

Or how about Dahna bint Mas-hal, from the 7th century, who complained to the governor (as you do) that her poet husband had not touched her or consummated their marriage, then chided her husband for his few feeble attempts at affection:

> *Lay off, you can't turn me on with a cuddle, a kiss or scent.*
> *Only a thrust rocks out my strains until the ring on my toe falls*
>   *in my sleeve and my blues fly away.*

Ohhhh my!

Here's the 12th-century poet Safiyya al-Baghadiyya, writing about her own hot bod:

*I am the wonder of the world, the ravisher of hearts and minds.*
*Once you've seen my stunning looks, you're a fallen man.*

Yesss, Safiyya!

Or finally this woman, known only as Juhaifa Addibabiyya, who made this complaint about her garbage husband:

*What a man you gave me, Lord of all givers.*
*He's a nasty old lump of wrinkles with shrivelled finger bones*
*    and a bent back like a croaking crow.*

What a sick burn. And it rhymes in Arabic!

Anyway, this brings us to Ulayya bint al-Mahdi, about whom only a bit is known. She lived from 777 to 825, and was the daughter of al-Mahdi, the third Abbasid Caliph to rule the Islamic world from the empire's seat in Baghdad. She was a singer and composer, like her mother before her, as well as a poet, and was brought up by her brother the Caliph Harun Arrashid after her father died when she was young. Her brother fostered her love of music and singing and poetry, but was less keen on the way she would brazenly identify her lovers in her poems, and so he asked her to be a bit more tactful by swapping their names for women's.

In one such poem, she wrote:

*Lord, it's not a crime to long for Raib who strokes my heart*
*    with love and makes me cry.*
*Lord of the Unknown, I have hidden the name I desire in a*
*    poem like a treasure in a pocket.*

124

And in another one:

*I held back my love's name and kept on repeating it to myself.*
*Oh how I long for an empty space to call out the name I love.*

Eventually her brother got over it and let her just name her lovers to her heart's content. You apparently can't keep a lover's name from a poet forever. When her brother died, Ulayya was devastated and swore off wine and music in her grief, until, that is, her nephew Caliph Amin came to power and missed having her music at his parties, and so she returned to poetic courtly life.

OK, one more from Ulayya before we go. But don't forget that for every cool woman we *do* know about in history, even just a little bit, there were countless more women out there whom we'll never know, but who did cool things and wrote lusty poetry.

*Love thrives on playing hard to get, or else it wears off.*
*A bit of unmixed love is better than a cocktail.*

# 37

# Sor Juana Inés de la Cruz

c. 1651–1695

As every woman knows, one of the most offensive things a young lady can do is be cleverer than the men around her. This was the crime that the Mexican nun Sor Juana Inés committed in the 17th century in Mexico City. How dare she garner acclaim for her genius in Spain and the New World, and critique such little things as the church and the status of women? How could she be so selfish as to produce brilliant literary works when the men were just trying to get on with the Spanish Inquisition? It's no wonder members of the clergy had to give her the sad news that her literary work was *causing natural disasters*. Sorry, Sister Juana. That's just science.

When the Spanish first arrived in what is now Mexico in the early 1500s, they found a thriving and educated civilisation. Naturally, they looked upon it and thought, 'this won't do at all,' and set about destroying the native populations with that classic

European combination of slavery, disease, rape, and starvation. Sor Juana was born in Mexico in 1651. She was a Creole – a Spaniard born in the New World – and also a *mestiza*, a person of mixed Spanish and indigenous heritage. She was of a privileged class in the hierarchical culture of New Spain, but not wealthy. Her mother, who never married her father, had earned the respect of her community by succeeding in the business of managing *haciendas*, but by the time Sor Juana was of age, there was no respectable route for a single woman of her class other than marriage or joining a convent. After a period of time chilling in court as a lady-in-waiting, she chose the convent.

While becoming a nun may not seem like a glamorous choice, the convent in Sor Juana's time was basically a woman-run charitable institution and business with considerable autonomy from the church. Like a sorority with less matching minidress photo shoots and a lot more God. Juana ended up in the convent of San Jeronimo and Santa Paula, a posh convent where she had the time and space to study and build up the largest known library in all of Spanish America. Plus, as a bride of Christ, she didn't have to marry an IRL man, who as we all know, can be terrible.

But no amount of female autonomy in Sor Juana's day could fully escape the watchful eye of that great exercise in male foolishness, the Spanish Inquisition. To the church in the 17th century, if you didn't fit a very limited and very confined definition of womanhood, you were probably a witch. Seventy-five per cent of those investigated and/or killed by the Inquisition in Spanish America were women, because women are well known to be witchier than men. If you didn't listen to the men around you and follow the strict religious commands of the clergy, you were probably a witch. If you became a celebrated poet and writer and philosopher, you were *definitely* going to make men suspicious. Sor

Juana was all of these things, and so of course, was publically denounced by a handful of shitty clerics who thought that if she was not a witch she was at the very least a ~scandal~ of the church.

To be clear: she wasn't running around naked, having wild affairs, smoking cigarettes and getting wasted in the middle of Mexico City (as far as we know). In fact, she was very religious. Sor Juana believed that to be a good Christian and true to Jesus's word, you had to not be an asshole. And fine, she may have written a bit of erotic poetry, but really, who hasn't? No, what made her so ~scandalous~ was her audacity to write publicly about secular subjects like philosophy and science. And so the clerics naturally thought: *Oh no, she likes science, she must be a witch!*

It hadn't always been this way between the church and Juana. Juana was born in either 1648 or 1651, and for a time, she was a treasure of the church. She was a brilliant child who wanted to go to school so much that when she was only three she followed her sister to school one day, and lied to the teacher and said that her mother had let her. Knowing she was making this up, but thinking she was pretty cute, the teacher gave her lessons anyway, and little Juana had learned to read before her mother even worked out what was happening. She went on to write carols and other religious writings that won her a prize from the church. As a young adult, Juana couldn't go to university because of her gender, so she set about educating herself instead. When she decided to marry Christ instead of some trash man, it was seen as quite the 'get' for the church. But it wouldn't be long before she began to make the religious establishment uncomfortable with her scandalous opinion-having.

From the comfort of her Goddy sorority, Sor Juana continued to write poems and plays and satires and treatises and more. She took to criticising the behaviour of clerics, challenging the idea that clerics were equal to God in their status, and believed that all individuals could have a relationship with God. She reinterpreted doctrine that she found sexist so that it would suit better her understanding of the equality of women before God. She also argued that women were not, in fact, intellectually inferior to men – another thing some people still haven't grasped in our current chaotic times. She wrote canticles (hymns) dedicated to great women of history like St Catherine of Alexandria. Perhaps best of all, she wrote a famous poem entitled *Hombres Necios* – 'Foolish Men', which was about how foolish men are. In a response to her public denunciation, she even wrote that though Jesus was a man, it was also ignorant men who were responsible for his death, just as ignorant men now pursued her unjustly, which is a pretty sick burn, tbh. 'Oh, how many abuses could be avoided in this land if only the women were as well instructed,' she wrote.

In the end, Sor Juana defended herself cleverly against the threat of the Inquisition. Being a whole lot smarter than any clergyman in her orbit, she wrote convincing arguments that the reason she primarily wrote on secular subjects rather than religious ones was because, oh dear me, she just wasn't smart enough to comprehend such important, otherworldly topics. Yes, she could learn Latin in a matter of weeks, and could write a 975-line mythic poem of epic proportions that would be celebrated in Spain as a literary masterpiece. But she just wasn't good enough with her girly little head to write the sorts of Goddy things that the church preferred.

Despite her eloquent defence, the only way Sor Juana could ensure she escaped torture was to sign a declaration repenting for her previous scandalous ways, a declaration which she wrote in her own blood and was compelled to sign, '*Yo, la peor de todas*' which can be translated as 'I, the worst of them all,' or even 'I, the worst of all women.' (Same.) The church took away and sold her immense collection of 1,000–2,000 books, as well as her musical and scientific instruments, and when she died treating illness in her convent in her 40s, they burned her writings so that her ideas wouldn't cast a salacious stain on the history of the church and New Spain.

Luckily, and to the great disappointment of any fans of the Spanish Inquisition, her works were rediscovered and published in the 1950s and beyond. In modern Mexico, Sor Juana has been reclaimed as the mother of Mexican and Latina feminism – and was declared in 1974 at a celebration in Mexico City to be 'the first feminist in the New World'. As the Mexican poet Octavio Paz has put it very nicely: 'It is not enough to say that Sor Juana's work is a product of history; we must add that history is also a product of her work.'

# 38

# Tarabai Shinde

## 1850–1910

*I*f you are a lady, a gentlewoman, a chick, a broad, a girl, or a person who considers themselves a feminist, you may have at some point in your life felt an uncontainable fury, a righteous anger, a screeching, burning fire of rage and indignation at the actions of some man or another. Whenever this occurs, there's not much to do to cure the affliction of your soul other than scream into the abyss, metaphorically or not.

The way that Tarabai Shinde coped with her rage in 1882 was to write a furious, sarcastic, stinging, shouty feminist rant of a booklet. It was titled 'A Comparison Between Women And Men' and subtitled 'An essay to show who's really wicked and immoral, women or men?' Spoiler alert: it was men.

Tarabai came from an elite family in the little town of Buldhana in what is now Maharashtra, India. Her particular rage in 1882 was in reaction to the news that a woman had been sentenced to hanging for killing a baby she had had out of wedlock. The woman was a widow, and women of her class weren't supposed to ever remarry or have more children after the death of their husband. The woman's punishment, and the public discussion that followed concerning the general immorality and wickedness of women, pushed Tarabai over the edge.

She was sick of men. Men who sold out to the British colonisers, male religious leaders who made up oppressive rules for women, all of male society who prevented women from receiving education or being allowed free movement, and forced them into terrible marriages. She was sick of not having a voice, sick of the conventions that confined her to her home, sick of the way women were written about in novels and plays and newspapers, and sick of women being blamed for matters out of their control. And so she put it all to paper in her blistering 'A Comparison Between Women And Men' polemic, thought to be one of India's first feminist tracts – though who's to say 19th-century India wasn't full of feminist tracts that we just haven't discovered yet? Quick everybody check your old cupboards!

OK, let's enjoy some highlights from this work, shall we? It's just so delightfully shady:

> Every day now we have to look at some new and more horrible example of men who are really wicked and their shameless lying tricks. And not a single person says anything about it. Instead people go about pinning the blame on women all the time, as if everything bad was their fault! When I saw this, my whole mind just began churning and shaking out of feeling for the honour of womankind. So I lost all my fear. I just couldn't stop myself writing about it in this very biting language. In fact, if I could have found even stronger words to describe how you men all stick together and cover up for each other, I would have used them in my clumsy way. Because you men are all the same, all full of lies and dirty tricks.

Tarabai writes that she is 'just a poor woman without any real intelligence,' and, speaking directly at the men she seeks to drag, we see that solid sarcasm can still work 140 years later:

With powerful intellects like yours you'll find all types of criticisms to level at it, and all sorts of ways to sing the praises of your own kind instead . . .

In another passage that doubles as a description of an office I once worked in, Tarabai absolutely destroys the men who talk a big game but don't have much to show for it. She critiques her compatriots who fancy themselves to be modernising India and fighting against the British, but are in fact as useless, as, well, you'll see:

> . . . but who actually does anything? You hold these great meetings, you turn up at them in your fancy shawls and embroidered turbans, you go through a whole ton of *supari* nut, cartloads of betel leaves, you hand out all sorts of garlands, you use up a tankful of rosewater, then you come home. And that's it. That's all you do. These phoney reform societies of yours have been around for thirty, thirty-five years. What's the use of them? You're all there patting yourselves on the back, but if we look closely, they're about as much use as a spare tit on a goat.

And as we all know, there's not much use for a spare tit on a goat.

One boy who lived in Tarabai's town remembered her in her later years as a cantankerous old woman. You know, the kind of woman who reads too much and isn't soft and maternal the way women should be. 'She had a very fiery temper,' he said. (No shit.) 'Whenever she saw small children, she would chase after them, hitting at them with her stick.' Whether or not the children Tarabai chased with her stick were punk-ass kids, however, remains unclear.

Tarabai faced criticism for what she wrote, and never published anything again, as far as historians can tell. Perhaps she'd just said everything she'd wanted to say. Perhaps a thousand proto-Internet commenters swept upon her house, insisting with their superior intellects that, *well, actually,* there are, in fact, many uses for a spare tit on a goat. In any case, she ended her tract on a positive note, no child-chasing to be found: 'I pray the lives of women in this world may at last become sweet and that all women find a place of happiness in this world and the other.' She then thanks God and signs off, retiring from her brief but flawless writing career in order to spend more time with the neighbourhood's children.

# 39

# Phillis Wheatley

c. 1753–1784

*I*know it's kind of the point of the book, but why doesn't everyone know about Phillis Wheatley? Why had I never heard of her before writing this? Why do I know all the words to the songs of the *South Park* movie that came out in 1999, when that square millimetre of mental real estate could have been filled with the poems of Phillis Wheatley? Why could we have not spent one less week on *Lord of the Flies* in school, since everyone already knows that kids are shitty, and used that time to study Phillis instead?

To get a sense of Phillis Wheatley's importance, we can start with Thomas Jefferson, who was very concerned that people should know that Phillis Wheatley was *not* important. In fact, he wrote in his 1781 book *Notes on the State of Virginia* that Phillis Wheatley was SO unimportant that, 'Religion, indeed, has produced a Phillis Wheatley; but it could not produce a poet . . .

The compositions published under her name are below the dignity of criticism.'

Yes, he believed her work to be 'beneath the dignity of criticism', while ironically bothering to criticise her in his book. 'I don't even LIKE her,' Jefferson wrote, before bursting into tears. 'I don't think about her at ALL. I'm not obsessed with her, YOU are. God,' he continued, snot dribbling out of his nose and into his mouth. 'I'M the only genius, that's why they'll put me on the $2 bill someday, the best bill ever!!!! MOM I WANT A GRILLED CHEESE SANDWICH GIMME IT I'M A GENIUS!!'

The source of Jefferson's fears? Phillis Wheatley was an enslaved black woman who also happened to be a genius. Her very existence as such threatened his entire world view, and indeed the justification for slavery: the imagined inferiority of her race. So where did this supposedly dangerous young woman come from?

Phillis Wheatley was captured and enslaved in West Africa sometime between the ages of seven and ten, and arrived in Boston aboard a slave ship in July 1761. (Smug East Coast types: a quick reminder that the American south was not the only place that benefited from, or enacted, slavery.)

Phillis was bought by a wealthy merchant, John Wheatley, for his wife Susannah. The Wheatleys set about giving Phillis a classical education. She learned English, Latin, and Greek, and within a matter of months was reading and writing poetry, had memorised the Bible, and had begun writing letters to religious leaders.

Her first poem was published in 1767, when she was just a teenager. Her owners helped publicise her work by introducing her to intellectual society in Boston – but let's not give them a cookie, because whether or not you teach your slave Latin, you're still a fucking slave owner.

Soon enough, Phillis's writings and skills as a conversationalist had made her something of a local celebrity in Boston. She grew influential in an incredible time in Boston – this was, after all, the years shortly before the Revolutionary War, and other than dealing with Jefferson's whinings, Phillis corresponded with the sorts of founding fathers American high school students are taught to revere as gods.

Despite her acceptance in white Boston intellectual society, the Wheatleys could not find Phillis a publisher for her first book of poetry, because, surprise, racism. Instead, Phillis was sent to London to meet a publisher there. In London, she met Benjamin Franklin, among others.

Phillis arrived in London just a year after the Somerset decision had outlawed slavery in England and Wales, though not throughout the empire, because, well, the empire's wealth and existence depended on slavery. But here was Phillis, arriving and turning from a local celebrity to an international one, while still enslaved. Phillis wrote that the graciousness with which she was received in London 'fills me with astonishment'.

Now, remember how we didn't give the Wheatleys a cookie? Good. The family's son, Nathaniel, forbade Phillis from meeting again with Benjamin Franklin, because she was still enslaved by his family and he was worried that Ben might give her ideas about freedom.

Finally, in the same year of her book's publication, 1773, Phillis was freed: 'My Master, has at the desire of my friends in England given me my freedom,' she wrote. Her American owners had been suitably shamed by members of English society into freeing their slave.

Phillis pointed out the hypocrisy of American revolutionaries for desiring freedom while carrying on enjoying the institution of slavery. She once wrote of this hypocrisy to a reverend about 'The strange Absurdity of their Conduct whose Words and Actions are so diametrically opposite. How well the Cry for Liberty, and the reverse Disposition for the Exercise of oppressive Power over others agree, – I humbly think it does not require the Penetrations of a Philosopher to determine.' Which is basically a fancy 18th-century way of saying 'You're a bunch of fucking hypocrites'.

Phillis's life and achievements were profoundly influential upon the society in which she mingled. In her short life, (she only lived to be 31), she became the first black person in the Americas to be published, she met with Washington, for whom she had written a poem of praise, and was praised in turn by Voltaire, who compared her writing to that of Catherine the Great, the empress of Russia.

In one poem, 'An Hymn To The Morning', Phillis wrote:

> *Aurora hail, and all the thousand dies,*
> *Which deck thy progress through the vaulted skies:*
> *The morn awakes, and wide extends her rays,*
> *On ev'ry leaf the gentle zephyr plays;*
> *Harmonious lays the feather'd race resume,*
> *Dart the bright eye, and shake the painted plume.*
> *Ye shady groves, your verdant gloom display*
> *To shield your poet from the burning day*

It's a lot more beautiful than most people's thoughts on the morning, which generally range from 'Shut up' to 'Five more minutes' to 'But I don't *want* to go to school.'

Writing influential tracts on the subject of liberty and freedom and religion in the first years of the American republic, and consorting with leading thinkers of the day, Phillis Wheatley could well be regarded as one of America's very founders – had history not Thomas Jeffersoned her.

But Phillis Wheatley *could not* matter to the founding fathers. She *could not* be a genius, despite her extraordinary gifts for learning and for writing. She couldn't be any of these things without unravelling the ideologies that the new United States depended on: a moral justification for slavery rooted in the inferiority of black peoples, and a concept of American liberty and justice for all that did not include that large proportion of the population which was enslaved.

Just by existing, Phillis was dangerous to the entire American project.

We should all know more about Phillis Wheatley. She should be on the $50 bill. Across the land, every payday, people feeling lush will say to one another: 'I've got a wallet full of Wheatleys.' Besides having a nice ring to it, just think how much it would piss off Thomas Jefferson.

# 40

# Nellie Bly
## 1864–1922

Nellie Bly is exactly the kind of name you'd want for a scrappy, go-get-'em, brassy lady journalist who tucks a pencil behind her ear and says 'I swear, mister, I'll get the scoop!' In fact, it was the name of a popular 19th-century song, and also was the pen name of Elizabeth Jane Cochran, born in 1864 in Pennsylvania. We'll call her Nellie here, though, because it's cooler.

When Nellie's father died, he left no will to look after his second wife and their family, and so his money went only to his first family and left Nellie and her mother impoverished. Nellie knew she had to find a way to support her mother. She went to school to train to be a teacher, as did pretty much every ambitious 19th-century woman in this book – teaching was seen as about the only job open to women at the time – but didn't have the money to continue beyond the first term. Desperate for a proper job, Nellie would finally find her calling when reading a column in the *Pittsburgh Dispatch* titled 'What Girls are Good for' which declared working women to be 'a monstrosity', written by a popular columnist who was probably sad and alone and had shit mutton chops. Nellie did what one does faced with a sexist prig, and wrote a letter to the paper saying that he was a sexist prig, and that women had to work to survive. The paper loved the drama of it all, and gave her a job.

Nellie threw herself head first into her dream job. She wrote about the conditions of women working in factories in Pittsburgh, and the awfulness of divorce laws for women in the State of Pennsylvania. She was just proving herself to be a natural investigative journalist when her editors, alarmed that this lady writer they had so carelessly brought into their midst should be *doing actual journalism*, relegated her to the women's section of the paper. Thankfully, this is something that has never happened again in the history of journalism, no sirree, nothing to see here.

They were right to do it, really. Girls don't like hard news! They like fashion and cupcakes and pretty little kittens. While these things are all actually great, to be fair, Nellie was not interested in writing about them, however, and convinced her bosses to let her report as a foreign correspondent from Mexico. She went, she wrote about the daily lives of Mexicans, she critiqued the Mexican government, she was thrown out of Mexico, she returned to Pittsburgh, and her editors were like, 'Aw, how cute of you. Back to the fashion pages!'

Feeling absolutely stuck, Nellie simply quit and left a note which read: 'I'm off for New York. Look out for me. Bly.' People just don't quit like they used to.

After six months of funemployment, which was actually less funemployment and more traipsing around New York begging for work from newspapers, Nellie scored a job at the *New York World*, edited by Joseph Pulitzer.[15]

Nellie wanted to be a real journalist. She wanted to throw herself headlong into stories with the explicit purpose of improving working people's lives. Pulitzer set her a challenge to prove she was tough enough: to get herself admitted to a notorious mental institution, the Blackwell's Island Insane Asylum, which is nearly

---

15. What an amazing coincidence that his name was Pulitzer and he was a journalist!

impossible to say, it turns out. But how would she get herself committed? She couldn't just walk up to the gates and say, 'Hello, I'm terribly mad, do please admit me to your fine institution!'

Well actually, it was the 1880s, and a woman expressing her own opinion could be enough to have her packed away for 'treatment'. A woman with ideas was dangerous, and must be interred for her own safety and the safety of the wider public, of course. 'I was left to begin my career as Nellie Brown, the insane girl,' she later wrote. 'As I walked down the avenue I tried to assume the look which maidens wear in pictures entitled "Dreaming". "Faraway" expressions have a crazy air.' In fact, Nellie only had to fake madness, pretending not to know who she was, for as long as it took to get to the asylum, after which she was just herself, which I suppose was alarming enough to 19th-century sensibilities.

For ten days, Nellie experienced the horrors of the asylum, its rotten food, its cruel employees, and the mistreatment of patients. She had buckets of icy water poured over her head for a 'bath', she saw rats everywhere and patients being beaten by the staff or tied up in ropes, and discovered that many women detained in the asylum seemed perfectly sane and had been sent there for dubious reasons by their husbands. She was eventually released at the request of her paper, and the report she published created a huge public outcry. She went on to write a book about the experience titled *Ten Days in a Madhouse*, in which she expressed her pleasure that as a result of her work 'the City of New York has appropriated $1,000,000 more per annum than ever before for the care of the insane.' Nowadays, that's around $25 million.

In a much more fun piece of reporting, Nellie set out in 1889 to try and beat the record of the Jules Verne character Phileas Fogg in *Around the World in 80 Days*. She made it in 72 days, and returned to cheering crowds in New York. (By the way, if anyone wants to pay me to try and beat this record, I would be super happy to give it a go.)

Nellie was crafting a whole new approach to journalism. As a woman in a male industry, she could go undercover in places her male peers never could. Clearly jealous, some of her male colleagues who undoubtedly also had shit mutton chops dismissed her work as 'stunt reporting'. Sure, bros. You're clever and important, so you must know what you're talking about.

However you feel about 'stunt journalism', and however shit your facial hair is, it's undeniable that Nellie's style of reporting drew in a huge audience, exposed dark and terrible injustices, and produced tangible change. If that's not real journalism, what is?

# 41

# Elizabeth Hart

1772–1833

*E*lizabeth Hart, also known as Elizabeth Hart Thwaites after she bagged her man, was one of two prominent sisters who lived in the late 18th and early 19th centuries on the Caribbean island of Antigua.

The sisters were free, mixed-race women of some property and social standing, living at a time shortly before the end of slavery in the British Caribbean. Both married white Methodist men, and so had matching husbands. They both worked in education and social work, founding a Female Refuge Society for enslaved and free needy women and running schools from the 1810s to the 1830s. And, of course, they both loved Methodism. They simply could not get enough of the Methodist church. But really, who can?

What we know of the Hart sisters, we mostly know from letters they wrote to a Methodist preacher about how much they loved Methodism (a classic Hart sisters pastime). In their letters they wrote about the evils of slavery, and denounced the practice of concubinage and the sufferings of enslaved women.

The reason this chapter is about Elizabeth and not her older sister Anne, however, is because Anne sounds like a bit of a narc, whereas Elizabeth was a bit more sinful, and so a bit more fun.

Elizabeth's sins, as detailed in an 11-page letter she wrote to a preacher, include:

1. Wavering in her faith as a youth.
2. Being 'lulled into Carnal security'. (Who hasn't been?)
3. Enjoying 'company, conversation and Books which did not tend to the Glory of God'.
4. Enjoying 'Music's charms'.
5. Dancing.
6. General youthful folly.

Dancing seemed to be a true weak spot for Elizabeth, who wrote of her guilty feelings when listening to one British preacher who had come to the Caribbean to talk about Jesus. She said she felt 'really ashamed of [her] conduct by the sermon which the Doctor Preached . . . in which he mentioned the evil consequences of Dancing in particular.' Uh oh.

Elizabeth also seemed to have a bit of an emo streak, writing a poem about her tormented spiritual journey after the death of another missionary, a Mr McDonald, who she may have fancied and we can only presume was a dreamboat.

*My solemn engagements are vain*
*My promises empty as air*
*My vows I shall break them again*
*And plunge in eternal despair.*

Meanwhile, big sister Anne wrote nothing of her carnal pursuits. If she had any, they have been lost in the sands of time. Or perhaps she was just nice and boring.

Beyond Elizabeth's forbidden love of dancing, good conversation and ungodly Books and company, she and her sister also wrote arguments against the racial stereotypes of their time. Elizabeth argued in her letter that enslaved people were in no way inferior or degenerate, but were simply suffering under the yoke of slavery. As well as their letters, the sisters wrote histories and biographies and manifestos and polemics against slavery. They were some of the first African female writers in the Caribbean.

Both sisters worked as the first educators of free and enslaved black people in Antigua, and focused all their energies on bettering their conditions on the island. They were both in a somewhat precarious social position, attempting to gain acceptance into Methodist society at a time when Christian interracial marriage was still taboo. They argued in favour of allowing free women of colour such as themselves to gain leadership positions in the Methodist church, pointing out how well placed they would have been to preach across racial lines on the island.

Elizabeth died in 1833, and her boring sister Anne died in 1834. We can only assume they are both now chilling in Methodist heaven, where perhaps Anne has been convinced to try a bit of dancing herself, and maybe Elizabeth has caught up with the missionary she secretly fancied, Mr McDonald.

# 42

# Jovita Idár

1885–1946

When United States Army Texas Rangers came to the newspaper where Jovita Idár worked in 1913, they ran into a bit of unexpected trouble.

After an editorial in the paper *El Progreso* criticised President Woodrow Wilson's intervention in the Mexican Revolution, the Rangers wanted to shut down the paper and destroy its office and printing press. Unfortunately for them, Jovita stood in their way, well aware that what they wanted to do was illegal. (Note to any interested parties/presidents: destroying newspapers that have said mean things about you is illegal, and has been for quite some time.) So she stood in the doorway, refused to stand aside, and sent them packing.

Early the next morning, they snuck back when she wasn't there, broke down the door and broke the press with a sledgehammer, also breaking the windows and scattering the type across the floor. But as it turns out, destroying a printing press and scattering a newspaper's type all over the floor like an angry toddler will never stop a woman like Jovita from saying what she wants to say – the Idár family simply picked up and kept on publishing more and more newspapers.

Jovita was born in 1885 in Laredo, Texas. The Idár family was made up of teachers, activists and muckraking investigative journalists. If you don't know the term, muckraking is exactly what it sounds like: digging up dirt on powerful people and institutions.

For a Mexican-American family in Texas, it was a dangerous job to expose the racism and economic injustices directed at their family and community.

The family paper was *La Crónica*, and its goal was the 'industrial, moral, and intellectual development of the Mexican inhabitants of Texas'. It was run by Jovita's father, who was the kind of guy you'd describe as a 'pillar of the community'. Every community, if it's lucky, has a pillar. Jovita and her father and brothers reported on the very worst issues facing Mexicans in Texas, from segregation to lynching, and Jovita took over running the paper after her father's death.

When not busy with her investigations or frightening off burly officers by standing in doorways, Jovita also advocated for better education for her community. In a state where powerful forces in agriculture wanted Mexican-American kids to be working in their fields instead of learning to read, the schools for Mexican children were worse off, and the teachers paid much less. Luckily in today's America, inequality in the education system has long since been eradicated,[16] and public school teachers are paid handsomely.[17]

Jovita believed that the answer to a better education system for Mexican children in Texas was not complete assimilation into white schools, but high-quality instruction in bilingual or Spanish-speaking schools, so that the kids could learn and preserve their culture, their language, and their history.

The other big Idár family activity was organising the First Mexicanist Congress, held in 1911 in Laredo, a gathering of activists from across Texas to discuss civil and human rights. From this congress came the League of Mexican Women, of which Jovita

---

16. It hasn't.
17. They're not.

would become president and lead charitable projects toward the development of education and the alleviation of poverty.

'Woman must always seek to acquire useful and beneficial knowledge, for in modern times, she has broad horizons,' Jovita wrote. She believed that women must be educated and become influential in all industries – and not spend their days 'living deceitfully on gossip and lurid tales', as fun as that might be.

Jovita participated in the Mexican Revolution of 1910, working as a nurse for La Cruz Blanca – a Red Cross-type organisation. She also served as a volunteer nurse with the American Red Cross in WWI.

So Jovita, as well as being brilliant and brave, was a teacher, a journalist, a nurse, a community leader, and just about every other thing you can be if you care to be of service to your community. Before she died in 1946, she founded a free kindergarten, and continued to found and edit more publications. In fact, in a classic bridezilla move, she postponed her own wedding to focus on getting a new paper, *Evolución*, off the ground.

As for the Texas Rangers, they never destroyed another of her printing presses. It would have been nearly as pointless as trying to get past her in a doorway.

Ladies: if a man tries to enter your house and you suspect he has designs on your printing press, whatever you do, don't let him in.

# 43

# Louise Mack

1870–1935

Like many of the women in this book, the Australian journalist and novelist Louise Mack is one whose writing remains so witty and charming today that reading her words may fill you with an urge to reach across space and time to be best friends. As it was, she was best friends with Ethel Turner, another famous Australian writer of novels and children's books. The two women would compete, support, and spur each other on to greater and greater things over the course of their lives and over the course of their deeply intense, intimate friendship. Get yourself a best friend who can do the same.

Louise was born in 1870 in Hobart, Tasmania to a large family as boisterous as it was poor. Despite being incredibly bright, Louise spent so much time during high school editing a student paper, having fun with her friends, and writing lovesick poetry that she didn't get into university as she had hoped.

Instead, she became a governess, which she absolutely hated. 'Teaching is so horrible,' she wrote. 'It takes the curl out of your hair and the backbone from your body and gives you dirty nails and a contemptible attitude and a bad temper.' When not teaching and thereby losing the curl of her hair, Louise spent all her spare time writing or else eavesdropping on strangers' conversations in order to come up with new characters for her stories.

In 1896, she published her first novel, *The World is Round*. It was a satirical look at Sydney society – which made things a bit awkward for Louise among her fancier friends. She decided to travel to London to try and make it as a writer.

On the long journey by ship between Australia and London, Louise wrote hilarious letters to her family, beginning with her disappointment at the boringness of her fellow passengers when she had expected great intrigue and conversation, and the way in which everyone on the ship drove each other mad as the weeks wore on.

'It is the third week of the journey that the unloveliness of the human race becomes most apparent,' she wrote. 'Every time the women pass each other they smile. They never pass without it. Soon it becomes worn to shreds, a mere painful pressing back of the lips. You learn to dread it as you see it coming towards you.' People who work in offices will recognise this phenomenon.

When the ship stopped in Naples, Louise went ashore and managed to miss the ship as it departed. She had to chase it by making a mad dash to Marseille, where the ship was due to dock. Louise revelled in the adventure of being alone and broke in a foreign country: 'Alone among all these Italians. The intoxication of moments like this is what your true traveller must ever seek. Without them one might as well stay at home. But with them the world is a glorious place.'

Upon arriving in London, Louise was instantly in love with the city. She signed off her letter to her family recounting her travels with total incredulity at her circumstances, hardly able to believe she could be so lucky as to be in London:

> Here I am in London!
> Is it really I?
> Walking down High Holborn

Unconcernedly?
Circumscribing Fleet Street,
Wandering through the Strand,
HERE I AM IN LONDON!
– So I understand.

More later. With love,
From Lou in London

Louise wanted to be a good writer. An important writer. The kind of writer that future hipsters would refer to at Dalston house parties while rolling themselves cigarettes of 'natural' tobacco. But she also had to pay the bills.

So while waiting to hear whether her second novel would be published, Louise, alone but not lonely in London, sucked it up and requested an interview with the fiction editor of the prominent publisher, the Harmsworth Press. After weeks spent holed up writing her novel, totally pale and barely able to afford food, Louise looked, in her words, 'an absolute FRIGHT.' Too weakened to walk the long way, and too broke to afford the taxi she took to the interview, she instructed the doorman to charge the taxi driver's fare to the fiction editor himself, then ran off into the building before either could question her. Luckily enough, she was offered the opportunity to earn some money by writing serialised stories with a mass appeal.

Though she knew she was writing absolute smut, Louise turned out to be a genius at writing the equivalent of today's trashiest soap operas. Able to feed and dress herself, and looking and feeling altogether less of a FRIGHT from the benefit of some money, Louise also received the good news that her novel *An Australian Girl in London*, that is, her proper writing, would be published.

The reviews were excellent. 'If all Australian girls are like Louise Mack,' one reviewer wrote, 'the more of them who come to London the better it will be for London and the world.' She had made it as a proper writer – though the public still scrambled for her serials, which she continued to write by pacing around her apartment, dictating thousands of words of ridiculous plot a day to a typist.

After a six-year stint in Italy working for an English language paper, and reliving what it felt like to be *alone among Italians*, Louise returned to London in 1910 to continue her reign as the Queen of Romance. Her preposterous stories were published in the *Daily Mail* and the *Daily Mirror*, and translated into French, Italian, and German.

When war broke out in 1914, the time came for Louise to prove herself as an entirely different kind of writer: a war correspondent. She went to her fiction editor, Harmsworth, and asked to be sent to the front. He agreed, thinking a woman might provide a good 'human interest' take on the war – a line still familiar to many women journalists today.

As it turned out, her incredible bravery and risk-taking would deliver a lot more than a 'human interest' angle, as she reported from places that her fellow male correspondents had fled in (justifiable) fear. Louise managed to travel inside German lines risking certain death should her identity be discovered.

Louise was one of only two correspondents to get to and witness the bombing of Aarshot in Belgium by German forces. 'It seems to me that the End of the World will be very like this,' she wrote of the experience.

Then in Antwerp, Louise took notes with a pencil and notebook while bombs rained on the city. 'When it comes to fear and curiosity, in ninety-nine cases out of a hundred curiosity wins,' she wrote, describing what it was like to feel the urge to report under such circumstances. 'You are not callous because you are curious . . . you are curious because you are alive . . . because you have a right to see and hear all the strange and wonderful things, all the terrors as well as the glories that make up human existence. Not to care, not to want to see, to know, that is the callousness beyond redemption.'

As German forces approached Antwerp, Louise met three English correspondents who implored her to leave with them. She decided not to, instead disguising herself as a Belgian servant in the very hotel that the Germans would soon occupy. And so she worked behind the bar in the dining room where she could overhear the victorious Germans in conversation and so complete her story. When one officer became curious about the silent barmaid – who could not speak without revealing her true identity – the Belgians of the hotel, who were protecting her, locked her in her bedroom for the entire next day so that she would not be exposed.

Finally, she disguised herself as the Belgian wife of one of her allies in the hotel, and strode through the corridor with him and his children all the way outside and into a waiting car to take them to safety.

Her book on the whole ordeal, *A Woman's Experience in the Great War*, was published in 1915, and remains a gripping and terrifying account of the horrors of that war. Nothing could be further from the ridiculous romantic serials she'd used to pay the bills in London. Luckily for Louise Mack, though, she could write just about anything.

# 44

# Beatrice Potter Webb

1858–1943

This chapter is not about Beatrix Potter, beloved author of *Peter Rabbit*, but Beatrice Potter Webb, the seminal sociologist. Sorry, I know! But we're here to learn some cold, hard facts, and not facts about lovely woodland creatures, but about the empirical study of poverty.

Beatrice was born in 1858 in Gloucestershire, the eighth of nine sisters born to a wealthy railway magnate, which was the profession of all wealthy Victorian fathers. Were you even a wealthy Victorian father if you weren't a railway magnate? No. Beatrice also had a brother, who died young, devastating their mother who only ever wanted a boy. Beatrice was the emo one of the family, who enjoyed hiding from her relatives and reading books in a pile of hay with only a cat for company, as we all do. She didn't like *Jane Eyre*, though, and complained, 'The author's conception of love is a feverish almost lustful passion,' which is actually the best thing about that book and says a lot about Beatrice's personality.

The future husbands of Beatrice's bevvy of sisters would refer to them as a 'monstrous regiment of women', the 19th-century version of a girl gang. In a time when it was thought that women couldn't possibly be clever, because their uteruses would get in the way of their brains, Beatrice and her sisters received fine educations. She was not without her self-doubts, though, as she tried to teach herself advanced maths and science and wondered, 'Why should I, wretched little frog, try and puff myself into a professional?' Beatrice also despaired at the absurdity of the marriage market each social season, when her sisters would be married off one by one.

As for Beatrice's love life, she made The Choice: the choice between a rugged hunk of man and a clever but kind of gross-looking little fellow. The rugged hunk of man was Joseph Chamberlain, future famous politician, and future father of future famous prime minister Neville Chamberlain. He was 20 years older than Beatrice and threw her into a world of turmoil. She said he set off within her a 'deadly fight between the intellectual and the sensual', lol. Ever the emo, she called meeting him 'the catastrophe of my life'. If Beatrice Potter Webb had lived in 2005 she would have dyed her hair black, straightened her fringe over her face, and ringed her eyes in a centimetre of eyeliner.

On the other side of the ring was Sidney Webb. You get a clue from his surname who won this contest of the heart, but thanks to Beatrice's fanatical diary-keeping we get to enjoy a few vintage sick burns about Sidney's physical appearance, aged a century to perfection. She recorded the fact that 'his tiny tadpole body, unhealthy skin, cockney pronunciation, poverty, are all against him.' Yes, she was a snob, but in the end realised that hunky Joseph was far too controlling of his female relatives for her taste and decided upon Sidney. After all, she reasoned, 'it's only the head that I am marrying.' Ouch. But, I suppose, it's a sensible choice to make given that when we're all withered and old, nobody's a rugged hunk of man any more, but you can still have nice conversations.[18]

They had to wait for her father's death to marry, because marrying into the lower middle classes would have been too much for a railway magnate to bear. In one of their many torrid love letters, Beatrice wrote to Sidney that 'the permanence and worth of a relationship depends on the consciousness in both partners that moral and intellectual growth rises out of it.' Phew! Is it getting hot in here?

OK, I need to talk about Beatrice's brain so that I don't get in trouble with her ghost for getting carried away with the telling of her underwhelming love life. The summary is, boy, was it a big one! Phew, check out the big ol' brain on her, I tell ya. And on him! A big fat brain on a tiny tadpole body. This was an intellectual power couple for the ages. They were a true partnership, despite their differences in personality (Sidney was chill and used to say to her, 'Keep your hair on, missus!' whenever she got *intense* – but in a cute way). They were a two-person think tank and their dinner table hosted the intellectuals and power players and policymakers of the day. They didn't have children but they did give birth to 18 jointly authored full-length books, and many more not-full-length books. 'Are the books we have written together worth (to the community) the babies we might have had?' Beatrice asked in her diary.

Beatrice and Sidney did many impressive things together. They spent their honeymoon researching trade unions in Ireland for a huge history they wrote together, one of their dozens of book-babies. They wanted to found a new, modern university in an urban

18. Mum and boyfriend, please don't read anything into this.

centre that wouldn't be a waste of space like Oxbridge, and so founded the London School of Economics, a place where rich people still go today to spend a lot of money on a masters because they don't know what to do with their lives. They galvanised the Fabian Society, one of the incubators of British socialism, and made the Labour Party suck less. 'The Labour Party exists and we have to work with it,' Beatrice once complained in one of her trademark draggings, calling it 'a poor thing but our own.' They also founded *The New Statesman*, for better or for worse, and worked to better the education of Londoners of all ages. Clement Attlee remembered them with the praise: 'Millions are living fuller and freer lives today because of the work of Sidney and Beatrice Webb.'

Beatrice got her start when she first came to London, as all well-meaning rich girls do, working in philanthropy in the East End. Through this work she came to believe that it would not be charity, but rigorous social science and socialist policies, that could improve the conditions of London's poor. Beatrice was interested in co-operatives, which were not pleasant mid-range supermarkets, but a sort of trade union for consumers rather than for producers.

As part of a royal commission to look into the alleviation of poverty, Beatrice wrote the dissenting opinion on what should be done, envisaging a national minimum income that was essentially the first draft of the future British welfare state. She said such a state would 'secure a national minimum of civilised life . . . open to all alike, of both sexes and all classes, by which we meant sufficient nourishment and training when young, a living wage when able-bodied, treatment when sick, and modest but secure livelihood when disabled or aged.' As you can see, Beatrice was a mad socialist.

Beatrice wasn't a proponent of women's suffrage at first, caring more strongly about what she thought of as economic democracy. She praised the role of women in the new Soviet Russia, where as she and her boo described it in one of their many book-babies, 'emancipation was never thought of as merely the removal of legal disabilities,' as in, women winning individual rights, but rather thought that 'the economic and even the household subjection of women had to be abolished.' (For more on what this looked like, see the paragraph in Alexandra Kollontai's chapter in which the family unit is abolished.) When the Webbs did eventually take up the issue of women's political representation in Britain, they saw it as a battle against 'an essentially masculine capitalism' as the movement expanded beyond its rich girl early proponents.

The Webbs felt caught between two systems: they disliked both unchecked American-style capitalism, which Beatrice wrote in 1913 in *The New Statesman* would lead to 'constantly increasing armaments and to periodical wars of a destructiveness that the world has never witnessed,' which is definitely bad; but also the dictatorial nature of Bolshevism in Russia. They were, however, fundamentally collectivists interested in radical reform, and in the mid-1920s visited the Soviet Union and wrote about 1,000 pages of propaganda about how great it was entitled *Soviet Communism: A New Civilisation?* Their support of Stalin (at least until he made a pact with the Nazis) was held in disregard by some factions of the British left who weren't so hot on Stalin's purges and gulags. The Webbs died before the post-war British welfare state came into being, but if it weren't for them, it may not have happened at all – the Webbs helped shape the people, the ideas, and the party that created it.

Anyway, if you'd still like to hear about Beatrix Potter and woodland creatures, you can find her delightful works in all good children's bookshops.

I'll stop now before I summon an intellectual haunting by both Webbs, angry that I may have misinterpreted the many fruits of their giant brains.

# 45

# Julia de Burgos

1914–1953

You'll notice there are a lot of poets in this book. The thing about poetry is that you can't be stopped from writing it. You can be poor, you can be marginalised, you can be trapped in your home, you can be barred from education or work because you are a woman, but nobody can stop you thinking up poetry. Unless perhaps they run up to you when you are in the middle of a poetic thought and shout 'BAH!'

Anyone can be a poet, but not everyone can be a good poet. As for Julia de Burgos, she is now regarded as one of the greatest female poets in Latin American history, and the most important poet of 20th-century Puerto Rico. And yet she was only 39 when she died, anonymously, in New York City, and was buried in a potter's field – a cemetery for unidentified people, usually poor.

Julia was born in 1914 in the town of Carolina, Puerto Rico, and was the eldest of 13 children. Her family suffered greatly from poverty and malnutrition, and six of Julia's siblings died. She became a teacher in 1935, and wanted a doctorate, but was too poor to afford it. Instead, she went to Old San Juan in 1936, and began publishing poems in papers and magazines. Her poems dealt with the subjects of Puerto Rican independence, US imperialism, and the unequal status of women, and she also wrote poems and essays for rallies of the Puerto Rican Nationalist Party.

Puerto Rico suffered terribly in the 1930s from the Great Depression, which started in the US with the 1929 stock market crash and spread across the entire world making everything Greatly Depressing. The island was consumed with protests and strikes, including strikes by women. In 1936, Julia published the poem 'Es Nuestra la Hora' ('Ours is the Hour'), which called for Puerto Rican workers to unite in the fight against US imperialism.

Julia left the island in 1940, and moved to New York City where she lived and worked in Harlem with African American artists and activists. Julia herself was African-descended. She wrote for the Puerto Rican nationalist paper *Pueblos Hispanos* in New York City, but eventually moved to Washington DC and worked as a secretary in the civil service. One day, FBI agents came and questioned her about her writings for *Pueblos Hispanos*. She denied leftist political leanings, and told them, '*Pueblos Hispanos* has become too Communist. I just want to see Puerto Rico be independent and free.' She was fired that same day, because while she had said she was anti-communist, they decided she was still too much of a lefty for 1950s tastes, when if you weren't the type with a white picket fence, who enjoyed shooting guns into apple pies, you were a socialist suspect.

Julia moved back to New York, suffered from depression and alcoholism, and spent her last years in a hospital. She once filled an intake form in hospital and wrote her occupation as 'writer', only for a hospital employee to cross it out and write 'suffers from amnesia' instead. Nobody could erase her writings, though. Julia's works laid the foundations for future Puerto Rican and Latino poets and feminists. One of her last poems, 'Farewell in Welfare Island', foreshadowed her death far from Puerto Rico. It ended:

*It has to be from here,*
*forgotten but unshaken,*
*among comrades of silence*
*deep into Welfare Island*
*my farewell to the world.*

# 46

# Marie Chauvet

1916–1973

I t's time to add another Very Bad Man to our growing mental list of Very Bad Men of History. Yes, it sucks to even have to think about Very Bad Men in as lovely a book as this, but in many cases to fully understand a Truly Badass Babe, you have to know how Very Bad the Very Bad Men in her life were.

And so our Very Bad Man in this chapter is Haiti's François Duvalier. Haiti is famous for being the first independent black republic. Enslaved Haitians seized control from France in 1804 – EIGHTEEN-OH-FOUR – more than half a century before the American Civil War. Duvalier came along a century after the Haitian revolution and independence. His nickname, 'Papa Doc', makes him sound more like the beloved proprietor of a small-town pizza restaurant than a brutal dictator. But a brutal dictator he was, remembered for the reign of terror with which he ruled Haiti from 1957 to 1971.

This absolute shitstain of a man wreaked violence upon his own citizens with total abandon. He instituted a volunteer militia force of loyal goons, the *Tonton Macoute*, who would receive an automatic pardon for any crimes they committed in its service. Duvalier's ideology, if a monster can be said to have an ideology beyond 'being a monster', played upon popular resentment of the country's mixed-race, lighter-skinned elite, who he declared enemies of the state, thereby attempting to justify his authoritarianism. But anyone could be the victim of his forces' arbitrary violence. Religious figures, sports clubs, writers, artists, and educators lived under constant threat of censorship, harassment, or murder.

So now you know what the novelist Marie Chauvet was up against.

Born in 1916, Marie Chauvet was a member of the mixed-race elite of Haiti. She would host gatherings of important poets at her home in Port-au-Prince, and wrote novels addressing race, class, and gender. Her works would criticise both the corruption of the elite society to which she was party, and the brutality of the government opposed to it – so basically, she pissed everyone off.

Marie wrote her most important work in 1968: *Amour, Colère et Folie*, which translates to *Love, Anger, Madness*. It was a devastating critique of the violence and totalitarianism of the Duvalier regime, and so, of course, put her in a huge amount of danger.

Remember the last time you decided not to rock the boat? 'Hmm, better not call out my Great-Uncle Martin for that sexist thing he just said. I wouldn't want to offend anyone. Best to just leave it.' Now imagine making the opposite decision, and not just calling out Great-Uncle Marty, but your entire set of friends and family, and also a dictator who would not hesitate to kill you. That's what Marie Chauvet was willing to do for her beliefs.

'Feel free to shriek at the top of your lungs if you ever see this manuscript,' she wrote of *Love, Anger, Madness*. 'Call me indecent, immoral. Sprinkle me with stinging epithets if it makes you happy, but you will not intimidate me anymore.'

She sent her work to that most chic of old-timey feminists, Simone de Beauvoir, who endorsed it and thus led to the manuscript's acceptance by a prestigious publishing house in Paris. This is where things should have gone very right. Everything was on track for Marie Chauvet to become a worldwide celebrity, if it hadn't been for a Very Bad Man of history.

Marie's family was terrified of the consequences of her novel's publication under a regime which would have your entire family killed for less than a full-throated denunciation of its rule. And so Marie's husband, Pierre, convinced her to buy up the entirety of the Paris publishing house's stock of *Love, Anger, Madness* upon its publication, and to forbid it from ever being printed again. She agreed. Her family – who had already seen loved ones tortured, imprisoned, murdered and disappeared by Duvalier – then destroyed all copies of the book, other than a few hidden copies left in Paris and elsewhere.

After all this, Marie decided to divorce her husband, and moved to New York City to marry again and write more novels. *Love, Anger, Madness* would not be reprinted until 2005, many years after her death in 1973.

Duvalier died in 1971, after his 24-year reign of torture and oppression. He was succeeded by his equally awful son, who ruled until a popular uprising caused him to flee the country in 1986.

Listen. This book is full of thwarted plans and missed opportunities for deserving women. Whenever you encounter such a frustration in a woman's story, take a moment to shake your fist at the sky in rage and disappointment. Shriek into a pillow like a wild banshee. Yell at a passer-by that 'IT DIDN'T HAVE TO TURN

OUT THIS WAY.' Then please pull yourself together and carry on, because if Marie Chauvet didn't give up after the destruction of her greatest work, but kept on writing, you certainly don't have an excuse to give up on anything.

# 47

# Zabel Yesayan

## 1878–1943

Zabel Yesayan is another example of a brilliant woman who lived in a time and place where to be intelligent and opinionated was the most dangerous thing to be. In fact, she managed to live in not one but two such places in the course of her life.

Zabel was an Armenian born in 1878 in Istanbul, then the capital of the Ottoman Empire. She published her first poem in a weekly paper at age 16, and by 17, had decided to become a writer professionally. So she did. That was that. There was no decade of umming and erring, no grand proclamations about the novel she had 'knocking about in her head' – she just did it.

As Zabel set out on her path she received a warning from Sprouhi Dussap, the first female Armenian novelist. 'When Madame Dussap learned that I wanted to enter the field of literature,' Zabel recalled later, 'she warned me that a woman's path to become a writer had more thorns than laurels. She said that our society was still intolerant towards a woman who appeared in public and tried to find a place of her own. To overcome this, one had to surpass mediocrity. Success came easily to the man who merely got his education, but the stakes were much higher for the intellectual woman.'

Zabel went to France to study literature, and married a painter at age 19, as one does when one moves to France. She returned to Istanbul, however, without her husband and against his wishes in order to continue to build her reputation as a writer there. What she found when she returned was one of the first great tragedies Zabel would witness in her life: Armenian refugees fleeing massacres in Adana, in what is now southern Turkey, and arriving in Istanbul. Zabel decided to travel to Adana to see for herself what had happened there, turning her findings into a book called *Among the Ruins*. The utter destruction she witnessed in that city changed her, and it would not be the last time she documented Ottoman crimes against the Armenians.

As a prominent Armenian intellectual, particularly one who had publically decried crimes against her people, Zabel knew she was in danger. In 1915, the first year of the Armenian genocide that would claim 1.5 million lives at the hands of the ruling Turkish party, the Committee of Union and Progress, she had a close call with Turkish officials. While exiting a building, an official asked her if she was Zabel Yesayan. 'No,' she replied coolly, 'she is inside.' She quickly made her escape and moved to safety in Bulgaria.

In Bulgaria and then back in France, Zabel found work with an Armenian newspaper and set about the grim task of documenting what was happening back at home, collecting testimonies of death marches, deportations and destruction from those Armenian refugees who had managed to escape. Zabel wrote under a male pseudonym, worried about the safety of her remaining family in Istanbul. She said in letters that the work nearly drove her to madness, yet without it, that history, however horrible, could have been lost. As it is, the Turkish government has to this day denied that the Armenian genocide took place, making such testimony all the more powerful.

In 1932, Zabel was invited to become a lecturer at Yerevan State University in Armenia, which had by then become part of the USSR. She had high hopes for life in Armenia but once again, the relentless awfulness of history caught up with her. In 1934, Moscow hosted the first Soviet Writers Congress, which gathered writers from across the USSR, for the unofficial purpose of allowing Stalin to work out who needed to have an eye kept on them. Zabel attended, and despite her initial enthusiasm for the Soviet project, ended up on Stalin's shit list. A few years later, when Stalin began to actively persecute Armenian literary figures, arresting writers as well as their families, Zabel was in danger again.

Zabel was arrested and thrown in prison where she was not allowed to read books or newspapers or listen to the radio, and so instead she hosted prison literary salons in which she discussed French literature from memory, as you do. It is not known exactly when or where she died during her imprisonment, but she left behind her ten books, countless letters and articles, and of course the testimony she gathered of the genocide.

For Zabel, writing was a deeply political act, and her novels dealt with women's place in society among other injustices. 'Literature is not an adornment or a pretty decoration,' she explained, 'but a mighty weapon or a means to struggle against all matters I consider unjust.'

# 48

# Mirabal Sisters

Patria Mercedes Mirabal Reyes 1924–1960

Bélgica Adela Mirabal Reyes 1925–2014

María Argentina Minerva Mirabal Reyes 1926–1960

Antonia María Teresa Mirabal Reyes 1935–1960

There were four Mirabal sisters, so this section really has four women, meaning this book actually has more than 100 women in it, which just goes to show that women can't do maths. Minerva, Patria, and María Teresa Mirabal gave their lives in the fight against the Dominican dictator Rafael Trujillo, who ruled officially and unofficially between 1930 and 1961. The fourth sister, Dedé, decided not to take part in their radical activities. If you would like to criticise her for this, please ensure you are living under a brutal dictatorship first.

Trujillo, who had a stupid Hitler moustache and a fat, round head, had been an army cadet before becoming the commander-in-chief of the Dominican army, and eventually president. The US had occupied the DR between 1916 and 1924 in the name of 'stability', like how it recently occupied Iraq and Afghanistan and now they're really stable. When Trujillo became president in 1930, the US liked him because he wasn't a communist, and they thought he was, as the saying goes, strong and stable. What did stability under Trujillo look like? Kidnappings, disappearances, murders, rape. You know, all that stable stuff which is so preferable to . . . what was it again? Oh yes, communism.

Trujillo's reign was terrible for women. He would send 'Beauty Scouts' around the country to find women and invite them to his parties or, failing that, to kidnap them. Listen, if you have to send your underlings to find women, you're doing it wrong, and also you're a sexual predator.

One day, the second-youngest and fiercest Mirabal sister, Minerva, was scouted and made to attend a party with Trujillo and her sisters. Trujillo propositioned her, and she refused his attentions. Trujillo, belonging to the school of thought that when you're a star they let you do it, carried on creeping on her. So what did she do? Well, the legend goes that she slapped him in the face. And this wasn't just any face: this was a face like a piece of old ham cut from a pig who hated his life. It was the face of a dictator who had killed people for less.

Minerva and her sisters left that night, but Trujillo would imprison and torture their father in retaliation, and then spend the next decade trying to get revenge for the harm done to his ego. He had made an enemy of the Mirabal sisters for life.

Minerva and her sisters enjoyed a comfortable middle-class upbringing, and were even allowed to attend university at a time when that wasn't the done thing, because as we all know, when women go to university they get ideas about assassinating dictators and socialist revolution. Which are very un-stable things, which Minerva in particular would take a keen interest in.

When Minerva returned for her second year of law school following the slappy party incident, she found she had been banned from classes unless she gave a speech about how great Trujillo was, which is the kind of petty thing only a man who looks like a crumpled, crusty sock would desire. She was eventually allowed to complete her courses – but was not allowed to practise law. Another time, when Minerva and her mother were staying at a hotel, they were locked in their room and told they would not be allowed out until Minerva agreed to sleep with Trujillo. Have you ever heard something more pathetic? But I guess that's what you would expect from a man with a personality like an angry, horny weasel. Minerva and her mother escaped.

Minerva had had enough, and so naturally began a movement to topple the dictator. María Teresa and her husband joined her quickly, and Patria joined after witnessing the June 14th massacre, when Dominican expatriates attempted to return to the island and take power but were all killed. Patria, who had been unsure about her little sisters' activities, then knew she had to do whatever it took to free her country. 'We cannot allow our children to grow up in this corrupt and tyrannical regime,' she famously said. 'We have to fight against it, and I am willing to give up everything, including my life, if necessary.'

The women called their movement the Movement of the 14th of June in commemoration of the massacre, and the sisters' code name was *Las Mariposas* – the butterflies. Together, they sat around the table at Patria's house and planned sabotage actions and a plot to assassinate Trujillo with bombs at a cattle fair he was set to attend.

Somewhere along the line, somebody was a snake and betrayed the plot to the authorities. The sisters were arrested and imprisoned. It wasn't a good look for Trujillo to be holding the sisters, who were just simple innocent wives and mothers after all, so in time he released them, but continued to hold their husbands. He moved them to a remote prison, to lure the women into a trap. At the end of 1960, on their way to visit their husbands, the women were stopped in their car and beaten to death, their bodies dumped in their car and pushed off a cliff to make it appear to be an accident.

People weren't stupid, though. Of all the crimes Trujillo had committed over the decades, this was the one that roused the public consciousness against him and sealed his fate. Not even the US liked Trujillo any more, as stable as he may have been, which, to be perfectly clear, wasn't stable at all. The death of *Las Mariposas* mobilised the rage of Dominican women, and in May 1961, Trujillo was assassinated in his car by a group of seven Dominican men. They did it with weapons supplied to them with CIA approval, as the US had finally changed its mind about supporting Trujillo's murderous regime.

Dedé, the surviving sister, took in the children of her lost sisters, and spent the rest of her life until her death in 2014 spreading their story. Some of the sisters' children are now in government in the DR. In 1999, the UN commemorated the sisters by naming November 25th the International Day for the Elimination of Violence Against Women.

On this day each year, remember the butterflies.

# 49

# Mary Wollstonecraft
### 1759–1797

There are two things to discuss when it comes to Mary Wollstonecraft: her brilliant philosophical mind, and the fact she shagged her way across Europe. We're going to start with her politics and philosophy, and then move on to the sex stuff, as God intended.

Mary Wollstonecraft was born in Spitalfields, London, in 1759. She was from a middle-class family, but her awful abusive father drank away what money the family had, leaving Mary, her mother, and her six siblings in a precarious position. Mary was the second oldest, and her brother, Edward, was her mother's favourite and was educated far beyond Mary's few years of schooling. Mary was rightfully annoyed at her brother's spoilt position, and the fact that she was considered troublesome for displaying the same qualities: 'Such indeed is the force of prejudice that what was called spirit and wit in him,' she wrote later, 'was cruelly repressed as forward-ness in me.' Parents, do not cruelly repress the spirit and wit of your daughters! Just don't.

Mary and her sisters had to go to work to support themselves and their family, but the only occupations open to women at the time all sucked ass. You could be a teacher, you could be a governess and raise some rich person's garbage children, or you could do needlework, and that was close to being it. Mary sucked at being a governess, as well as a teacher, and when she and her sister opened a girls' school in Newington Green, London, it struggled and failed. Although nowadays the site of the school is a Pokéstop, so that's good news at least.[19][20]

Anyway, there was another way women could make money in the 18th century: writing. Mary got a job writing for the boringly-named periodical the *Analytical Review* about everything from travel to satire to politics. She published her first work in 1787, *Thoughts on the Education of Daughters*, and was so pleased with herself that she wrote in a letter to her sister: 'I hope you have not forgot that I am an Author.' (I'm pretty sure these boasting rights are the only reason to write a book.) By the 1790s, she was the most famous female political writer in Europe, having shot to fame for her biting reply to the conservative writer Edmund Burke's *Reflections on the Revolution in France*. She critiqued his apologia for the French aristocracy who had had their asses handed to them in her *Vindication of the Rights of Men*. She was a fierce defender of the French Revolution, at least in its early years before things got more

---

19. Greetings, future Earthlings. If this sentence left you wondering what a Pokéstop is, please understand that for a very short time in the summer of 2016, there was a game called Pokémon Go that many people cared about very much. In this game, a Pokéstop was a location where you could gather items for your quest to capture creatures called Pokémon, in an augmented reality superimposed on the world. After a few months, however, human beings tired of this game, as they tire of all things, and abandoned their Pokémon in the empty void of cyberspace where all faddish apps go to die. In the now cold and desolate wasteland of the Pokémon universe, millions of lost creatures languish and expire, deserted by their once devoted masters. Disused Pokéstops now mark this dead universe like so many tombstones, and Mary Wollstonecraft's former school is one of them. She was pretty goth though so I feel like she'd be into it.
20. OK technically she wasn't goth in the sense of gothic literature, which can be seen as a reaction to exactly the kind of ~reason~ that old Mary was famous for. But she was definitely emo.

behead-y. She captured the mood of the time with optimistic spirit: 'Reason has, at last, shown her captivating face . . . and it will be impossible for the dark hand of despotism again to obscure its radiance.' Suddenly, Mary was more than the founder of a Pokéstop: she was one of the most important philosophers in a time absolutely crammed with important philosophers.

Gather round now, and say it with me: WOMEN WERE THERE IN HISTORY! THEY DID THE THINGS MEN DID! THEY INVENTED THE WORLD! There is no reason you shouldn't know about Mary Wollstonecraft, the way they teach you in high school about Jean-Jacques Rousseau and Thomas Paine and all those other Enlightenment fuckers who were her friends and contemporaries, whose names you dutifully memorised the night before the test, and then forgot. You should have had to memorise and forget Mary Wollstonecraft, too. She deserves to be taught to bored 17-year-olds who are mostly thinking about boning each other but will at least retain a vague familiarity of her name moving on. This is what education is for. This is what Mary would have wanted. But no, of course we can't teach children that women can be, and have been, leading intellectual figures. The girls might get ideas, and think that they, too, might be incredibly smart. It'd be chaos.

Mary's most important work was without a doubt *A Vindication of the Rights of Woman*. Enlightenment thinkers were all about vindicating things. 'The civilised women of the present century, with a few exceptions,' she wrote, 'are only anxious to inspire love, when they ought to cherish a nobler ambition, and by their abilities and virtues exact respect.' Mary Wollstonecraft would not have been a fan of reality television in the 21st century. Unless there was some kind of show where women pit their intellectual virtue against one another, and instead of winning a muscled man called

Brooks, you win a tenured professorship. Someone please create this show. It can be called *The Bachelorette of Arts*.

*A Vindication of the Rights of Woman* was an international bestseller, with the wives of gentlemen passing it round and debating its ideas that, hey, maybe women are people, and if they appear 'weak and wretched' it is because society made them so. Not all women were fans of Mary's critique of gender. One evangelical writer, Hannah More, explained in a letter why she had not read it: 'There is something fantastic and absurd in the very title . . . there is no animal so much indebted to subordination for its good behaviour as woman.' Good one, Hannah!

Other detractors decried Mary's appearance, because as we all know, how you do your hair determines whether you're a good writer or not. Mary would wear plain, unfashionable clothes with her hair loose around her shoulders, leading some to call her a 'philosophical sloven', which would make for a great Tumblr username nowadays.

Mary was committed to equality above all, not only between sexes, but between social classes. With the decline of the feudal system and the rise of capitalism in England, Mary warned that 'the tyranny of wealth is still more galling and debasing than that of rank.'

Some of Mary's sickest burns of her career were levelled at Rousseau. She admired his philosophy of reason, but she couldn't stand for his ideas about women. He believed that women were naturally inclined to servitude and born 'to submit to man and to endure even injustice at his hands.' One merely had to look at the toys children played with, which of course they selected in a vacuum without any cues from the society around them about what they should enjoy, to see the natural order of things: 'Boys want movement and noise, drums, tops, toy-carts; girls prefer things which appeal to the eye, and can be used for dressing-up – mirrors, jewellery, finery, and specially dolls. The doll is the girl's special plaything; this shows her instinctive bent towards her life's work.' Yes, exactly, this is why little girls grow up to be mothers, and little boys grow up to be drums.

He also deduced with all his magnificent reason that women should only be educated insofar as it helped them look after men at home, and, you know, maybe make a small, containable amount of witty conversation at dinner. Otherwise, they should rely entirely on their husbands' brilliance.

'To reason on Rousseau's ground,' Mary responded, 'if man did attain a degree of perfection of mind when his body arrived at maturity, it might be proper, in order to make a man and his wife one, that she should rely entirely on his understanding; and the graceful ivy, clasping the oak that supported it, would form a whole in which strength and beauty would be equally conspicuous. But, alas! husbands, as well as their helpmates, are often only overgrown children; nay, thanks to early debauchery, scarcely men in their outward form – and if the blind lead the blind, one need not come from heaven to tell us the consequence . . .'

This was a very sick burn in 18th-century Enlightenment circles. RIGHT, TIME FOR SOME SEX!

You've already heard that Mary Wollstonecraft was a 'philosophical sloven'. She was also, it turns out, a bit of a libertine – at least by 18th-century middle-class English standards. Really her great scandal was that she had, like, three boyfriends total, and maybe a girlfriend too, so who are we modern harlots to judge her?

Mary's first great love was Henry Fuseli, who sounds like a pasta but was in fact a man. A married man, no less. They met in 1788. He was a painter and writer, which should have been a big red flag, but Mary fell passionately in love for three years. Unable to live without him any longer, Mary asked Henry's wife, Sophia, if she could live with them and be Henry's 'spiritual spouse'. Sophie was, uh, not cool with this, and so Mary moved to France alone, as one does to deal with heartbreak and make radical friends.

The French Revolution was in full swing, in its fun prison-storming years rather than its scary guillotine-y years. She met an American Captain Gilbert Imlay, fell in love again, and got preggers. As things got more guillotine-y, though, Gilbert left France on 'business' and left her alone and pregnant to fend for herself. She had the baby, named her Fanny (lol), and wrote with pride to her friend that, 'My little Girl begins to suck so MANFULLY that her father reckons saucily on her writing the second part of the Rights of Woman'. Nice one.

While the whole being-abandoned-while-pregnant thing should have been another red flag, the heart wants what it wants, and Mary's heart still wanted this fuckboy Gilbert. He sent her on a trip to Scandinavia to sort out some business drama for him and she happily obliged, but when she returned to him in London, she found him with a new mistress. There was nothing left to do but throw herself off a bridge into the Thames, where she was thankfully rescued.

Fucking Gilbert. At least she got a beautiful literary work out of it, writing *A Short Residence in Sweden, Norway, and Denmark*, a collection of fictionalised letters detailing heartbreak and despair.

Eventually, though, Mary would meet her equal in William Godwin, the philosopher and historian. They had met previously at a dinner party and had a loud argument about religion. Five years after their contentious meeting, Mary brazenly turned up at his home with a Rousseau novel to discuss. They became lovers, and wrote erotic letters to each other, which were mostly about blushing and probably too ensconced in allusion and metaphor to produce any 21st-century boners. It did the trick for them, though, and soon Mary was pregnant again. They married, shocking all their friends, who hadn't realised Mary had never married that absolute waste of space, Gilbert.

The couple were happy as can be, enjoying each other's company, playing with Mary's first child, and engaging in intellectual debates and whatever it was that made them blush so much. It was all cut short, though, after Mary gave birth to their child, and died of an infection. William was bereft, and wrote to his friend: 'I have not the least expectation that I can now ever know happiness again.' If only they had found each other sooner and had more time, instead of the years with Gilbert. If only women's healthcare didn't suck, then and now.

After her death, William published the memoirs of Mary's life, including all the scandalous stuff about her ~liberated~ sexuality. As soon as the prudes got their hands on it, they held her sexual freedom up as proof that suffragists, women's rights advocates, feminists, and women generally were all just sluts. And so she was sidelined by more conservative women's rights activists in the 19th century who found her *three entire boyfriends* altogether too scandalous for their tastes, but by the 20th century, wilder women held her up again as a hero.

Mary Wollstonecraft's daughter, the inventively named Mary Wollstonecraft Godwin, grew up to write *Frankenstein* under her married name, Mary Shelley. What a shame the Marys never got to meet each other properly – who knows what they could have done together?

# 50

# Ida B. Wells-Barnett

1862–1931

The thing about Ida B. Wells is that she accomplished not one, not two, not three, but one billion remarkable feats in her 68 years of life. Each one of these billion achievements should have been enough to earn her the right to eternal fame and glory, and yet today not every journalist in America has the words 'IDA BELL WELLS-BARNETT' tattooed on their body – as they should. And so we must say once again that a brilliant woman has not earned her due recognition in history.

Ida Wells was born in 1862 in Mississippi. Her parents, James and Elizabeth Wells, gained their freedom after the Civil War and became involved in Republican politics in the post-emancipation South. (Remember, at this point in American History, the Republican party was interested in the reconstruction of the South and the extension of rights to formerly enslaved people, rather than its focus today on giving guns to foetuses.)

The immediate aftermath of the Civil War was a time of great hope for black people in the South, who suddenly found themselves at the centre of political life as the majority of voters. With great energy, freed people like Ida's parents began working to take their place as full citizens after centuries of being denied their very humanity, let alone the right to vote. Ida's parents campaigned to elect black people to political office, while encouraging their eight children to take advantage of their educations. Ida later described her duty as a child: 'Our job was to go to school and learn all we could.'

Ida's duty would become much greater in 1878, when she lost her parents and a sibling to a yellow fever epidemic. Her extended family planned to divide the siblings and institutionalise one of her sisters, Eugenia, who was paralysed from scoliosis – but Ida said her parents would 'turn over in their graves to know their children had been scattered.' And so at 16, an age at which a girl's only concern should be hiding her pimples from her crush, Ida took responsibility for her entire family.

She lied about her age in order to get a job in a rural school six miles' ride by mule from home, but after a few years of her tiring schedule, she decided to move the family to Memphis, Tennessee, where she continued to work as a schoolteacher.

In 1884, the course of Ida's life changed forever. She was travelling in the Ladies' Coach of a train from Memphis to Woodstock, Tennessee, as she'd done many times before. The conductor approached her and asked her to leave the coach, which was full of white women, and go and sit in one of the shittier carriages instead. Ida refused. He tried to force her, so she did what she had to do, and bit his hand. The conductor ran away in fear to find backup. It ended up taking three grown men to drag Ida from the carriage, while the rest of the passengers cheered.

Ida was of course enraged by the incident, but what she did next, most people would never dream of: she decided to sue the railroad. And, amazingly, she won. She was ecstatic, and wrote about her experience in a Baptist publication called the *Living Way*, calling on black people to stand up for the rights granted them by Reconstruction era laws, thereby solidifying them. It was her first entry into the world of activist journalism – but would not be her last.

As the years had progressed since the end of Reconstruction, though, white people were fighting more and more against the gains black people had made in the South. Their tactics included outright voter fraud, finding new 'legal' ways to disenfranchise black people, instituting segregation, and lynching men who they claimed had committed crimes. In 1883, the year before Ida's train incident, the US Supreme Court had nullified the Civil Rights Act of 1875 – which had guaranteed equal treatment of African Americans in such public spaces as public transport, among other protections. By overturning this law, the Supreme Court said that private citizens, businesses, and organisations COULD discriminate according to race.

Ida's case was the first example of a black person challenging this ruling, as she had been discriminated against by a railway company. When Ida won her case, it threatened legality of segregation in the private sphere – so the Tennessee Supreme Court stepped in to overturn her victory in the lower court. Ida was distraught. The ruling to overturn her victory was clear proof that there would be no justice for black people in the South. The system could not be trusted.

But Ida was not done fighting. She doubled down in her activist journalism, and began writing a weekly column for the *Living Way* under the pen name Iola. Her bold, political writing grew so popular that it was picked up by nearly 200 black publications across the country. She may have lost her case, but now she had a platform.

'She has plenty of nerve,' one of Ida's editors wrote of her. 'She is smart as a steel trap, and she has no sympathy with humbug.' Having no sympathy with humbug, I suppose, is the 1880s equivalent of giving no fucks.

Her male editors at the *Washington Bee*, meanwhile, described Ida as a 'remarkable and talented schoolmarm, about four and a half feet high, tolerably well proportioned and of ready address.' Which, I suppose, is the 1880s equivalent of calling someone an absolute babe. Ida was the whole package: tolerably well proportioned with no sympathy for humbug. She also had a seemingly infinite supply of energy, and she was going to use every single drop of it to fight for the rights of black people and women.

As white backlash against Reconstruction grew, so did Ida's prominence as a journalist, but she was not without further setbacks. An exposé of Memphis' segregated school system would get her fired from her teaching job by the Tennessee Board of Education. She was devastated once more, but picked herself up and spent more time on her journalism. She began to be invited to give lectures and attend conferences across the country, becoming a leading figure on the women's rights circuit and gaining national prominence for her writing on race.

Ida saw the potential of journalism to make political change – and never would her writing have more of an impact than her work in the 1890s to document, denounce, and analyse the rising phenomenon of lynching in the South. She was compelled to take on this work by the brutal lynching of three of her friends in 1889. A group of white grocery store owners had attacked the black men's grocery store, resenting that it took business away from them, and the ensuing fight left several white men injured. Ida's friends were arrested, but before they could even face a trial, a white mob raided the jail house, took away the men, and tortured, beat, and hanged them.

Grieving and enraged, Ida wrote in the black press that black people should leave the city of Memphis, which obviously did not value their lives. Thousands followed her advice, crippling the local economy. She also organised a very effective boycott of the city's trolley service. Where Ida led, others followed.

She then set about researching her most ambitious project yet. She travelled across the South and documented 728 lynchings from the previous decade. She came to understand lynching to be a means of social control. Her work set off a firestorm for proving that most of the 'crimes' for which black men were lynched – especially claims that they had raped white women – were fabricated.

'The more I studied the situation,' she wrote, 'the more I was convinced that the Southerner had never gotten over his resentment that the Negro was no longer his plaything, his servant, and his source of income.'

Ida was travelling when her lynching work was published, and heard the news that her newspaper office had been destroyed in a fire. She received threats that men would be waiting for her at train stations should she try to return to Memphis. She knew she couldn't go back to the South.

So she stayed where she was, in New York. In 1892 she gained the support of 250 prominent black women who gathered for an event at New York's Lyric Hall to raise the funds needed to publish her reporting on lynching as a pamphlet titled *Southern Horrors: Lynch Law in All its Phases*. Those women included Frances E.W. Harper, who you'll hear about next.

Even after all this – the threats to her life, the deaths of her friends, the trauma of her alienation by a country that had for a time in the 1870s seemed to her and her family so promising for free black people – Ida B. Wells, being Ida B. Wells, carried on. She travelled to London and formed the first English anti-lynching society. She shamed America in the international press for its treatment of black people, and turned lynching from something that white Southerners could 'justify' as retribution for imagined crimes into an international, public, politicised debate. An opinion piece in *The New York Times* denounced her as 'slanderous and nasty-minded' for her criticisms of the United States. Thankfully Ida, as we know, had no sympathy for humbug.

Ida also did grassroots community organising in Chicago, never afraid to get her hands dirty. She advocated on behalf of black men in Arkansas who had been imprisoned for rioting during a union-isation effort, and secured their release. She co-founded the National Association for the Advancement of Colored People, the NAACP, which carries on its work to this day. She even met President McKinley and called him a dick. In so many words.

In 1895, Ida married Ferdinand L. Barnett, an attorney with a similar love of strong middle initials, and became Ida B. Wells-Barnett. She was one of the first women in the country to keep her own last name after marriage – something women sometimes still get shit for today, so imagine how bold a move it was over a century ago. Fellow women's rights reformer Susan B. Anthony apparently judged her for getting married, saying it would divide her time from her activism. But Ida, it turns out, didn't care much about the fears of Susan B. Anthony.

Ida B. Wells did so much in her life. She experienced unprece-dented victories as well as heart-rending tragedies and defeats. But she never gave up. She never just decided, 'That's it, I'm done,' and lay on the floor staring at the ceiling. Well, maybe she did – those moments don't usually make it to the biographies. But whether or not Ida ever felt unable to go on, she always picked herself up soon after, and got back to work.

# 51

# Frances Ellen Watkins Harper

1825–1911

Frances Ellen Watkins Harper was good at most everything she did. Born in Baltimore in 1825 to free parents, she made a career of being on the right side of history, and for this her writings and poetry should be taught in every school in America. Can someone with the ability to make that happen get on it? Excellent.

Frances was orphaned early on and raised by her aunt and uncle, the educator and abolitionist William Watkins, who instilled in her a profound sense of justice that she'd carry with her through life. She published her first book of poetry in 1845, entitled *Forest Leaves*. In 1854 she published another book of poetry, with the less whimsical but nevertheless accurate title, *Poems on Miscellaneous Subjects*. It was a bestseller, and made her a star.

One of her most famous poems is 'Bury me in a Free Land', first published in 1858, which begins:

*Make me a grave where'er you will,*
*In a lowly plain, or a lofty hill;*
*Make it among earth's humblest graves,*
*But not in a land where men are slaves.*

Right. It's time for a truth bomb. In the 19th century and beyond, prominent white suffragists like Susan B. Anthony and Elizabeth Cady Stanton fought to win votes for women, but in doing so, resorted to some racist bullshittery. Despite this, Frances managed to win prominent positions in white-dominated suffragist organisations like the National Woman Suffrage Association.[21]

Tensions over race came to a head most acutely in debates surrounding the passage of the 15th Amendment to the Constitution, which would extend the right to vote to black men. Stanton, Anthony, and most white women suffragists were opposed to the enfranchisement of any more men without also winning the vote for women.

These white suffragists argued that they had sufficient maturity and therefore the right to vote by claiming they were more evolutionarily developed than all black people. A popular theory in biology and social science at the time stated that people's development from youth to maturity reflected the advancement of the species as a whole. The theory postulated that white men reached maturity and independence (and thereby the right to vote) at age 21, while white women and all black people never did reach the same height of evolutionary maturity.

21. By the way, Frances believed strongly in the prohibition of alcohol, and was a prominent member of the Women's Christian Temperance Union. So please set aside your cold, refreshing brewski for the remainder of this chapter, should you so happen to be enjoying one at this moment, as I am.

Instead of assuming that anyone who believed in this theory was a complete, irredeemable idiot, white suffragists like Stanton and Anthony argued *within* its framework that white women were in fact as evolutionarily mature as white men – and more so than all black people.

Frances, on the other hand, rejected this theory and argued that all people, according to the principles of democracy and of Christianity, were truly equal and deserving of equal rights. Frances would not abandon black people and jeopardise the passage of the 15th Amendment for the sake of a racist ideology that would empower white women. 'When it was a question of race,' Frances said, she 'let the lesser question of sex go.' She would, however, also criticise those black men who championed their own rights and allied themselves with white men at the expense of black women. 'It is no honor to shake hands politically with men who whip women and steal babies,' she wrote in the *Anglo-African Magazine* in 1859.

The argument surrounding the 15th Amendment led to a split in the American Equal Rights Association, of which Frances was a founding member, and whose stated goal was suffrage for both black men and for all women. Harper and her allies would go on to found the American Women's Rights Association, while Stanton and Anthony would found the National Woman's Rights Association.

Here's a quote from Frances that everyone should have up their sleeve the next time they hear some racist or sexist nonsense – which is likely to be imminent, because the world is bad: 'We are all bound up together in one great bundle of humanity, and society cannot trample on the weakest and feeblest of its members without receiving the curse on its own soul.'

Frances Harper's profound faith in the equality of people regardless of race, class, and gender was, at the time, quite revolutionary.

The equality of all people is, hopefully, obvious to most today. Other than perhaps dodgy uncles at family reunions, who are inevitably the last demographic to ever come round to a new idea. The next time you face a dodgy uncle, remember Frances, and in everything you do, try to end up on the right side of history.

# 52

# Ethel Payne

1911–1991

*E*thel Payne was born in 1911 and grew up in Chicago dreaming of becoming a writer. She took night classes at Northwestern's journalism school, and in 1948 took a job as a hostess at a social club for American soldiers posted in Japan. She kept a diary while there about her observations and about the experience of black soldiers in a segregated military – General Douglas MacArthur had ignored an executive order from President Harry Truman to deseg-regate the armed forces. Ethel shared her writings from Japan with a reporter for the *Chicago Defender*. They put together an article on black GIs, and when she returned to the US, she was hired by the *Defender*, whose motto was very much to the point: 'American Race Prejudice Must Be Destroyed'.

Ethel worked as the *Defender*'s Washington correspondent in the 1950s and 60s, and became known as the 'First Lady of the Black Press', covering the front lines of the civil rights movement. As one of only three African American reporters with accreditation in the White House press corps, Ethel had the opportunity to directly grill presidents on civil rights issues, and carefully planned her questions so as to put them on the spot. She once asked President Eisenhower if he intended to ban segregation on interstate travel, which was within the remit of the federal government's abilities. As you can imagine, Eisenhower was not pleased with this question, and his angry man-baby response made national news: 'You say that you have to have administrative support,' he snapped. 'The administration is trying to do what it thinks and believes to be decent and just in this country, and is not in the effort to support any particular or special group of any kind.' It was a very 1950s 'all lives matter' moment – and he was criticised for it. Eisenhower, who fought in wars but was afraid of this black woman reporter, simply stopped calling on her. The press secretary even looked into revoking her accreditation, and investigated her to try and find some dirt. There wasn't any – her only problem was that she was asking a bunch of racists about how racist they were. Her direct and relentless questioning on 'awkward' topics earned her the reputation of, surprise, being 'aggressive', which is interesting given that when white male journalists ask blunt questions, they're seen as being 'good at their jobs' and are rewarded with whisky and promotions.

Ethel Payne was the first African American woman to give commentary on national TV and radio, and Kissinger called her 'that woman who gives me hell on CBS'. In the course of her career, she travelled to every corner of the globe; she reported on black troops in the Vietnam war; and she interviewed Nelson Mandela, Martin Luther King Jr. and JFK. She was a reporter, but Ethel was fully committed to the idea that her purpose as a journalist was deeply tied to activism, as she explained to an interviewer a few years before she died, quoted in a 2011 *Washington Post* article, 'Ethel Payne, "First Lady of the Black Press," Asked Questions No One Else Would':

> I stick to my firm, unshakeable belief that the black press is an advocacy press, and that I, as a part of that press, can't afford the luxury of being unbiased . . . When it comes to issues that really affect my people, and I plead guilty, because I think that I am an instrument of change.

# Women who wore Trousers and enjoyed Terrifying hobbies

# 53

# Annie Smith Peck

1850–1935

According to science, there is a small but very important part of the brain which clearly instructs human beings to be terrified of precipitous cliff edges, pointy rocks, slippery, stabby, near-vertical slopes of ice, great big jaggedy crevasses, and swirling, blizzardous death-storms. It has ensured the continued survival of the human race.

Annie Smith Peck, however, seemed to lack this bit of her brain, and so became famous in the late 19th and early 20th centuries for climbing murdery-looking mountains, laughing in the icy face of death, and other such ~girly things~.

Born in Providence, Rhode Island in 1850 to a fancy-enough family, young Annie spent her early years furiously studying the classics, snogging her dreamy boyfriend Will (shout-out to Will), and fangirling over the young suffragist Anna E. Dickinson, who toured the country giving lectures about how women were actually quite good at things.

Eventually, Annie wanted to go to university, as her older brothers had. Unfortunately, however, it was the 1870s, a time when many great men of learning and science firmly believed, in their logical and rational way, that higher education for women would lead to their infertility and early deaths. A very popular 1873 book by one Edward H. Clarke, a Harvard professor with a presumably large and important willy, stated that women's attendance at university would 'shut the uterine portals of the blood up, and keep poison in, as well as open them, and let life out.' Sorry, girls, that's just science.

If Annie hadn't been a woman and therefore a highly illogical being, she might have heeded such wise and important willy-given advice. However, she persisted against the warnings of such learned men, and wrote to the president of the University of Michigan, which had in 1870 begun to admit women and even treat them as equals. She was accepted, and had a grand ol' time studying classics.

After university, Annie was once again warned against the dangers of ~a lady~ moving around the country to different teaching jobs, let alone to Europe to carry on her studies, which she very much wanted to do. Her mother warned her what it might look like for a young woman to travel alone to Europe like a giant slut. But Annie, according to Hannah Kimberley's biography *A Woman's Place Is At the Top*, was not bothered what others thought of her, and replied: 'I have lived long enough to have got beyond trying to make all my actions satisfactory to my numerous friends and acquaintances.' Whack that over a sunset and put it on Instagram, friends.

But now to the murdery mountains.

Being outdoorsy, Annie got a taste for mountain climbing when she found that she was not only good at it, but that it was excellent for her *humours*. She began mounting moderately murdery mountains like Mount Shasta in California and the Matterhorn in Germany. She drummed up press interest in each of her attempts to increase her own celebrity enough to make a living on the lecture circuit after her climbs. In these lectures, she would show rooms of elegant ladies and gentlemen slides of her journeys and describe the mountains' beautiful views, as well as their 'chasms of unknown depth where a few inches more of slipping would have meant farewell to earth's pleasant scenes'.

Listen. We all have our strengths. Annie could scale perilous mountains with hands and feet numb from impending frostbite, keeping a cool head at mind-bending altitudes, and staying stead-fast despite the possibility of a terrible death at any moment. And I can hold my pee in for a really long time.

Annie, ever the PR girl, made enough of a name for herself that the media would sometimes exaggerate the heights of the mountains she'd climbed, or say she'd been the first woman to climb them when she actually wasn't. (Just some more of that FAKE NEWS we've been hearing so much about lately.) Annie didn't always make a huge effort to correct them, preferring to increase her own noto-riety, and therefore her desirability on the lecture circuit. Feel free to judge her for this, but just make sure you've climbed at least 21,831 feet in ice and snow first. Then go right ahead.

Mountain climbing was of course a sausage fest in Annie's time. As well as our time, I suppose. Throughout her career, Annie would have to deal with men doubting or belittling her achievements. And while many climbing clubs and outdoorsy societies included women, some, like Britain's Alpine Club, would not admit women, even those as accomplished as Annie. 'I was told the presence of ladies would spoil their dinner,' Annie wrote of that club. Which makes sense. The presence of a woman at dinner would lead to mass hysteria and the early deaths of all, surely.

Even more shocking to 19th-century sensibilities was a widely circulated portrait of Annie posing in her climbing outfit – wearing trousers LIKE A COMMON HARLOT. This fashion choice created quite the stir in a time when American women were literally being arrested for wearing trousers. Which also makes sense. Imagine being forced to know that women had two separate legs, and not just one big tree-trunk leg hidden under a voluminous skirt? Yes, everything made sense in the 19th century.

Annie's most famous climb was in 1908 when she reached the summit of the northern peak of Peru's imposing Huascarán mountain, where she and her climbing team reached her career record altitude of 21,831 feet (aka the height you have to beat to be allowed to talk shit about Annie). This altitude made her the record holder of any man or woman in the entire Western Hemisphere. And she did it at the sprightly age of 58.

Annie achieved all of her mountaineering feats without the high-tech Patagonia gear that dads pretend they need to go camping for a night. Her supplies included woollen socks, a wool face mask with a moustache painted on, and bars of chocolate. She said that 'chocolate is absolutely essential' for climbing. Amirite, ladies?! No really, it's good for altitude sickness, apparently.

After her achievement at Huascarán, Annie thought for a time she had achieved the altitude record for the entire world, but one woman would set out to prove her wrong: Fanny Bullock Workman. No, I didn't make up that name. Once upon a time in the 1800s, two parents looked at a baby girl and thought, 'She looks like a Fanny Bullock.'

An aside: in 2011 my best friend Emily and I (hey Emily) decided we should stop referring to other women as bitches. Now, should we ever feel tempted to call a woman a bitch, we instead pause, take a deep, calming breath, and say: 'I'm sure she's lovely.'

Since Emily is reading this book (you better be reading this book, Emily) I shall simply say of Fanny Bullock Workman that she was, I'm sure, a very lovely person. Perhaps the loveliest!

Fanny was ten years younger than Annie, and from a much wealthier and better-connected family. While Annie had to scramble for funds for each trip she took, Fanny and her husband travelled all around the world's highest peaks with all the best gear and the best guides. Hearing Annie's estimates that she had reached anywhere from 22,000 to 24,000 feet or above on Huascarán, Fanny took it upon herself to hire a team of engineers to 'triangulate' (idk, use maths) the mountain's exact height and thereby debunk Annie as FAKE NEWS. Fanny spent the equivalent of $300,000 to prove that Annie was not, in fact, the Queen of Climbing, and rather it was she, the lovely Fanny, who was Queen.

But it wasn't enough for Fanny to spend huge amounts of money triangulating mountains. No, this Fanny was an insatiable fanny. She was an old-timey Regina George. She went on to talk shit in the press about Annie's physical appearance and, of course, her slatternly trouser-wearing. One interviewer recorded that Fanny 'alluded with a smile of subtle scorn to the fact that the scaler of the Andes (AKA OUR ANNIE) invariably climbed in knicker-bockers.' Fanny added, 'I have never found it necessary to dispense with the skirt.' OK, Fanny. OK. Cool. I'm sure you were lovely.

When Annie learned that Huascarán was in fact lower than Aconcagua – which Fanny had climbed with her dirtbag husband – her reply was ice cold:

> I always hoped Huascarán would prove to be the highest mountain in the Western world, but now it seems that Aconcagua is highest. But anyone can climb that. It's just a walk. No cliffs. No glaciers.

Fanny left her alone after that.

Annie's second great rival would come in the form of Hiram Bingham III, a fancy Yale man said to be the inspiration for Indiana Jones. Hiram disapproved of women climbers, especially middle-aged women climbers in knickerbockers like Annie, and decided to outdo her by climbing what was thought to be a higher peak than Huascarán, Coropuna in Peru. Annie had set her sights on the very same mountain. As the headline blared in *The New York Times*: 'MISS PECK GOES OUT TO CLIMB THE HEIGHTS: Huascarán Not Being the Top of America, She's Going to Find the Top and Stand on It'.

Of course, Hiram was too proud to admit that he was in direct competition with a woman 25 years his senior. He wrote to his wife: 'Of course we are not racing for Coropuna but she thinks we are – which makes it amusing.' Ha ha yes, very amusing, dearest Hiram. I'm sure you were lovely.

Annie and Hiram set off from New York to Peru in a rush, even ending up on the same boat for one deeply awkward bit of the journey. After a race across South America that should probably be the inspiration for the next Indiana Jones film, Annie and her crew made it to the mountain first. She planted a flag near the top which read: VOTES FOR WOMEN. It may as well have read: SUCK IT, HIRAM.

Annie spent her later years actively involved in the suffragist movement. As a seasoned expert in pan-American relations, she also wanted to be a diplomat to a South American country, but, naturally, women weren't allowed to be diplomats in those days. On the plus side, in her old age she began to hang out with a girl gang of other overly daring women such as Amelia Earhart, who cited Annie as an inspiration. Earhart wrote of Annie: 'I am only following in the footsteps of one who pioneered when it was brave just to put on the bloomers necessary for mountain climbing.'

Annie would continue to climb until the age of 82, and after a lifetime of travel and exploration, always living by her motto that 'home is where my trunk is,' she died at 84. Her gravestone in Providence reads: YOU HAVE BROUGHT UNCOMMON GLORY TO WOMEN OF ALL TIME.

# Jean Batten

1909–1982

*I*f you've ever been on a plane, you're probably aware that they make no sense. How do they get off the ground? How do they know which way to go? How do they stay up? They're so heavy. These are just some of the questions that mankind will never be able to answer.

But none of this bothered Jean Batten, the mega glam 1930s aviator from New Zealand who set multiple world records for her daring long-distance solo flights around the world. Jean was born in Rotorua, New Zealand, in 1909. She was a gifted musician and ballet dancer, but what she really wanted, like all teen girls, was to fly planes. And so she moved with her mother to London to join the London Aeroplane Club, learn to fly, and find out how to make planes stay up.

Jean and her mother were laser-focused on their goal: for Jean to attain international superstardom by hurtling across oceans in tiny tin cans in a state of constant peril. And to do so while maintaining a glamorous image. Just how glam are we talking? Well, Jean would carry a make-up bag in her tiny planes so that her lipstick would be camera-ready as soon as she got out of her plane after each heroic feat. Jean would have been amazing at Instagram, and her mother would have been the first to comment each time she posted.

Jean's first feat was to try and break the record of Amy Johnson, the British aviator who was the first woman to fly solo from England to Australia. Jean wanted to do the same, but faster. On her first attempt, she flew into a sandstorm and went into a terrifying tailspin, but managed to pull out in time to make a safe landing near Baghdad. Back in the air, she carried right on, as if she hadn't just nearly died – and hit ANOTHER sandstorm, this time forcing her to land in Balochistan, in what is now Pakistan. At this point, her tiny plane was knackered, and the engine gave out entirely. She crashed near Karachi, but crawled out of the wreck just fine, presumably with her make-up looking absolutely 10/10.

A word on planes in the 1930s: Jean was flying a plane known as a Gypsy Moth. It wasn't even enclosed, guys. Have you ever been on a motorway and had to roll up the windows because the wind was getting a bit much? OK, now imagine flying through a series of sandstorms in an open-top plane, alone, from England to Australia. Also, you have no way of communicating with anyone on the ground. Also, your lipstick looks great.

Jean, instead of deciding after her first failed attempt that the ground was actually a quite nice place to be, decided to give it another go. On her second attempt, Jean ignored warnings not to try and fly against a strong headwind across the Mediterranean Sea, and ran out of fuel. She knew it was her own silly fault, and recorded thinking at the time: 'A watery grave is what I deserved.'

If it's what she deserved, she didn't get it, instead crash-landing on the outskirts of Rome without breaking a bone, and even finding a kind Italian gentleman to lend her some spare wings to get her plane back to England.

Still, Jean thought to herself that, yes, she'd quite like to try it again. She wasn't, after all, enough of an international superstar yet. And so, in 1934, Jean finally made it from England to Australia, through a monsoon in Burma, in just under 15 days – breaking Amy's record by four and a half days. She was the world record holder, and a media sensation. The headline of the *Daily Express* read: 'THE GIRL WHO HAS BEATEN ALL THE MEN'. To drum up continued press for herself and her sponsors, she undertook tours across Australia and New Zealand with a little black kitten named Buddy.

Jean's next feat was becoming the first woman to fly herself across the South Atlantic, and then in 1936, incredibly, to fly the first direct-ish flight from England to New Zealand. A flight from England to New Zealand nowadays is punishing enough, and at least you get to watch a few movies and have a look through the skincare section of the duty free catalogue. Jean, meanwhile, had to stay focused all that way on the difficult task of not plummeting to her death. At least by this time she was flying a plane with a top.

The last leg of the New Zealand feat was the most dangerous, crossing the Tasman Sea between Australia and New Zealand. 'If I go down in the sea,' she said, 'no one must fly out to look for me.' This was a 1,200 mile crossing with only a watch and a compass to guide her, and yet she was such a keen navigator that she managed to land within 100 yards of where she'd planned.

To sum up: Jean Batten was a madwoman who escaped death over and over flying teeny tiny planes through perilous storms that would make most people shit themselves in terror. But shitting yourself in terror is not very glam, and Jean was a very glam woman.

Here's the other thing about Jean, though, that comes up in anything you watch or read about her. Beyond her nutso solo flights in tiny tin-can planes, Jean Batten was also famous for charming men, taking their money to buy planes, crashing those planes, returning the bits of broken plane to the men, and then dumping the men. This, and the fact that she became a recluse and died alone, having never married, always ends up as the shameful denouement in the telling of her life story. Her critics will stress that she was too vain, too aloof, and too cruel to the men who loved her. And she cared too much about her lipstick, after all.

One man gave her his life savings, £400, to buy her first plane. He wanted to marry her, and clearly saw this as the deal – a deal which she reneged on. A quick word to my gentlemen readers: if you give someone £400 to buy a plane, it doesn't oblige them to marry you.

What Jean loved was flying. She loved 'the intoxicating drug of speed, and freedom to roam the earth'. If she wanted to be remembered and beloved as a legend, I propose that we let her. It may be a tired line of argument, but truly, would history begrudge a man for his vanity at wanting to be a legend? Would we judge a man to be cold, and deserving of a lonely death, rather than remember him as a romantic and enigmatic confirmed bachelor, if he had wronged a few lovers in his 20s?

The truth is, Jean *did* want to marry, once – a fellow aviator named Beverley Shepherd. But one day, his plane went missing. Jean took off in her plane to help in the search, to no avail. While some of those in the plane survived, Beverley did not. Jean remembered reading the news: 'I bought a newspaper and forced myself to read it. It was almost as if I deliberately drove a dagger into my heart.'

Later, she fell in love again, with an RAF pilot. He died, too, in World War II, which also marked the end of her flying career.

Is a woman not allowed to be cold after suffering all that? Or do women have to keep smiling to their graves? Do even the great female adventurers have to end up domesticated in order to earn the well wishes of history?

Wait, don't go! Come back. I'm done ranting. Mostly. My point is, if Jean Batten was an asshole, let her be an asshole. Nobody cares that Winston Churchill was an asshole. So many famous men of history were probably assholes, but we remember their assholishness as their *not giving a damn*, their romantic rejection of the social pleasantries that would have held them back on their quest to greatness.

OK. That's Jean. You have heard her story, and if you'd like to criticise her for not marrying some men who made some poor financial decisions, please do so after setting a world record and crash-landing in a sandstorm. Then go right ahead.

# 55

# Khutulun

c. 1260–1306

*S*hould you ever find yourself at a party speaking to someone new, maybe someone you want to impress, and are totally at a loss for what to say, you should tell that person the story of Khutulun. Their reaction to it will determine if they are worth a moment more of your time.

Khutulun was a Mongol princess who lived from 1260 to 1306, and this was her deal: any man who wished to marry her would have to beat her in a wrestling contest first. Should the suitor win, then YOLO, they'd get married. Should he lose, he'd have to fork over like 100 horses. Needless to say, after years of this policy, Khutulun had amassed great herds of lovely horses, and the Mongolian steppes were littered with the debris of shattered male egos. Eventually, Khutulun did decide to settle down – though she remained undefeated in wrestling, of course. At a certain point a girl runs out of space to keep all her horses, you know?

What we know about Khutulun comes mostly from the guy who invented Backpacking Through Asia For A Summer After College, And Then Bragging About It For The Rest Of Your Life: Marco Polo. He said that Khutulun was 'so well-made in all her limbs, and so tall and strongly built, that she might almost be taken for a giantess.' But how much we can trust of his history is hard to tell, because you know how men are with their travelling stories.

Khutulun was the daughter of Khaidu, who led the Chagatai Khanate, a section of the Mongol Empire. In those days, it was NBD for Mongolian queens and princesses to be active in politics and battle, though as a woman, Khutulun couldn't succeed to the throne. She did, however, remain involved in politics after her father's death by serving as an adviser and general to her brother Orus, until he was defeated and things went south for the whole family.

That aside, would Khutulun's story not make for a perfect romcom, in which Jennifer Aniston wrestles Ryan Gosling nearly to his death then rides away, triumphant, upon his herd of beautiful stallions? 'Looks like the only thing I'll be riding tonight,' Khutulun turns to camera, 'is this magnificent steed.' *She winks and gallops into the sunset.*

Get in touch, Hollywood. We've had enough stories about underwhelming white men dating super hot women. Give us a wrestling princess blockbuster, please!

# 56

# Pancho Barnes

1901–1975

ancho Barnes was a hard-drinkin', swearin', love-makin', plane-crashin' stunt pilot who ran a wartime club in the Mojave desert that may or may not have been a hotbed of prostitution. Pancho was born Florence Leontine Lowe in 1901 and grew up in incredible wealth and privilege in a massive southern California mansion with 32 rooms. What do people do with 32 rooms? Do they know 32 people? Or are most of them just filled with boxes of old school essays that they don't want to throw away 'just in case'?

Whatever they did with those 32 rooms, Pancho preferred to spend her days outside riding horses and eventually learning to fly planes, which as we know is every little girl's true ambition. Her grandfather was an inventor and one of the founders of the California Institute of Technology, today known as CalTech, a place where students go to bid farewell to the sun forever, retreat to their labs, and transform into mole people in the name of science. Pancho was never much of a 'Florence', and got her nickname when a friend misremembered the name of Don Quixote's companion, Sancho; in any case Pancho stuck.

Pancho was meant to be a good, religious society girl, and so was married off to a wet blanket of a husband, the Reverend C. Rankin Barnes. On their wedding night they had a go of it, after which the good reverend announced: 'I do not like sex. It makes me nervous. I see nothing to it. We shall have no more of it.' And that was that. Thankfully, though, Pancho's sexual days were not over as she took a series of lovers and had wild affairs all across the greater Los Angeles area, which were mostly great, except for one guy who stole her plane.

When Pancho learned to fly, her instructor told her, 'I've had thirty-three women students so far and not one of them has soloed,' as in, flown alone without the instructor there to take over if things went south, or, I suppose, directly downward. 'I've been getting a little discouraged,' he said, 'but if you want to learn I suppose I'll have to try and teach you.'

Pancho proved that whiny loser well wrong, and not only quickly learned to fly solo, which she described as, 'one of the highlights of my life,' but became a stunt pilot for Hollywood in the 1930s in films like *Hell's Angels*. She'd got her start in the film industry first as a stand-in, then a script girl, and an animal handler, hiring out her horses that she'd taught to run alongside moving trains as cowboys leapt on their backs, and other horsy stunts. In fact, Pancho herself was the stunt double from time to time for cowardly cowboy actors. (To be fair, I probably wouldn't want to jump off a moving train onto a horse either.) In the same year, Pancho founded the Motion Picture Pilots' Association, the first ever union for her profession, which she set up because she was pissed off by how little she and other stunt pilots were paid to risk their lives on set.

Pancho flew all over the south-west, and into Mexico where she charged $10 per ride to pick up pleasure-seekers and fly them around a bit. Once, annoyed by an instructor giving her a 'check ride' to verify her pilot's licence, Pancho cut the engine mid-flight to freak him out and demonstrate how far beyond him she was in skill. Her fame grew steadily as a 'lady pilot', which is like being a pilot, but you're not a man. She entered women's flying competitions, including the first ever women's race in 1929, known as the 'Powder Puff Derby'. She competed against Amelia Earhart, who'd become a rival when Amelia called Pancho a 'marginal' pilot in her book. Pancho had beaten Amelia's air speed record in 1930. Classic women, always at each other's throats, getting jealous of other women's air speed records.

Pancho fell on hard times during the Great Depression of the 1930s, as almost everyone did. She bought some property in the Mojave Desert, and eventually opened up a club on it that came to be cheekily known as the Happy Bottom Riding Club. During World War II, airmen and Pancho's Hollywood pals would come to the desert to drop their rank and military hierarchies and unwind, as Pancho supplied them with liquor. Once, after hearing the Feds were on their way, she buried a load of smuggled Mexican booze in the desert to hide it – but a storm overnight hid the booze's location, and it was lost forever. Good news for anyone who lives near the Mojave Desert and wants an excuse for a treasure hunt.

Pancho also supplied her club patrons with young aspiring Hollywood starlets, leading to the accusation by some that she was actually running a brothel. She replied by putting up the following sign in her club:

WE ARE NOT RESPONSIBLE FOR THE BUSTLING AND HUSTLING THAT MAY GO ON HERE. LOTS OF PEOPLE BUSTLE AND SOME HUSTLE, BUT THAT'S THEIR BUSINESS AND A VERY OLD ONE.

Another critic, Bill Bridgeman, decried her establishment in his book, saying the place was 'run by an extremely ugly old woman'. She replied with quite a sick burn, according to the biography *The Lady Who Tamed Pegasus*: 'Ugly, I'll accept, but extremely ugly is taking it too far. I'll get that sonofabitch when I write my book. Problem with Bill was that he was chasing one of my girls and having trouble catching her. He asked me to give him a little help or put in a good word for him, so to speak. I told him that he was a big grown man and that he shouldn't have to have any help in his girl chasing. He really got pissed off and has been sorta mad at me ever since.' Pancho remained fundamentally chill though, conceding that, 'Bill is a damned good pilot and after I take my pound of flesh for his smart ass remarks we'll have a few belly laughs and everything will be OK.' She reportedly also said of the critics moralising about her club: 'We had more fun in a week than those weenies had in a lifetime.'

Pancho was pretty relaxed about everything she did. She even ran to be a member of the LA County Board of Supervisors, an election she lost despite the fact that she'd written her name in skywriting every afternoon of her campaign. What more could voters want from a candidate? She said of her opponent Buron Fitts: 'I used to razz Buron because he blushed so easily.'[22] She wasn't bothered when she lost, though, saying that she 'didn't take

---

22. We need to bring back the word 'razz'. Can everyone make an effort to drop this word into conversations at least once a week please? Thank you.

anything too seriously, including or perhaps particularly, politics.' Maybe she was only ever in it for the opportunity to write her name in the sky.

The top military brass weren't keen on the Happy Bottom Club, and so authorities eventually tried to seize the land to build up an air force base. Pancho would fight a lengthy court battle to contest the move, which became known as the 'Battle of the Mojave', but the club mysteriously burned down before she could win her suit. The club was never rebuilt, and the land today comprises the Edwards Air Force Base – which may, come to think of it, make your search for the mysterious lost Mexican liquor a little more difficult.

# 57

# Julie D'Aubigny

c. 1670/1673–1707

Julie D'Aubigny lived in 17th-century France, and her interests included impaling men with her sword, having affairs with hot men and women, and opera singing, presumably not all at the same time.

Her father was a secretary to an important member of the court of Louis XIV, the Compte d'Armagnac, who was in charge of all the king's horses. Whether or not he was also in charge of all the king's men, or putting Humpty Dumpty together again, is unknown. History is full of paedophiles, and so when young Julie was either 13 or 15, she became Armagnac's 'mistress', which is gross.

Julie was taught by royal tutors, so received an uncommon education for a girl of her station. We know that her dad liked swords and women, but her mother's identity has been lost to history. A love of swords (and women, as we'll see) passed straight on to Julie, as her father insisted she learn to fence, perhaps in order to protect herself, or perhaps because it was cool. She was described as having a fiery personality, which is often just a way of saying a woman had a personality.

After about two years of grossness, Armagnac found Julie some wet blanket of a husband, Jean Maupin, whose last name would later be her stage name, La Maupin. But Julie was not about to settle into domestic life. Within about five minutes of marriage, she'd fallen in love with a swordsman, Henri de Seranne, who whisked her away to Marseille where he said he had property. Once in Marseille, or perhaps even en route to Marseille, Henri turned to her and said, 'So, babes, when I said I had property in Marseille? What I actually meant was that I *don't* have property in Marseille.' Ladies: if your man says he has property in Marseille, make sure you double check it's true before you buy your plane tickets!

Instead of enjoying a relaxing life of property ownership, then, the couple got to work, performing in fencing and singing exhibitions for cash. Julie often dressed in men's clothing, for the practicality of it but also 'cause it's an absolute *look*. Once while fencing before a crowd, some punk in the audience shouted out that he, a man, believed that Julie must also be a man, and not a woman, as had been advertised. The story goes that Julie proved him wrong by swiftly whipping her tits out. Sometimes you have to do whatever it takes to make a man shut up.

The couple's fortunes improved when they were accepted to the Marseille Academy of Music, promoting them from the world of haphazard theatre to that of legitimate musicians and performers that rich people pay money to see. Julie, however, would throw away this fine opportunity in hot pursuit of a young lady named Cecilia Bortigal, who was perhaps from Bortugal. Cecilia's parents took fearful note of Julie's courtship of their precious Ceciliakins, and sent her to a convent for her own protection from this lesbian menace. Joke's on them, though, because convents are *full* of women.

Determined to rescue her fair Cecilia, Julie went to the convent and said that yes, she absolutely wanted to be a nun. She loved Jesus and everything. Wanted to marry him, yup, that's why she was there. Once inside, Julie plotted a MAD ESCAPE in which she laid the DEAD BODY of a RECENTLY DECEASED NUN in Cecilia's cell, then SET FIRE TO IT so that everyone would think she had died. They then fled over the convent's walls and into the world, triumphant to be reunited, until they got bored and broke up. Burning a body and breaking out of a nunnery would be hard to top in a relationship. Their plot discovered, Julie was charged with all of the bat-shit crimes her escape had necessitated.

Julie was then on the run from the law for a while, and not wanting to face justice for the Burning Nun Incident, lay low in various towns around France. Julie's version of lying low, however, entailed singing, fencing, and getting in brawls. Once, near Tours, she fought off three men in a tavern fight, stabbing one straight through the shoulder. It's OK, though, because they became lovers after that.

Eventually, Julie wanted to get back to Paris. Luckily her creepy old paedo friend, Armagnac, was mates with the king and arranged for her pardon. Thanks to her paedos in high places, Julie returned to Paris and scored an audition at the Paris Opera along with her lover du jour, Gabril-Vincent Thervenard. When he was accepted into the company, he said he'd only join if his weird-ass stabby sexy singing girlfriend got in too, and so they were both accepted, and rose to stardom in the opera.

Let's just stop here for a second to consider our own boring lives. Yes. Wow. OK, carry on.

Julie's *fiery* personality carried her through her years of stardom and further affairs. Once, she was creeped on by a tenor in the opera company who thought he was hot shit. Wanting to settle scores, she went out at night dressed as a man and challenged him to a fight, which she won, pocketing his watch and snuffbox. He hadn't recognised her, which is pretty ridiculous no matter how manly her clothes may have been, and the next day at work described the story of how he had been menaced by a gang of burly men. At this point, Julie was like, 'Surprise, bitch!' and produced his stolen watch and snuffbox.

Julie's most over-the-top duel, however, occurred at a ball at the Palais-Royal in 1696. Dressed as a fancy man as usual, Julie had been letching on a pretty young marquise, possibly even kissing her, when three of the girl's suitors marched over to defend her honour and challenge Julie to a duel. She was like, 'OK meet u outside lol,' and then grievously harmed, or even killed, the gallant defenders of the marquise. Julie strode back into the ball, shouted out to everyone 'Hey, someone should probably get these three assholes a doctor,' and then went to Brussels to lie low for a while. Sometimes you just have to remove yourself from a hot situation till things chill out a bit.

Julie spent some years shagging her way round Europe like a posh kid on a gap year, until enough time had passed since the Ball Incident for her to safely return to Paris and to the stage, in 1698. Her stardom was unblemished, and only rose to greater heights. She took on 41 acting roles, and performed for the king and nobility. When some guy talked shit about one of her female co-performers, Julie stuck her sword through his arm. Julie was a good friend.

Things were going well when she once again fell in love, this time with the Marquise de Florensac. They were happy together for a few years until he suddenly died from a swift illness, leaving Julie devastated. So unhappy was Julie with the loss of Florensac that she retired from the stage, and retreated into a life of, surprisingly enough, prayer and repentance.

She died a few years later, in 1707, at the age of 37. Perhaps only then did all the men who she'd stuck holes in finally feel safe.

# 58

# Lilian Bland

1878–1971

There are plenty of ladies in these pages who enjoyed the time-less pleasure of flying around in tiny, perilous planes, so we must take a moment to recognise the one who may have been the first woman to fly, Lilian Bland. Lilian was born in Kent in 1878, but in her 20s went to live with her widowed father in Carnmoney in what is now Northern Ireland. Her plane, which she built herself, was called the Mayfly, and was about as delicate as its insect name-sake. When she finally got it off the ground, she managed to get up about 30 feet in the air and fly a quarter of a mile before running out of steam and landing, which may not sound like much to us land-dwellers but is undoubtedly higher than if any of us tried to fly in an aircraft we'd built ourselves.[23]

---

23. Unless this is actually something you know how to do. If so, amazing! Well done. Be my friend.

Lilian first got a taste for certain-death flying as the passenger of a pilot boyfriend she had, who wouldn't let her have a go at the controls, which is a big red flag, ladies! She then asked the pilot Louis Bleriot, who had flown across the Channel from France to England, if she could come along as a passenger some time. He also said no, at which point Lilian knew if she wanted to hurtle through the air toward the certainty of grievous injury, she'd have to do it herself, and so in 1909 set about building the Mayfly. At first it was an unpowered glider, but then she installed a 20-horsepower engine, which just doesn't seem like enough horses to get a girl into the sky. The engine's petrol tank was late to arrive, so she fashioned one out of a whisky bottle and used her deaf aunt's ear trumpet as a funnel for the fuel.

What makes Lilian Bland wonderful is not only her pioneering flying, but the absolute lack of fucks she gave in her day-to-day life. She was born into a wealthy family as, let's face it, you'd have to be if you wanted to take up the hobby of crashing planes for a laugh, but she was far from an elegant lady. Lilian wore trousers – *ANOTHER ONE, SOMEONE CALL THE POLICE ALREADY* – shot rifles, smoked, did martial arts, drank, gambled, rode horses but DIDN'T do it the ladylike side-saddle way, and enjoyed a casual swear from time to time. Her father was so stressed about Lilian's flying that, in the manner of posh fathers, he offered to buy her a car instead. Unfortunately for him, she was also a reckless driver. She ended up working as a car dealer for Ford, as well as a photographer and a journalist, which is cool, but not as cool as flying planes tbh.

She eventually moved to Canada with her husband, who was also her cousin, 'cause why not keep it in the family? She died at age 92 in 1971, a surprisingly old age for someone who gave as few fucks as she.

# 59

# Lotfia Elnadi

1907–2002

Listen, I know there's lots of gals flying planes in these pages, but I just still don't understand how planes stay up and am too impressed with the women who not only worked it out but did it for themselves. So here's one more.

Lotfia Elnadi was born in Cairo in 1907. As a young woman, she read about a new local flight school and knew it was for her. She learned to fly in just 67 days, paying her fees by working as a secretary at the school, and became the first woman in Africa and the Middle East to get a pilot's licence. Her dad was mad at first, as she had told him she was just off to a study group twice a week – that classic excuse that most people use to go snog their teenage boyfriends and girlfriends – when she was in fact off to flight school. He soon got over it, however, when he saw the worldwide acclaim she received.

When she was in her 80s, Lotfia told an interviewer for the aviation magazine *Ninety-Nine News: Magazine of the International Women Pilots* about her first, much-publicised solo flight in 1933 in a Gypsy Moth, an open-air biplane: 'I not only flew to circle the pyramids in the Egyptian desert, I dipped my wings to fly between them! I was a show-off, was I not?' Look, if you knew how to do that you'd be an idiot *not* to be a show-off. And luckily she was a skilled flyer, because it would have been pretty awkward to put a dent in your country's most precious landmark.

'It was such a feeling of freedom,' Lotfia explained. 'The Moth, with its open cockpit, meant that the wind blew around my face. I flew for the sheer pleasure of it,' she said, much in the same way that people fly Ryanair today: for the sheer pleasure of it. The first person she ever flew was her father. Afterwards he said, 'he'd been frightened, but then he decided that he was in the hands of his daughter,' Lotfia recalled. 'He knew that if we crashed, we would crash together, so he relaxed and began to enjoy the flight.' Sure, that would be reassuring, in a way. Maybe?

Lotfia became a national celebrity, flying all across the country and up and down the Nile. She once had to make an emergency landing in the middle of the desert after an engine failure. She was found by some Bedouins who lent her a mule to take in search of help. She eventually had to quit flying due to an injury, but not before winning medals and honours as the first lady of the Egyptian skies.

Yes, there have been lots of pilots among these women. But there's something wonderfully alluring about their symbolism, fighting against sexism and stereotype to gain the skills to literally fly off the face of this hell earth and take their lives into their own hands. Ladies, we must all learn to fly before we can be truly independent. I will see you all at flight school – tell your parents you're off to a 'study group', it works every time.

# Women who fought empires and racists

# 60

# Queen Nanny of the Maroons

c. 1686–1755

Sometimes it's difficult to find out very much about a woman's life from hundreds of years ago, particularly when the historical references we have about her were written by racist men whose asses she roundly kicked. So it is with Queen Nanny of the Windward Maroons. Most written references to this incredible Jamaican leader's life were recorded by the British colonial soldiers whom she fought in the early 18th century. There is however enough oral history to add to dodgy British records, so that we can learn more about the excellent Queen Nanny.

Jamaica was settled by the Spanish in 1509, soon after its 'discovery' in 1494 by one of the absolute shittest men of history, Christopher Columbus. In the 150 years following his arrival, the native Arawak people were nearly completely wiped out by the colonisers, who meanwhile began to bring enslaved people from West Africa to the island. When the British invaded Jamaica to take it from the Spanish in 1655, most Spaniards left to Cuba and elsewhere, disappointed that the island didn't have gold anyway. In the struggle between the two colonial powers, the people the Spanish settlers had enslaved escaped to their freedom in the mountains and forests of Jamaica. A 'Maroon' is a word first used by the British in the 1730s to describe these communities of free and escaped slaves.

The free Maroons survived by living off the land as well as raiding the plantations run by the British, who'd come to Jamaica for a pleasant colonial experience of slavery and exploitation only to have their weapons, food, and livestock disappear in the night. The presence of the Maroons inspired and assisted uprisings and desertions from these huge, brutal sugar plantations – and nothing inspired a slave revolt like the example of successful revolts at the plantations next door. The escapees went to join the free Maroons, and so the community grew.

British officials had to keep writing back to England that things weren't going very well, and that the Maroons 'are like to prove as thorns and pricks in our sides'. One British governor, D'Oyley, who was oily, tried to get the Maroons to stop their raids by offering them 20 acres a person (of the land which they already lived on) as well as their freedom (which they had already claimed for them-selves). Some white settlers just gave up and left the island altogether, though most stayed, bringing hundreds of thousands more enslaved people to Jamaica for more than another century. The community of Windward Maroons, who lived on the Eastern side of the island, however, successfully kept their freedom and fought off the British – at the time the most powerful empire in the world – for 83 years. Queen Nanny was one of their most important military and political leaders.

Nanny was born in the 1680s in the Asante Empire, present-day

Ghana, and was likely transported to Jamaica as a free person, or became free soon after arriving. One British soldier who may have encountered her, Captain Philip Thicknesse, who was thick, claimed he'd seen her wearing a girdle of knives around her waist, 'many of which I have no doubt had been plunged in human flesh and blood.' Was it her? It's not clear. He also called her an 'old Hagg', so he's probably not to be trusted on anything to do with women.

Nevertheless, Nanny's achievements are remembered in oral history, Thicknesse or no.

Firstly, as a military tactician, Nanny instructed her fighters in the proper use of the *abeng*, or cow horn. Using a secret code system, the Maroons could relay complex information across long distances. These messages, passed from hill to hill, meant the Maroons could prepare for a British attack a full six hours in advance, as they slowly approached, unable to communicate over distances, crashing through the forest in bright red coats like an obvious horde of twats.

Once those twats arrived, they faced another disadvantage: a town built with a single narrow entrance, so that no matter how large the number of British troops, they had to enter battle single file, like a queue of pricks tutting at each other in Waitrose. Nanny had also devised systems of camouflage so effective that a British soldier might go to hang his coat on a tree, only for that tree to turn out to be a fighter about to kill him. Camouflage, good construction, and long-range communication were only three of Nanny's devices in her defensive strategy.

In the end, the Windward Maroons signed a treaty with the British in exchange for a grant of land and the right to be left the fuck alone (to this day!). It's a remarkable example of resistance, if only in one small community, on an island that felt the full force of British colonial evils.

A final legend about Nanny said that she could catch bullets. It's said that at the treaty signing with the British, Nanny caught bullets out of the air and said, 'Take these, good friend, there is peace; so now I am free to show you that only one man's bullets can harm Nanny' – pointing at heaven to indicate which Man. If you're boring and want another theory to explain this legend, it could be that Nanny would *recycle* bullets, which is much less cool but definitely practical.

In any case, today in Moore Town, residents leave glasses of water for Nanny at her memorial, and still use the phrase, whenever someone starts acting up: 'Granny Nanny didn't catch bullets for you alone.'

# 61

# Njinga of Angola

c. 1583–1663

Njinga (which can also be spelled Nzinga) was the queen of Ngongo and Matamba, in what is now Angola, southern Africa, and I'll say it once more: there is no reason for you to never have heard of this incredible shining powerful queen of history. No non-racist reason anyway. European chroniclers and other enemies in the 17th century vilified her as a bloodthirsty tyrant, which is funny, because they were busy being fucking slave-trading fucks, weren't they? Also, sorry but who the fuck wasn't a tyrant in the 1600s?

But listen. Njinga was such a boss, where do we start? Her birth. She was born in 1583, and from her childhood, Njinga was trained by her father, the ngola (ruler), in the art of governing and war, alongside her brother, Mbandi. When her brother became the new ruler, Njinga left the kingdom as she was seen as his rival and they didn't really get on. In fact, it's possible she killed him in the end, but that may just be a rumour spread by her enemies. Everyone knows how enemies love to spread rumours, it's their favourite thing to do.

Before he died (RIP) Mbandi got his sister to return and act as his envoy to the Portuguese, who were in the area and up to no good. He wanted her to negotiate a peace treaty of sorts with them that would ensure Ngongo's independence. Njinga was like, 'Sure bro,' and in 1622 went to negotiate with the Portuguese governor and live out one of her all-time most iconic moments. She arrived bedecked in clothes and jewels and attended by her ladies-in-waiting, to find that the Portuguese motherfucker, who sat in a velvet-covered, gold-embroidered chair, had only arranged for some carpet for Njinga to sit on at his feet.

Given that Portugal's goal was for Ngongo to submit to them entirely, Njinga clocked that this was not a good look, especially for a future queen. She immediately gestured to one of her attendants to get on all fours and be her chair for the several hours of negotiation. The move had the intended effect. They hammered out a peace treaty to maintain Ngongo's independence, which the Portuguese of course did not honour, and carried on looting Ngongo's territory and raiding its villages and enslaving people. Njinga had, however, refused to submit Ngongo to Portuguese rule.

One concession Njinga did make to the Portuguese was also a savvy diplomatic move: she was baptised and converted to Catholicism. The Portuguese goals in the region were twofold: to recruit new Christians and to kidnap people into slavery to be transported to the Americas, as Jesus clearly instructs all good Christians to do. If Njinga could say she was a fellow Catholic, she had recourse directly to Rome for political support against the Portuguese. Did she truly 'mean' her conversion? That's between Njinga and God, leave them alone.

Speaking of things that are between Njinga and God, she *may* have had a hand in killing her brother, but also he may have wanted to commit suicide. Also she may have killed his son. Who's to say who did and didn't kill whom? Whatever, their beef went way back. The point is, Njinga was elected queen by the court, and successfully kept the independence of the Ngongo and then the Matamba kingdoms against the Portuguese, and more or less maintained power for herself from 1646 until her death in 1663. Even in old age, she led fighters in skirmishes with the Portuguese. Basically the Portuguese had a terrible time as long as she was in charge. She reconquered lands from them, and the people they had enslaved escaped to her territory. She made alliances with the Dutch and the Kingdom of Kongo to keep the Portuguese out, and was accepted as an official Christian ruler by the Pope, making things awkward for the Portuguese.

Let's discuss Njinga as queen. She would occasionally dress as a man and was, like so many, a fan of young men and women, romantically speaking, and so naturally kept herself a sort of harem. It had to go in one of her negotiations however, since as a good Catholic she was compelled to give up her concubines and pick one to marry. Ugh, fine. So she picked a hot, significantly younger man, and married him.

Her death took her people by surprise. She was one of those people everyone just assumed would never die, like my grandma. Her legend lives on, however, in Angola and also in those places some of her people had been transported to as slaves; in Brazil, Cuba, and even the US – as some of the enslaved people first brought to Virginia had been captured by British pirates from Portuguese traders who had originally taken them from Njinga's Ngongo.

So should you ever find yourself thinking about queens in history, don't only think of Queen Elizabeth I or Queen Victoria – remember the reign of Queen Njinga.

# 62

# Rani Chennamma

1778–1829

Chennamma was the Rani (queen) of Kittur, in southern India, in the 18th to 19th centuries. When she was a girl, she received training in the things all little girls must be educated in to this day: how to ride a horse, how to shoot an arrow through the chest of your enemy, and failing that, how to destroy him in a swordfight. All of these skills would come in handy over the course of her life.

When Rani Chennamma's young son died, the British came along and tried to take control of Kittur. She tried to adopt an heir to carry on her husband's line of succession, but the British said it was not legal, according to some BS laws they'd just made up. In fact, these were the laws that the British would use again and again to dispossess rightful rulers across India, until the shit really hit the fan, as we'll see in Rani of Jhansi's chapter.

The British tried to expel Rani Chennamma, as well as her adopted son. She was like, 'Fuck this,' and attempted to keep Kittur independent. She went to war with the British, who attacked with 200 of their men and attempted to confiscate the state's jewels. See, this is why all daughters must be taught to wield a sword and use a bow and arrow: Rani Chennamma was ready. Her forces killed the British collector and took other officers hostage. What did they expect, honestly? She agreed to release them on the understanding that it would lead to peace; however, the British, never known for keeping their word about literally anything, regrouped with more forces and continued the fight.

When Rani Chennamma was captured and killed, her lieutenant carried on fighting until he was also captured and killed. She was the first (but not the last) female leader to take up arms against British colonialism. Her legacy of telling the British to fuck off, with her words as well as her actions, would soon be taken up by our next lovely warrior, Rani of Jhansi.

# 63

# Lakshmibai, Rani of Jhansi

## 1828–1858

akshmibai, also known as the Rani of Jhansi, is probably the most famous Indian woman who resisted British colonialism in India, though certainly not the first one, as we've already seen. She is often depicted as she spent much of her life: riding a horse, resplendent in jewels, and wielding a large sword.

When Lakshmibai's husband, the Maharaja, died in 1853, the state of Jhansi was under threat of British annexation. The British Governor-General of colonial India at the time, the Marquess of Dalhousie, a posh prick, had instituted something called the Doctrine of Lapse. This was basically the formalised version of the same law used to fuck over Rani Chennamma in the previous chapter. What it meant was that if the ruler of an independent Indian state died without an heir, the British could just *have* it (though many of these princely states were already British puppets). Before Lakshmibai's husband died he had adopted a son, Damodar

Rao, and insisted to the British that he was the rightful heir and that Lakshmibai should rule until he came of age.

Dalhousie, though, saw an opportunity and refused to recognise Damodar Rao's adoption, annexing Jhansi, collecting the profits of its land, and evicting Laxmibai from the palace. She was furious. Jhansi had long been friendly with the British, autonomous but loyal. And so with this in mind, Lakshmibai hired an eccentric Australian lawyer, John Lang, and the two talked from 6pm till 2am one evening in 1854 to draw up an appeal to the ruling according to multiple treaties that had been previously signed between the British and Jhansi. The lawyer later described the most important thing about their collaboration, Lakshmibai's appearance: 'Her face must have been very handsome when she was younger, and even now it has many charms – though according to my idea of beauty, it was too round.' Shut the fuck up and get back to your lawyering, John.

Dalhousie, being a prick, rejected the appeal, and Lakshmibai railed against the 'gross violation and negation of British faith and honour.' Jhansi officially lapsed to the British in 1854, as British rule in India grew ever more autocratic and dismissive of local religions and customs. After decades of oppression, tensions mounted and the last straw came in 1857 when a rumour spread that the bullets for a new kind of rifle to be used in the Indian army, whose use required the soldier to bite them, were coated in cow and pig fat, offending Hindu and Muslim soldiers alike. The British did not expect 'loyal' troops would ever rebel, but they did, breaking out in what is now known as the Indian Rebellion of 1857.

Lakshmibai was primarily concerned with the autonomy of Jhansi above all else, and even as the fighting spread she attempted to find diplomatic arrangements with the British. She built up the city's defences and recruited an army of 15,000 soldiers, which she originally meant to do on behalf of the British against the rebels. In the chaos of the uprising, though, she had been left once again with autonomy over Jhansi, and the city and its queen both saw the potential to claim independence once more. So she hoarded food and munitions, and even had the land surrounding her fort cleared of trees so that if and when the British came, they would be roasted in the sun, like so many British pensioners in Spain. She began dressing as a warrior, but still adorned herself with diamonds and pearls, because she was a queen, after all.

Soon, the British came under the direction of Sir Hugh Rose, another posho. They fired cannons at the fort's city walls, and Lakshmibai rode her horse among her troops who were resisting the siege with their ancient guns. Without the arrival of reinforcements, Jhansi fell to the British and was destroyed. The better version of the story has it that Lakshmibai made her escape by leaping on horseback from the walls of the fort, her son on her back, but it's more likely she just rode out normally at night.

Lakshmibai was finally killed in June 1858 in combat with Hugh Rose's soldiers. She is supposed to have said, when rallying her troops: 'If killed in battle we enter the heavens and, if victorious, we rule the earth.'

# 64

# Yaa Asantewaa

c. 1840–1921

Oh look, it's the British again. Where are they now, with their little pink pricks? They're in Asante kingdom, in part of what is now Ghana. It's 1900, just a few years since they seized power and abolished the Asante monarchy and government, trying to make their little pink pricks feel better. But, oh no! The Asante kingdom is divided after five years of civil war, and while some Asante factions have sided with the British, many have not – including the queen mother, Yaa Asantewaa.

Yaa Asantewaa was born around 1840 in central Ghana, and her little brother would become the chief of the Edweso people. When he died (RIP little bro) she took over as Queen Mother to her grandson and heir – whom the British exiled in 1896. To add to their fuckery, the British governor then demanded to have the Golden Stool, the throne and symbol of the Asante people. The British also wanted to stop sharing profits from mining concessions they had rented from the Asante. As the remaining non-exiled Asante leaders faffed about, unable to decide what to do, Yaa Asantewaa had words for them:

> I must say this, if you the men of Asante will not go forward, then we will. We the women will. I shall call upon my fellow women. We will fight the white men. We will fight till the last of us falls in the battlefields.

The men were like, 'Oh shit,' and so Yaa Asantewaa became the leader of the war effort. It's not known if she fought alongside their troops, or directed them like a general, but she led them one way or another throughout nearly two years of fighting. She masterminded deception techniques such as pulling strings through brush so that the British would waste their bullets on empty thickets, and strung up bells and bottles in the trees in order to hear them coming. The Asante and the British had fought many wars throughout the 19th century, but this would be their last.

The Asante had the British forces cornered, laying siege to the British fort and cutting off food and supplies – but along came more pink-pricked reinforcements to break through the blockade. It's rumoured that when she was captured, Yaa Asantewaa spat in the face of a commanding officer. She and more than 50 of her lieutenants and advisers were then exiled to the Seychelles, where she died in 1921. She has since become a national hero to Ghanaians and a symbol across Africa of resistance and leadership.

# 65

# Jind Kaur
## 1817–1863

Jind Kaur became the ruler of the Sikh Empire of Punjab, which is now mostly in Pakistan, in 1839. When her husband the Maharaja died (RIP), she became the regent for her young son, Duleep Singh, who would grow up to be dreamy. Before that, however, mother and son would have to deal with those tea-drinking, whimsical flying-umbrella-nannying, quaint little bloodthirsty murderers, the British.

The death of the Maharaja was seen by the British as an opportunity to finally stick their greedy, pink, stubby little fingers into the Punjab and annex it. They found an obstacle to their greedy pink finger plans, however, in the shape of Jind Kaur, who would defend the sovereignty of the Punjab through two Anglo-Sikh wars in 1845–6 and 1848–9. Unable to easily rid themselves of Jind Kaur, the British desperately tried to smear her reputation, saying she had a string of affairs with her ministers and calling her the 'Messalina of the Punjab'. Messalina was a Roman empress who had *also* had her reputation smeared by allegations of sexual impropriety. Whether or not such rumours are true, we can confidently assume that those who spread them, both in the past and now, are lonely virgins.

Jind Kaur was only in her early 20s when she led her forces into battle with the British, doing away with conventions concerning the proper behaviour of a woman of her station and instead holding court and giving counsel to her ministers and generals. When the

British at last defeated her, they separated her from her son and sent him to England aged nine. They saw the pair as a threat to the legitimacy of British rule, which is a funny thing to worry about, since there was none to begin with. But you know, nine-year-olds can be very scary.

As for Jind Kaur, she was imprisoned in a number of forts until one day when she disguised herself as a servant and fled. She travelled across 800 miles of forest, and upon finding safety in Kathmandu, Nepal, wrote the British a letter saying that she had escaped by magic. Her son, who had received such a gentlemanly education in England that he was in correspondence with Queen Victoria, eventually arranged for their reunion more than 13 years after their separation. She joined him in London, and died far from her home in 1863. See, with any story involving the British Empire, the story ends with sadness and dispossession. But oh, don't the British just have such cute accents, aren't they all so gentlemanly!

# 66

# Lozen

### 1840–1889

As a Native American woman living in the late 19th century at a time when United States troops were rounding up tribes, evicting them from their land, and incarcerating them in crowded reservations far from their homes, Lozen faced an undue level of fuckery in her life.

Lozen was born in 1840, a member of the Warm Springs band of the Apache people who lived in the area covering south-west New Mexico, south-east Arizona, the north-western bit of Texas and the Mexican borderlands.

The Apache believe that each person is granted a unique set of powers from their supreme deity, Ussen. In Lozen's day, Apache girls and boys alike underwent intense physical training and when Lozen came of age, she uncovered her own special powers that were to make her well suited to battle: a power over horses, a power to heal wounds and most importantly, the power to detect the direction and distance of enemies. This was divined by performing a special ritual in which she held out her arms, turned in a circle, sang a prayer and interpreted the tingling of her hands. And so, instead of getting married and settling into a domestic role, she became a warrior.

For the Warm Springs Apache, enemies were everywhere. Despite efforts on the part of native people to make peace, clashes with Mexicans and the US army increased, heightened by the growing population of prospectors searching for gold. When the US took territory from Mexico, they set about moving native peoples to a small number of reservations in order to take their valuable lands – paying no attention to the tribe or where they were from or how they lived.

In another classic white-people move, the US government would sign treaties with different tribes only to screw them over later. In 1870, the Warm Springs Apache had agreed to live on a reservation within their traditional lands in south-west New Mexico, Ojo Caliente – but in 1875, the US government wanted to concentrate all the tribes of the region on the San Carlos reservation, described by one Apache as 'the worst place in all the great territory stolen from the Apaches'. Its landscape was barren of grass and game, the river water brackish, and the whole place infested with insects, rattlesnakes, and malaria.

By 1877, Lozen's band had had enough, and wanted to move back to Ojo Caliente. Continually pursued by the US army, in 1879 they fled to the mountains, following their leader and Lozen's brother, Victorio, to a life of freedom. Constantly on the move to avoid the authorities, they carried out raids for horses, food, and ammunition. When it came to stealing horses, no one was better than Lozen. As one member of her band, James Kaywaykla, remembered it, she was an 'expert at roping', and 'no man in the tribe was more skilful in stealing horses or stampeding a herd than she'.

That's not all she could do. According to Kaywaykla, Lozen could 'ride, shoot, and fight like a man' and likely 'had more ability in planning military strategy than did Victorio.' She was the only woman who sat on war councils, and was highly respected by other warriors who saw her as their equal and by her extended tribe who followed her fearless lead.

Native Americans weren't allowed to leave their reservations, which is a pretty ass-backwards rule, if you think about it for even a half a second and you aren't a racist. So in 1879 Lozen's band fled under the cover of night. They found themselves trapped at a river, and seeing the women and children fearful to cross the rapids, Lozen led by example, driving her horse straight into the water, holding her rifle over her head, and swimming across to the other side. They followed her, and after Lozen rescued one horse and rider who had run into trouble, she told the women and children, 'I must return to the warriors.'

Lozen and her brother were an indomitable pair: he as chief, she guiding military strategy with her intuition and power to detect enemies, and both skilled in battle. With their powers combined, their band of about 60 warriors and their families managed to evade thousands of US army soldiers.

In September 1880, Lozen had to separate from Victorio and their band because one of their number was about to give birth. Luckily for the expectant mother, Lozen was the kind of protector whose skills ranged from delivering a baby, to seeking food and water, to murdering a soldier should the occasion call for it. And, of course, she could steal horses.

Separated from their tribe and with the US army in pursuit, Lozen, the young woman, and her newborn baby survived for weeks on the run. Lozen couldn't use her gun without attracting attention, so killed a longhorn cattle using only her knife, which is NOT AN EASY TASK, given the longhorn's, well, long horns. She used the longhorn for dried meat to last them a long journey across the desert; took its stomach for water, and its hide to make a bridle.

Then, by the Rio Grande, she observed a Mexican camp and one night swam across the river, waited for a guard to turn his back from his horses, cut a huge, strong horse free, casually leapt onto its back and rode it straight into the river, dodging gunfire as they swam back to safety. In the weeks it took to get back to the reservation where the mother and her baby needed to be, Lozen would steal a second horse for good measure. Listen, if you're not going to guard your horses properly, what else should you expect? Oh, she also killed a soldier and took his supplies. RIP.

When Lozen finally made it back, she heard the devastating news that Victorio had been killed. His band had crossed the border to Mexico but were pursued by US soldiers thanks to a new treaty between the nations, and were finally ambushed. Lozen was filled with regret. She believed that if she had been with them, they might have survived.

When Lozen was reunited with the band, the Warm Springs chief Nana said that 'Victorio died as he lived, free and unconquerable.'

'We are not to mourn for him,' Nana said. 'He has been spared the ignominy of imprisonment and slavery and for that I will give thanks to Ussen. His courage is to be the inspiration of those left to carry on our race and fortunately there are enough women and children that our People might increase. It is for us to rally and carry on the struggle.'

The struggle, though, would only get worse. The rest of Lozen's Apache band – even those who had stayed on reservations as commanded, and even those who had served as scouts for the US army – were rounded up and sent as prisoners to military forts in Florida, where many died from heat, humidity, and disease. The Apache wars were over. They were then moved on to Alabama, and from there were given their 'freedom' in Oklahoma. Some chose to return to New Mexico and their ancestral lands. Lozen would only make it as far as Alabama before dying of tuberculosis.

So remember Lozen the next time you hear that all-American

phrase, 'Liberty, freedom, and justice for all.' Not just for the way she died, a prisoner of the US government, but for the way Kaywaykla remembered her, 'a magnificent woman on a beautiful black horse,' fighting and staying free for as long as she could.

# 67

# Funmilayo Ransome-Kuti
1900–1978

*I* hope you're ready to welcome some excellence into your life, because it's time to talk about the Nigerian nationalist and women's rights activist Funmilayo Ransome-Kuti.

Taxes, as everyone knows, are boring. But women's tax revolts, it turns out, are anything but. Especially if we're talking about the Abeokuta women's tax revolt of 1947–48, which we most certainly are. Abeokuta is now a Nigerian city and the capital of Ògùn state, but was once more of a city-state, located in south-west Nigeria in Egbaland.

Not to oversell this tax revolt, but it was a completely fabulous historical event. It had everything. Cooperation among ladies of different social classes? Tick. Abusive songs? Absolutely. A lasting legacy of women uniting for common political goals? Yup. Old ladies taking their tops off? Indeed.

So what was this tax revolt about? Well, like many things, this one can trace its origins to that great wank stain upon the pants of history, the British Empire. You know, that empire that makes old English people say 'When I was a boy, things were different,' before boiling some potatoes to have cold later, and voting Brexit. That empire.

In the 1940s, that empire was at war. The British turned to their West African colonies for resources after the fall of its Far Eastern ones in 1942 to Axis powers. The Nigerian colonial government began to intervene heavily in the economy, taking steps like banning exports to Germany, setting quotas, and purchasing rice at below market prices – or just confiscating it.

These policies wreaked extra havoc upon market women, who obviously wanted to sell their rice at a good price and not have it confiscated by colonial officials. Market women were subjected to special taxes, rents, and fines, and faced lots of idiotic and terrible behaviour from tax collectors. For example, some tax collectors believed they could judge if girls were 15 and therefore old enough to be taxed by stripping them and looking at their breasts. I would try and explain the logic of these assholes to you, but I fear it would do irreparable damage to both of our brains.

In fact, the market women were facing three sets of puckered assholes: the tax collecting types, colonial officials, and the Alake Ademola II, the king of Abeokuta, who was basically a puppet of the colonial government. These assholes were all closely linked in their twattery. The Sole Native Authority, aka the British, gave the Alake arbitrary powers which he wielded with impunity. In setting things up this way, the British gave themselves plausible deniability whenever things went wrong. 'Oh, it's not us doing terrible things!' they could say, while brushing their teeth with sausage meat. 'It's the Alake!'

Enter Funmilayo Ransome-Kuti, who was not a market woman, and certainly not a twat, but rather a fancy lady. She was president of the Abeokuta Ladies' Club, a club of other fancy ladies who met to discuss fancy lady activities and concerns.

Seeing the injustice faced by the market women, and after personally intervening in defence of rice sellers, Ransome-Kuti encouraged her fancy ladies' club to start meeting with the market women and to widen their interests to include social justice issues like women's literacy and better education for children. The new, bigger group of women decided to form the Abeokuta Women's Union, with Ransome-Kuti elected president. The group's founding document clearly stated that 'no member of the Union should think herself better than others, all must move freely and happily.' This meant that the fancy ladies shouldn't dress too fancy for meetings, and shouldn't be snobs about the market women, who were very well organised as it was. The group, once united, quickly became a force to be reckoned with vis-à-vis all the assholes.

Things came to a head in 1947, when the women started camping out in front of the Alake's kingly compound to demonstrate against higher taxes, singing abusive songs at him.

Let us now enjoy the words to one such abusive song – which are remembered, by the way, in the memoirs of the great Nigerian playwright and poet Wole Soyinka, who was a young lad at the time, and doubtlessly learned a lot from the protesting women:

> *O you men, vagina's head will seek vengeance;*
> *You men, vagina's head shall seek vengeance*
> *Even if it is one penny. If it is only a penny*
> *Ademola, we are not paying tax in Egbaland*
> *If even it is one penny.*

Now please look upon the following emoji:

💯

The AWU's protest against the Alake's taxes and abuses would last a full nine months. When a woman was arrested, others would turn up at the jail and protest there as well. They'd close the markets altogether in a display of their united power. They organised food and water deliveries so that women could stay put outside the palace, trapping the Alake inside. They were joined by some supportive men (#notallmen) and pretty much brought the whole town to a standstill. They signed petitions and wrote letters to the press dragging the Alake's name. There was not much he could do, it turned out, when faced with so many well-organised vaginas seeking vengeance.

At one point, an angry council member came out and yelled probably the most ill-advised thing you could ever yell at a group of jubilant, protesting women: 'Go home and mind your kitchens and feed your children. What do you know about the running of state affairs? Not pay tax indeed! What you need is a good kick on your idle rumps.'

Well then. What do you think happened next? Soyinka describes the scene that followed: 'The women stripped his fellow council members down to their shorts and used the men's chiefly regalia to beat them.'

Let's throw in a few more of these bad boys:

💯 💯 💯 💯 💯 💯 💯

What happened then, however, was the most 100 moment of all. The older women of the group started to strip off, and hang out in front of the palace, nearly or completely naked, just chilling. At this point, the Alake lost the support of his council. He gave the fuck up, friends. He couldn't take it any more. He couldn't deal with the songs and the bad press and all the naked old ladies trapping him inside.

He left the compound on 29 July 1948 and went into exile. Not only that, but the protest forced the colonial government to abolish taxes on the women, at least temporarily. It just goes to show, girls, that with enough good pals, a bit of organisation, and a naked grandmother or two, you can do anything.

By the end of the protest, Funmilayo was pretty famous throughout the land. And what a fabulous thing to be famous for. We should all want to be famous for something exactly like this. Her role as a leading activist was cemented, and the success of the AWU led to the foundation of the Nigerian Women's Union, because if one town's women can get together and cause that much mayhem, what can a whole country's women do?

Ransome-Kuti ended up being one of the few women at the top of Nigerian nationalist politics, and agitated for independence from Britain. She advocated for women's right to vote, and was the first woman in Nigeria to drive a car. She wrote that 'no country can rise against its womenfolk,' and that women 'should be conscious of their womanhood and set a value on it, for only in this way will they be able to free themselves from intimidation and terrorism.'

When she saw that nationalist parties in Nigeria did not support women (yet wanted their votes), she started her own party, the Commoner People's Party. She and her hubby founded multiple students' and teachers' unions, and worked their whole lives in the name of trade unionism, nationalism, and anti-colonialism.

She also raised a family of activist and musician sons – including Fela Kuti – and had more famous musicians among her grandsons, Femi Kuti and Seun Kuti. In his 1981 song 'Coffin for Head of State' Fela commemorated his mother's death following a brutal raid on their compound in 1977. She died the next year from injuries after being thrown from a high window by soldiers. After her tragic death, Funmilayo's family carried on her legacy of activism and political agitation.

# 68

# Queen Liliuokalani

1838–1917

*I* am sorry to have to be the one to inform you that this is another tale of terrible white men being terribly terrible. We can't seem to escape them on this journey around the world. Even worse, it's *businessmen*. How dearly I would have liked to ban them from these pages, but alas, here we are again. Men have a way of making everything about themselves.

White people came to Hawaii in the late 18th century, beginning with the fabled Captain James Cook, who was promptly killed for attempting to kidnap the head Hawaiian chief in retaliation for a stolen boat (RIP). I don't know why he thought this would work out just fine, but anyway, there's a famous painting of the whole sorry incident for you to admire entitled *Death of Captain Cook*. The first missionaries arrived in the 1820s, led by one Hiram Bingham I. Remember Hiram Bingham III, who raced Annie Smith Peck to the tops of mountains? This guy was his grandfather.

Fast-forward 70 years, and a continued stream of European missionaries and sugar growers had made their way to the islands and decided that they were very clever and good and therefore should be in charge. They created the Hawaiian League and forced the Hawaiian King Kalakaua to sign a new constitution which would limit his powers, and disenfranchise the Asian and native Hawaiian residents of the islands by way of land ownership and literacy requirements. Only 3% of the population ended up with the ability to vote and stand for office – all of them fancy white educated clever men who were good and noble and therefore allowed to be bastards, because, I dunno, they think they look the most like God. The constitution came to be known as the Bayonet Constitution, and it perfectly paired the colonial penchant for violence with its interest in rules and the illusion of legitimacy. 'Well it says right here, in the thing that we wrote to give ourselves power, that we have all the power. You can't argue with that logic!'

Kalakaua died in 1891 and was succeeded by his sister, Liliuokalani. She was a gifted composer and musician, and would be the last Queen of Hawaii, ending a monarchy begun with the unification of the islands in 1795. Hoping to undo the shittiness of the Bayonet Constitution, Liliuokalani proposed restoring her powers and extending the franchise to native Hawaiians. Horrified at the thought, a group of 13 white businessmen created the Committee of Safety, and by 'safety' they meant 'organise a coup to remove the queen by military force.' Another example of old white men clinging to their safe spaces like the special snowflakes they are.

The aim of the men was to achieve annexation to the United States. However the president at the time, Grover Cleveland, known for serving two non-consecutive presidential terms and also for having a pudding instead of a face, ordered the men to restore the Queen to power and chill the fuck out.

In 1895, Hawaiians attempted a counter-coup to restore the Queen, but it failed and 100 men and the Queen herself were all arrested. The government of the newly declared Republic of Hawaii implemented martial law and accused the plotters of treason. You know, treason against the state they just invented by overthrowing the former one. Yes, it is all perfectly logical in the timeless manner of logical white colonisers. The government, under one Sanford Dole, who had a long, forked beard that you have to see to believe and was related to the Doles of banana fame, found everyone guilty and sentenced some to death.

The Queen was presented with a document of formal abdication and told if she would sign it that the lives of the men on trial would be spared. She signed, hoping to spare their lives, but, surprise! They carried on with the trials and the death sentences – though amid international outcry they would later be commuted. As for the Queen, they had found guns and bombs buried under her flowerbeds, and found her guilty of treason as well. It's like if I suddenly invented a state, the Republic of Memes, and found the Queen of England guilty of treason for not being into it. Or if I walked into your house and said, 'I declare this house mine,' and then called the police to come arrest you for breaking into your own house.

After a period of house arrest, Liliuokalani went to DC to petition the White House against annexation to the United States – but in 1898, Hawaii became a US territory. She continued to work trying to win back compensation and land from the government, and was eventually given a small pension. She continued to make public appearances until her death in 1917 at the age of 79. In 1959, Hawaii became the 50th and last state of the

United States, at least until it claims the moon once and for all. It wouldn't be until 1993, nearly a hundred years after the fact, that Congress apologised for the overthrow of the Hawaiian monarchy.

# 69

# Fanny Cochrane Smith

1834–1905

We are inhabitants of a time in which we take careful photographs and written records of every above-average lunch we have ever eaten, so that our grandchildren will not be denied these precious memories of their forebears. For the Aboriginal people of Tasmania, Australia, however, nearly every memory of their heritage was wiped out when British colonisers arrived in 1803 and brought along with them their trademark gifts of disease, deportation, displacement, massacres and broken promises. The British have always been so quaint and charming!

When the Aboriginal woman Fanny Cochrane Smith spoke into the large brass trumpet of an Edison phonograph between 1899 and 1903, she would record and preserve the oral history, traditional songs, language, and artistic legacy of her people. She called herself 'the last Tasmanian Aboriginal', which she was not, however she was among the last to fluently speak a native Tasmanian language, of which there were at least nine, and to remember the songs from before the time of white fuckery.

Fanny was born in 1834 on Flinders Island, in a settlement where survivors of disease and fighting on the main island of Tasmania had been sent to live in even worse conditions. As a child, she moved to Hobart and was trained in European settler institutions to become a domestic servant for appalling and abusive employers. When Aboriginal survivors were moved once again to Oyster Cove, Fanny went too and there married an Englishman who had been sent to Australia for stealing a donkey, which as far as British crimes go is pretty tame. The family lived off timber and ran a boarding house, and converted to Methodism. Fanny would cook traditional Aboriginal food and sing traditional Aboriginal music at Methodist functions, and became known for her witty hosting.

Fanny was in her 70s when the phonograph recordings were made on wax cylinders engraved with tracks, like a vinyl record, which are so delicate that every time you play them they break down a little more, much like me. Because of this, they have only been played between six and ten times, but have since been trans-ferred to more modern equipment so that they can be heard now, 120 years later. Their sound quality is poor, but clear enough if you consider the scope of history that has passed between Fanny uttering those words, her *own* words, and us listening to them today. They are considered the first recorded oral history, in sound, of an Aboriginal person recounting their own stories – and the oldest recording of an Aboriginal language. The original wax cylin-ders still exist at the Tasmanian Museum and Art Gallery, a rare example of an indigenous person getting to speak for herself, and still speaking for herself 120 years later.

# 70

# Lillian Ngoyi

1911–1980

South African apartheid was one of the most extreme examples of white idiocy and violence ever to grace this good green earth, and Lillian Ngoyi was one of the many incredible women who fought to end it. If you're not familiar with the word, 'apartheid' was the official state segregation policy that governed South Africa from 1948 until the early 1990s – yes, that recent – instituted by ever more fucked-up laws passed by the country's white government. South Africans were divided into four racial groups – you could be 'black' or 'white' or 'coloured' or 'Indian', and your classification determined everything from whom you could marry and where you could live to whether or not you were even a South African citizen – by the 1960s only white South Africans were allowed to vote.

It's incredible to think about the sheer *effort* required to maintain the apartheid system; the time and money and bureaucracy it took to prop up a segregated society when it probably would have been much easier to just not be fucking racist. But, well, some people adore their deep, long, historical, political and economic commitments to being racists and will go to great lengths to preserve their own destructive ignorance. Meanwhile, the US and Britain happily continued to defend, support and sell arms to the apartheid government right until the bitter end, because they are freedom-loving and enlightened western countries who know what's best for the world.

Lillian Ngoyi was born in 1911 to an extremely poor family in the capital city of Pretoria. Her father was a mine worker who died when she was young, and her mother worked in the households of white families at various domestic tasks. One of Lillian's earliest and most affecting memories was of a time when she and her brother went to deliver laundry to the house of one of her mother's white clients, and were not allowed inside – but a dog was.

After she left school, Lillian married, and worked as a trainee nurse in Johannesburg until her husband died and apartheid laws forced the uprooting of black South Africans from city suburbs and into crowded segregated 'townships' away from the cities. She ended up in Soweto, which would be the site of some of the most important uprisings in the fight against apartheid.

Lillian got a job as a seamstress, joined the Garment Workers' Union, and soon became a labour organiser among the women in her industry. In 1950, she joined the African National Congress, or ANC, now the ruling party of South Africa but which began as a resistance movement in the early 20th century. One of the many fucked-up features of apartheid were the 'pass laws' which required black South African men to carry internal passports with them in order to prove their reasons for entering white areas of the country. In the 1950s, as the government intended to extend the pass laws to women as well as men, the ANC organised the Defiance Campaign against these laws. Between June and October 1952, 8,000 people were arrested for protesting the pass laws – and hundreds were killed when police officers opened fire at a protest that came to be known as the Sharpeville Massacre.

Lillian took part in these actions, purposefully using the 'white facilities' of a post office in an act of civil disobedience. She was arrested, but quickly rose up through the ranks of the ANC as a gifted leader and public speaker. Within a year of joining, she became the first woman elected to the national executive committee, and went on to lead the Federation of South African Women. In 1956, Lillian and others led a march of over 20,000 women to the offices of the Prime Minister to deliver a petition with over 100,000 signatures against the proposed pass laws for women. It was the largest protest that South Africa had ever seen, and it was Lillian who would rap on the door of prime minister Johannes Geradus Strijdom, who was a real bastard on the scale of great bastards of history, to deliver the petitions.

In her 1966 memoir *Tomorrow's Sun*, the anti-apartheid activist Helen Joseph recalls how, after handing over the petition, Lillian led 30 minutes of solid silence at the head of the 20,000 person-strong crowd, in response to a government law forbidding speeches at rallies:

> As we stepped on that rostrum again and faced them, our hands empty now, those thousands of women rose spontaneously to their feet, lifting their hands in the Congress salute . . .Thirty minutes, and still the arms were raised. Lillian began to sing.

At an ANC women's conference in 1956, Lillian gave an incredible speech issuing a warning to Prime Minister Strijdom directly:

> Strijdom! Your government now preach and practice colour discrimination. It can pass the most cruel and barbaric laws, it can deport leaders and break homes and families, but it will never stop the women of Africa in their forward march to freedom during our lifetime. To you daughters of Africa I say, Praise the name of women; praise them.

Lillian died in 1980, and so did not live to see the dismantling of apartheid, which was brought about by an international protest movement to boycott the South African regime, in tandem with the daring activism of men and women like her. Among the many lessons to take from this struggle, here are two: never assume that just because something is the law, that it is right, or worth respecting. And secondly, the next time someone asks you with an air of false and cynical knowingness, 'What have protests ever achieved?' banish them from your life.

# 71

# Miriam Makeba

## 1932–2008

*I*f you've heard just one of South African singer Miriam Makeba's songs, it's probably her greatest hit, 'Pata Pata', which was released in 1967. 'It's a song with no meaning at all,' she once explained to an interviewer, laughing. 'Because it's about a dance. A dance called Pata Pata . . . I would have preferred another song to be popular than "Pata Pata". But people choose what they want.'

Miriam's music was in fact so much more meaningful than the fun hit 'Pata Pata' that it was considered dangerous by the apartheid South African regime and banned, and Miriam was forced to spend most of her life in exile from her home country.

Miriam was born in 1932 in Johannesburg. Her father died when she was young and she had to get a job as a domestic servant, while her mother worked for a white family and was forced to live far from her own children. Miriam's beginnings were rough, as she dealt with the most depressing trifecta of apartheid, an awful husband, and breast cancer, but her talent as a singer would lead her to a life of international celebrity.

Miriam's big break came in the 1950s when she sang with several bands including the all-woman group The Skylarks. She gained international recognition when she performed two songs in the 1959 anti-apartheid film *Come Back, Africa*, which had to be filmed in secret and was smuggled out of the country by the filmmaker, Lionel Rogosin. Though black artists were not allowed to travel from South Africa, Lionel bribed some officials to allow him to bring Miriam to the film's premiere at the 1960 Venice film festival. The film shot Miriam to fame. She embarked on a tour across Europe and America, and moved to New York where she was taken under the wing of the singer Harry Belafonte.

Her music combined American jazz with South African styles, and was a huge hit. Miriam sang about love and heartbreak, but she also sang about the brutal reality of being a black South African. She had a wide smile and was completely glamorous, and she sang with a clear and heart-stopping voice that trembled with a delicate vibrato to convey the deep emotion of her songs. Things were going well for her career when Miriam heard that her mother had died. She wanted to return to South Africa to attend the funeral but discovered that the apartheid government had revoked her passport and she couldn't go back. The exile lasted for decades, as she painfully recounted it to the author Hank Bordowitz:

> I always wanted to leave home. I never knew they were going to stop me from coming back. Maybe, if I knew, I never would have left. It is kind of painful to be away from everything that you've ever known. Nobody will know the pain of exile until you are in exile. No matter where you go, there are times when people show you kindness and love, and there are times when they make you

know that you are with them but not of them. That's when it hurts.

In New York, Miriam's star continued to rise, as she met some of the biggest musical American celebrities of the day such as Louis Armstrong, Marlon Brando, Sidney Poitier and Ray Charles. Since her exile, she began to take a more political stance in her work, though that is not how she would phrase it. 'I do not sing politics,' she said. 'I merely sing the truth.' While she lived in America, she also criticised segregation there, relating it to her struggle back home. 'There wasn't much difference in America,' she said. 'It was a country that had abolished slavery but there was apartheid in its own way.' When an interviewer asked her to compare the two countries, she explained that 'the only difference between South Africa and America is very slight. South Africa admits that they are what they are.'

In the 1960s Miriam testified several times at the United Nations about the reality of South African apartheid. She spoke about the Sharpeville massacre of 1960, in which police opened fire on thousands of anti-apartheid protestors. She decried mass imprisonment of activists such as Lillian Ngoyi and Nelson Mandela and said that 'My country has been turned into a huge prison.' She told the UN that South Africa should be put under economic sanctions and an arms embargo. For this, South Africa revoked her citizenship altogether, leaving her stateless. By this point, though, she was an international celebrity, and was offered passports and honorary citizenships all over the world.

The United States government didn't think of her so fondly. In 1968 Miriam married the leader of the Black Panthers, Stokely Carmichael, alienating those white audiences who had enjoyed her music but apparently weren't fans of her anti-racist politics. Her white audiences turned their backs on her, radio stations stopped playing her music, and the US government began spying on her. When she and her husband were out of the country, she was once again banned from returning, this time to the United States, who had revoked her visa. The couple moved to Guinea instead, and remained there for 15 years.

Exiled first by South Africa and then by the US, Miriam went on tour with her band across Europe and Africa and grew ever more famous, and ever more critical of both countries. The US began censoring the political aspects of her concerts shown on television, and her music in South Africa remained banned. The more the US and South Africa tried to diminish Miriam, the more outspoken she became in her criticisms and activism, and the more popular her music became around the world. She became known as 'Mama Africa'.

As the apartheid system began to be dismantled, Miriam was finally able to return to South Africa in 1990, a few months after Nelson Mandela was released from prison. The first place she visited was her mother's grave, where she could finally sit and grieve with her after so many decades.

Miriam carried on performing and singing all the way until her death in 2008, when she collapsed shortly after a joyful performance in Italy, aged 76. Mandela described the impact she had had on black South Africans living under the oppression of apartheid, saying that 'her music inspired a powerful sense of hope in all of us'. It turns out you can't ban someone's music from your country. People will find a way to listen to the songs that their government doesn't want them to hear – especially when they are as beautiful as Miriam Makeba's.

# 72

# Te Puea Herangi
### 1883–1952

For those who find it hard to coordinate a night out with your friends via the group Whatsapp, the story of Te Puea Herangi will be an especially humbling study in what it takes to be a true leader.

Te Puea was born in 1883 in the Waikato region of New Zealand's North Island. She was a leader in the King movement, or Kingitanga, which sought in the 1850s to unite certain Maori tribes in the North Island under a single king. In the face of land confiscations by European settlers of New Zealand, known in the Maori language as *Pakeha*, the Kingitanga provided a way for Maori peoples of the Waikato region to organise and preserve their autonomy and their land.

Though she never held the kingship, or a formal role in New Zealand's parliamentary government, none would do more in the first half of the 20th century to fight for the Kingitanga, the Waikato, or Maori rights in general than Te Puea did in her lifetime.

Even as a child, Te Puea had a commanding presence and displayed uncommon intelligence. When her mother died in 1898, she was recalled from school to come home and take up a bigger role in her community. When her older sister moved away from the region, Te Puea found herself the effective head of her tribe.

Still just a teenager, Te Puea suffered from chronic tuberculosis and did not expect to live a long life. Believing her time to be limited, she spent her teenage years enjoying herself, smoking and drinking and having plenty of sex. She was incredibly beautiful as well as bold and charming, and it was said that she could merely point at any man at a *hui*, a Maori meeting or social gathering, and he would be all hers. (In later years, Te Puea would devote herself to keeping young Maori on the straight and narrow, hoping they'd avoid the same excesses of her youth.)

As she began to mature, Te Puea turned her seemingly limitless energy to organising, leading, and bettering the lot of Waikato people.

Te Puea believed in cooperation among Maori tribes and was fiercely loyal to her people and the kings whose reigns she lived under. She herself was the granddaughter of one king, Tawhiao Te Wherowhero, and the niece of another, Mahuta. In 1913, a smallpox outbreak devastated Maori populations, who were more susceptible to the *Pakeha* disease and unable to receive treatment from hospitals that did not allow access to Maori people. Te Puea responded by setting up open-air hospitals to nurse the sick people herself.

At the outbreak of World War I, she would face an incredible test of leadership when the New Zealand government tried to impose conscription on the Maori of the Waikato, as British colonial administrations would on native peoples throughout the empire. While some Maori politicians believed their people should serve and so prove that Maori fighters were equal to their European counterparts, Te Puea was a firm pacifist, and what's more, did not see it as just or right that her people should have to offer up their lives for a colonial power that had broken its promises to them and taken their land. 'They tell us to fight for king and country,' she said. 'Well, that's all right. We've got a king. But we haven't got a country. That's been taken off us. Let them give us back our land and then maybe we'll think about it again.'

Angry that Waikato tribes refused to serve, the government

implemented mandatory conscription on Maori in 1917 – but only enforced it in the Waikato. Waikato men between the ages of 17 and 30 faced arrest if they did not comply. Te Puea invited these men to join her, and promised to shelter them. 'If we die,' she said, 'let us all die together.'

When the police came to try and enforce conscription on the group of men, she told them, 'I will not agree to my children going to shed blood.' The police took her youngest brother, who was only 16, but throughout the encounter the Maori remained passive and non-violent. So passive, in fact, that one very large man proved a bit of a challenge for the police: 'One of them was enormously fat,' Te Puea recorded. 'He just lay on the ground. The police had much difficulty in carrying him to the motor car. Of course no one would help them. We had to laugh, despite our tears.'

These men were detained, and subjected to what the officials called 'dietary punishments' – being given such small amounts of bread and water as to try to break their spirits. But they remained strong in detention, and Te Puea would come to sit outside the prison to join them.

Unable to break the solidarity of Waikato, the government tried another tack: implying that Te Puea's pacifism was in fact due to her being of German extraction and loyal to the Germans in the war. (Her grandfather, whom she never knew, had a German surname but was in fact English.) She replied to the smears in style: 'What if I am German? So is the British Royal Family. In fact I am neither pro-German nor anti-British. I am simply pro-Maori.' After the war ended in 1919, all of the Maori prisoners were quietly released from detention.

Her leadership in the face of the conscription struggle shot Te Puea to ever-widening fame. Te Puea led by example and never cared what people thought about her getting her hands dirty. She once again nursed people through the devastating Spanish Flu epidemic, and adopted many orphans. If manual labour was ever needed, she would simply begin the work herself and others would follow. When many years later she was awarded a CBE for services to the Maori and to New Zealand, she would nearly miss the ceremony because she was busy in the kitchens helping prepare food for the event. She accepted the award while still wearing the slippers she worked in.

Te Puea's community organising would reach more and more Maori tribes and more corners of New Zealand. Faced with flooding in their ancestral home, she led her tribe to relocate to a new village at Turangawaewae, where she would set up a community so well organised that it would come to be a key stopping place for VIP visitors to New Zealand. She began a performing troupe that toured the country to raise money for the community, putting on performances of traditional Maori music and *haka*. As her fame increased, so did the Kingitanga, the King Movement, and the perceived legitimacy of the king – though not all Maori tribes supported the movement. Te Puea became something of a diplomat both to other tribes and to *Pakeha* politicians and even prime ministers, whom she lobbied on behalf of Waikato relentlessly. She revived traditional Maori spiritual practices, and oversaw the construction of important Maori meeting houses and canoes.

In WWII, she remained a pacifist, but adopted the policy that any of her people who desired to enlist would not be stopped from doing so. Meanwhile, she contributed to the war effort in other ways, fundraising for the Red Cross and entertaining American troops stationed in New Zealand with her performing troupe. And year after year, she worked to improve education and health care for Maori people.

At the heart of the struggle of the Waikato people for the decades of Te Puea's life, however, was the unresolved issue of land. 800,000 acres of Maori land had been confiscated in 1864, and Te Puea was central to the fight for reparations of that land. Land reparations were – and remain – a controversial issue.

Te Puea negotiated a deal for monetary reparations, explaining her thinking thus: 'Money can never wipe away the blood that has been shed. No settlement can ever efface the tears that have fallen. And those who suffered most are no longer with us. No, money is not everything. But it means as much to know we have been proved right.' For Te Puea, what mattered more than the money was the government's admission in granting reparations that a historic crime had been committed against her people.

OK, how the hell did she manage all this in a lifetime? And she did it while battling poor health for most of her life. Her entry in the 1951 edition of *Who's Who* may hold the answer: 'Have no recreations. When I am not working I sleep.' And yet she enjoyed life – and not just in her wild teenage years. She loved her community and called all who followed her her children. She was unfailingly honest, loving, and forthright – though very strict about cleanliness, morality, and drinking.

Over 10,000 people came to pay their respects in the week after Te Puea died at age 68 in 1952. Though she is gone, so much of what she created in her lifetime has lasted to the present day. The buildings she built, the movement she shepherded so carefully, and the community she protected and advanced, give credit to her immense life's work.

# 73

# Whina Cooper

1895–1994

*(front left)*

Whina Cooper, the Maori leader known as *Te Whaea o te Motu* or 'Mother of the Nation' in New Zealand, got her start as an organiser at a young age. She was born Whina Te Wake in 1895 in the Hokianga region of the North Island. When she was a teenager a white New Zealander, or *Pakeha*, farmer began to drain 20 hectares of mudflats on Maori land in order to use it for farming. He had obtained the lease to do so from the government, who granted it because the land was not being 'used'. In fact, it was a source of shellfish for the Maori, as well as a perfect place to race horses in the summer when the mudflats dried. And anyway, if the Maori only wanted the mudflats in order to do absolutely nothing with them but go for squidgy walks from time to time, it was their land.

The local Maori met to discuss what to do. Whina's father,

Heremia Te Wake, wanted to find a solution through political lobbying, but the young Whina had an idea that wouldn't take weeks, by which time the mudflats could already be drained. She proposed instead to lead a group of workers down to the mudflats to fill in the drains as the *Pakeha* farmer dug them. She was charming and polite, no matter how pissed off the farmer got, and simply followed him filling in the ditches he'd dug. The farmer was furious, and called the police to arrest them – but Whina's effort had bought enough time for her father to convince the MP to revoke the lease. All the Maori who'd taken part in the protest were summoned to court, except for Whina. After all, what could a teenage girl have had to do with it?

Whina's boldness served her in many ways. At a dance for local young men and women, Whina met the handsome young surveyor Richard Gilbert. After World War I there was a shortage of young men, so Whina acted fast before the other girls could get in there, and asked him to marry her the very next day. He was like, YOLO, I guess, and they did. As Whina remembered it when she was old: 'I beat all the dancers and all the girls wanting to get at him . . .' She borrowed a ring from a shopkeeper to get married the next day. Lean in, Whina!

At the end of the 1920s, when it first became possible for Maori to get loans to develop their lands, Whina led the initiative. When Whina's husband died, though, she took up with one William Cooper, who was already married. It was a huge scandal, and led to her alienation for a time from her very Catholic community.

The 1950s saw a huge migration of Maori from rural areas to the cities of New Zealand. Whina moved to Auckland and was elected the head of the Maori Women's Welfare league, whose goal was to assist those who had moved and support the education and development of women. Whina surveyed slum housing in Auckland to reveal the exploitation of Maori families by *Pakeha* landlords. She worked to encourage breastfeeding and discourage drinking among Maori women in the city, and to improve health care generally. She opened the first urban *marae*, or Maori community centre, carrying on the legacy of the hero of the previous chapter, Te Puea Herangi, with whom she had been close.

Whina cemented her reputation as a fearless but controversial leader in the Maori Land March in 1975 aged 80. Angry at a series of laws that continued to dispossess Maori people of their lands, the decision was made to march from the top of the North Island all the way to its capital, Wellington, on the island's southern tip. The 700-mile journey would protest the huge loss of Maori lands. Out of 66 million acres of land in New Zealand, Maori owned 2.5 million, cut from 4 million ten years before. The march comprised about 5,000 people, led by the stirring sight of Whina, aged 80, with arthritis and a cane which she would wave about while giving speeches to the *marae* along the way.

Whina explained the importance of the march in her biography by Michael King:

For me it was several things going on. I wanted to draw attention to the plight of Maori who were landless. I wanted to point out that people who were landless would eventually be without culture. I wanted to stop any further land passing out of Maori ownership, and I wanted the Crown to give back to Maori land it owned that was of traditional significance to Maori. The march itself was to dramatise these things, to mobilise Maori opinion, to awaken the *Pakeha* conscience. And I agreed to lead it because the great leaders of the past were dead – Carroll, Ngata Buck, Te Puea, Tau Henare, Paraire Paikea. I was the last one that had known all those people. I had gone around with them, watched

273

them, listened to them, and filled up my baskets of knowledge from them. I wanted to put that knowledge to good use.

Whina was accused in her life of being too autocratic, and throughout the march she would kick anybody off who snuck away in the evenings to go drinking – it was meant to be a highly spiritual and symbolic journey. Once they arrived at parliament, Whina led the marchers in a show of unity among Maori tribes, having success-fully turned the national conversation to Maori land loss. At the conclusion of the march, however, younger and more radical marchers began to camp out in front of parliament and demand to see concrete results from the government. Whina, who was more conservative, was non-confrontational – (other than the part where she, well, led a 700-mile march, waving her walking stick at people along the way). This angered some of the marchers, and even more so when she accepted honours from the British government, who eventually made her a dame. Some more radical Maori disrupted that ceremony, believing her to have sold out to the *Pakeha* by accepting their honours.

Nevertheless, it cannot be denied that Whina was a once-in-a-generation community organiser and activist, having personally visited the *marae* of every Maori tribe to wave her walking stick at them and convince them to join the march. She had faced initial resistance from the Maori affairs minister in government, who at first considered the march to be an affront to his representation of the Maori in the New Zealand government. He asked her for a meeting, and she said no because the decision had already been made to march. His secretary then said: 'Very well. We'll close down all the *maraes* on your way,' so that they'd have nowhere to stay along the journey. Whina replied: 'That's all right, as long as the road isn't shut we'll sleep there.' The minister backed down.

Whina even managed to get permission for the marchers to be the first pedestrians to cross the Auckland Harbour Bridge. She became a media sensation and a figurehead for New Zealand as a whole. Along the way, the marchers collected the signatures of Maori leaders and elders across the whole of the island, and carried a stake at the head of the march known as a *pouwhenua*, which is meant to declare the tribal ownership of land. The protestors never allowed the stake to touch the ground along their journey, showing how much land had been lost by Maori.

Right to the very end of her 98-year-long life, Whina wanted to be in charge. When Whina was 87, a reporter wrote that, 'The sound of Whina Cooper's determined voice on the phone can still make a civil servant's heart shrink.' She was relentless, and when she wanted something done it would be done – whether or not others agreed with her. Whina believed that New Zealand should be one nation, Maori and *Pakeha* together, while other Maori wanted (and want) a separate Maori national identity within New Zealand. Her legacy remains a controversial one, but her leadership shaped the conversation for a nation dealing with its colonial legacy.

Perhaps Whina has given us the best way to remember her complicated and divisive history. As she explained to her biographer Michael King, she was '*he wahini riri, he wahine awhina, he wahine aroha* – an angry woman, a supportive woman, a loving woman'.

# 74

# Susan La Flesche Picotte

1865–1915

When Susan La Flesche Picotte was a child, she watched a woman die at the Omaha Reservation in Nebraska when a white doctor refused to treat her because he cared more about being an evil racist than saving a person's life. She decided to become a doctor herself, so that members of her community would not have to depend on the whims of evil racists for medical care.

When she was 14, her dad, the Chief Joseph La Flesche, or Iron Eyes, encouraged her to continue her education as far as possible, which meant leaving the reservation for a while. She went to study at the Hampton Institute in Virginia, a historically black college attended by many Native Americans who were not welcome at white universities, due to the inscrutable fears and superstitions of white people. Susan went on to the Women's Medical College of Pennsylvania, one of the few places women could study medicine at the time, and casually graduated at the top of her class.

She's thought to be the first Native American to receive a medical degree.

Susan returned to Nebraska, where she was the only doctor for nearly 1,300 Omaha people across 1,350 square miles. She ran public health campaigns against drinking and in the prevention of tuberculosis. She worked day and night helping her community in more ways than medicine, intervening in financial and family troubles. She married in 1894 and moved to Bancroft, Nebraska, where she ended up opening a private practice that treated both white people and people of colour, because she wasn't an evil racist. In 1913, she opened a hospital on a reservation in Nebraska.

When her husband died, Susan had to go head to head with the federal government in order to inherit his land. It had gone to a male relation rather than her, because it couldn't possibly be the case that a woman would be competent enough to handle the land of a man. She became an advocate for other Omaha people locked in struggles with the Office of Indian Affairs over land and money owed to them. She wasn't just a doctor, but a leader of the community, and one of those people with a seemingly infinite, glowing orb of energy inside of them – even as she dealt with chronic illness herself. In Susan's lifetime, it was almost unheard of for a woman to carry on working after marriage, and especially after having children, but thankfully, Susan didn't give a fuck about that, and saved a lot of lives because of it.

# 75

# Sojourner Truth

c. 1797–1883

You can find recordings on YouTube of the actress Kerry Washington performing Sojourner Truth's famous 'Ain't I a Woman' speech, made to the Women's Rights Convention in Akron, Ohio in 1851. It is a sublime rendition of this 19th-century abolitionist's witty and cutting speech about the intersections of the anti-slavery and women's rights struggles, punctuated every few lines with the question, 'Ain't I a Woman?'

It's an amazing, theatrical, emotional monologue, which asks over and over whether she, a formerly enslaved black woman, would 'count' as the kind of woman that a supposedly hostile crowd at the women's conference sought to liberate.

So it is frustrating to find out that this speech passed down to us in all its glory is not, in fact, anything like the real speech Sojourner Truth made. In a baffling but not surprising example of dramatic irony, the transcript performed by Washington and others was actually written 12 years later by the white suffragist Frances Dana Gage, who had been the conference's organiser.

And what she did – like a posh white person today enthusiastically singing along to rap – was publish Sojourner's transcript in an invented Southern dialect, (including two invented uses of the n-word). This is the version most people know, and what Kerry Washington bases her performance on. Here's an extract:

> Dat man ober dar say dat women needs to be helped into carriages, and lifted over ditches, and to have de best place eberywhar.
>
> Nobody eber helps me into carriages or ober mud-puddles, or gives me any best place.
>
> And ar'n't I a woman?

In fact, Sojourner was a Northerner from New York. She was born into slavery in 1797, and only spoke Dutch until she was nine. Her accent, if she had one, was Dutch, and in any case she prided herself on her clear English diction. After all, she toured the entire country delivering lectures and debating.

Sojourner gained her freedom in 1826, or rather took it for herself. New York State was set to abolish slavery in 1827, and her owner said he would let her go the year before, but reneged on his promise. So one morning, she took her infant and left at dawn. In the dictated memoirs she published in 1850, *Narrative of Sojourner Truth, A Northern Slave*, she recalled that when her former master came to find her and accused her of running away, she told him, 'No, I did not run away; I walked away by daylight, and all because you had promised me a year of my time.' He demanded she return with him, and she refused.

Once free, she went to court to try and get back one of her children who had been sold to the South – which was illegal at the time. She told her former mistress, 'I have no money, but God has enough, or what's better! And I'll have my child again.' In 1828, she successfully secured the return of her son, and was the first black woman to win a case like this against a white man.

Sojourner gained fame travelling around the country, moved by her religious convictions to preach about abolition, women's rights, prison reform, and against capital punishment. She helped recruit black soldiers to join the Union army in the Civil War, and afterwards worked to resettle formerly enslaved people attempting to start new lives. She lobbied the federal government for seven years to grant land to emancipated people, and even met with President Ulysses S. Grant, but was ultimately unsuccessful.

There is another transcript of Sojourner's barnstorming 'Ain't I a Woman?' speech, from only a few weeks after she gave it, published in collaboration with Sojourner in an anti-slavery newspaper. There are some overlaps between the two versions, but notably the 1851 version is likely much closer to Sojourner's own words, and in any case was published with her approval. A website called The Sojourner Truth Project has compiled readings of this original version of the speech by women with contemporary Afro-Dutch accents, to get a bit closer to Truth's truth. Here is an excerpt:

I have heard much about the sexes being equal; I can carry as much as any man, and can eat as much too, if I can get it.

I am as strong as any man that is now.

As for intellect, all I can say is, if women have a pint and man a quart – why can't she have her little pint full?

You need not be afraid to give us our rights for fear we will take too much, for we can't take more than our pint'll hold.

The poor men seem to be all in confusion, and don't know what to do.

The poor men! It's always a treasure to read sarcasm which works just as well more than 160 years after it was first uttered.

We should refrain from making the misconception about Sojourner's most famous speech another *'actually Frankenstein is the name of the scientist'* stick with which to beat each other. It's just a shame, and an ironic one, that her own words were lost. Everything that was uttered by brilliant people before the technology existed to record sound depends on the foggy memories of witnesses, journalists, and ethically dubious activists. Even the 'Gettysburg Address' speech by Abraham Lincoln, whom Sojourner also met, exists in multiple versions, but I suppose what really matters is the version carved in marble in Washington DC beside a 19-foot-tall statue of the president. (President Lincoln, that is. We haven't yet got a statue of the current president, though it's only a matter of time.)

So listen to both versions of 'Ain't I A Woman', and be inspired by them to get up, go outside, scream at the sky in a righteous fury, and then join an anti-racist activist group or two.

Women who knew how to
have a good-ass time

# 76

# Empress Theodora

c. AD 500–548

*L*et us now marvel at a lady who achieved one of the most impressive glow ups in the thousand-plus-years of history of the Byzantine Empire: Empress Theodora. If you don't know what a glow up is, you're about to find out.

Theodora was born in 500 AD to modest circumstances: her mother was an actress and a dancer, and her father was a bear-keeper for Constantinople's centre of debauchery, the Hippodrome – a job which, though awesome, didn't exactly make them rich. But the Hippodrome was a place for more than bear-related debauchery, and it was there that Theodora and her sisters were put to work as 'entertainers' after the death of their bear-wrangling father. In those times, being an actress was basically the same thing as being a prostitute, though being a prostitute was perhaps less of a *big deal* than it is nowadays.

By the age of 15, Theodora was an acting ~star~ of the Hippodrome. As well as her, er, *private* performances, she would dance for audiences with only a ribbon to cover her lady bits, and was also known for, well . . . Look. I don't know what your average Byzantine gentleman was into, and who are we to judge what got people's rocks off 1,500 years ago? It was a different time. In any case, Theodora *may* have had a fun circus 'act' in which geese pecked food out of her fanny.

It is true? Well, what we know of her is mostly recorded in the various histories of one contemporary historian, Procopius, who may have kind of hated her and her future husband. He said that she had many lovers, all at once, and that she wished she had more sexy bits in order to sex more dudes at the same time. Procopius, who frankly sounds jealous, may have meant to posthumously slander her name, but the joke's on you mate, all of this fun slander just makes us like her more.

After her early teenage years spent in a series of orgies and goose-related sexual performances (you can't libel the dead!), Theodora shacked up with a Syrian official and settled in Alexandria. She'd eventually get dumped, have a religious turn, and then move back to Constantinople in 522.

She came back a reformed, pious woman, and replaced her former line of *entertainment* work with the more low-key occupation of spinning wool, assuring people that, 'NOW I SPIN WOOL, GUYS. MY BAD ABOUT ALL THE STUFF WITH THE GEESE.'

But Theodora's life was only about to get more exciting. See, the place where she spun wool ever so innocently happened to be quite close to the royal palace, where she managed to catch the eye of the emperor-to-be, Justinian, by being like, 'Heyy, I'm just a pious wool spinner . . . with a *sexy past*.' And Justinian was all, 'I'm into it.'

Theodora was, as the Byzantines used to say, well fit. Procopius, in a more generous mood, said that 'painting and poetry' were insufficient to capture her ravishing beauty. Anyone who's cute but looks awkward in photos will relate.

Theodora became Justinian's concubine, as you do. But Justinian was so smitten that he wanted to marry her. Justinian's auntie, the current empress, knew of Theodora's less-than-salubrious past, and needless to say, didn't see her as marriage material. But unfortunately for her, she died, so they married anyway. RIP.

Theodora became empress in 527, and adorned herself with

magnificent dresses, furs, and jewellery. She bedecked herself in purple, visited hot springs and treated herself to luxurious beauty treatments, enjoying the rare gifts that Justinian brought her from across the empire. If officials forgot to kiss her feet, or otherwise failed to treat her with all due respect, they risked exile. It was a long way from spinning wool and, er, *performing*.

Justinian sought Theodora's advice in all stately affairs, and viewed her as an equal. (Shout-out to Justinian, original woke bae <3.) Under their reign, they won loads of wars which reconquered far-flung lands from Vandals and Ostrogoths and health goths and sport goths and skateboarding hooligan types. They rewrote Roman legal codes, some aspects of which survive in civil codes today.

Things were going well across the empire, but there was trouble brewing at home. In order to fund their imperial exploits, Justadora, as we will refer to Justinian and Theodora jointly, raised taxes on the wealthy. And if there's anything the wealthy don't like, it's sharing.

At this point in history, Constantinople was divided into two rival gangs: the 'Blues' (poshos who thought that Christ had a human AND a divine nature) and the 'Greens' (a worker's party who thought Christ had only one nature). The groups had originated from rival Roman chariot racer teams, but by the 500s they were mostly just shouting about Jesus. (Someone really should have asked Jesus about his nature, it would have saved a lot of trouble.)

Theodora was firmly team Blue, as they had helped out her family in the past. But the Blues weren't happy about the raised taxes, and the Greens weren't happy about the general Blue-ness of Justadora, and so everyone decided to riot. Aside from setting things on fire, the angry mob also took it upon itself to say that some dude called Hypatius should be the emperor, and that Justinian, instead of being emperor, should be dead.

Things were looking pretty grim, and Justinian was about ready to get the fuck out of town. But ho! The empress literally stood in his way, and gave him a speech about how not to be a tiny, scaredy baby.

'If you my lord, wish to save your skin,' she proclaimed, 'you will have no difficulty in doing so. We are rich, there is the sea, and there too are our ships. But consider first whether, when you reach safety, you will regret that you did not choose death in preference. As for me, I stand by the ancient saying: the purple is the noblest winding sheet.'

I have no idea what a purple winding sheet is, or why it is noble, however, the speech clearly worked, because Justinian decided to stay and fight it out. He ordered his troops to see off Hypatius, and took out another 30,000 demonstrators for good measure. This indirectly gives Theodora the highest kill count of any woman in this book. (Look, it's called *Nasty Women of History*, not *Nice Fluffy Bunnies of History Who Wouldn't Hurt A Soul*.)

In any case, if it weren't for Theodora's intervention, Justinian would have been surely overthrown – and then we'd all be sorry.

In the rest of the time they ruled together, Justadora completed the Hagia Sophia, a truly top-notch church, which was the largest in the world for nearly a millennium. Theodora also founded a monastery to house 500 women who had ended up in prostitution, and lobbied to reform the law to make it easier for women to bring suits against men, divorce, and own property.

Theodora died at 48 years old. Her life, friends, was a glow up for the ages. Should you ever find yourself fallen on hard times, perhaps sitting beside a lake, looking upon a goose and considering your options – remember Theodora, who rose from the lowliest station to become one of the two most powerful people in an empire at the height of its glory.

# 77

# Wallada bint al–Mustakfi

c. 994–1091

Wallada bint al-Mustakfi had the good fortune to be born to the Caliph Muhammad III of Cordoba in about 994, and the even better fortune for her father to be murdered, thereby inheriting his wealth and gaining total independence.

What would you do with wealth and independence, had you lived in Cordoba at the height of the Muslim conquest of Spain? This was a time and place celebrated for its running water, its gardens, its public baths, its university, its booksellers, its high literacy, and its all-around pleasantness – all during a period when the rest of Europe was thigh-deep in raw sewage, clubbing each other over the heads with sticks.

Well, Wallada did the classy thing: she opened a literary salon. It served as a school for women from all walks of life, from slave to royal, and she invited Jews, Christians, Muslims – and her lovers, naturally – to compete in fierce poetry competitions. She herself was a brilliant poet, and master of ~sensual wordplay~. Which everyone knows is the best type of wordplay. She never married, because who needs a husband when you have a literary salon well stocked with lovers and entertainment?

Speaking of lovers, one man had the good fortune to experience a long and particularly tortuous affair with Wallada. His name was Ibn Zaydun, and he has come to be known as one of the most famous masters of Arabic poetry of all time, because blah blah blah men get to be remembered by history, good for them, isn't that nice.

When times were good between Wallada and Ibn Zaydun, they'd wander the gardens at night, as Wallada wrote:

> *Wait for darkness, then visit me,*
> *for I believe that night is the best keeper of secrets.*
> *I feel a love for you that if the light of heaven felt, the sun*
>     *would not shine,*
> *nor the moon rise, nor the stars begin their nightly journey.*

Why the secrecy, other than the fact that secrets are hot? Well, Ibn Zaydun was a political rival of her family, and he and her dad absolutely hated each other. They probably shared some crushing handshakes.

Anyway, the poetry that made Ibn Zaydun famous was the cry-dicky stuff he wrote out of longing for Wallada after she'd cast him off for cheating on her. It's not known if the cheating took the form of criticising her work, or actually sleeping with someone else – though both are equally bad to a poet, I suppose.

After this incident, the poetry got petty. Ibn Zaydun pleaded to her: 'Remove your mask of anger, so that I may be the first to bow down and worship.'

Wallada replied: 'You are a pansy, a bugger, a fornicator, a cuckold, a swine and a thief. If a phallus could become a palm tree, you would turn into a woodpecker.' Nice.

Wallada eventually pulled the time-old revenge tactic of hooking up with Ibn Zaydun's worst enemy, this guy called Ibn Abdus, whom she'd stay with till she was old. And holy hell, did she live to be old! Wallada was nearly 100 when she died. In the mother-fucking 11th century! Shit.

Anyway, Ibn 'Cry Dick' Zaydun then wrote some insulting poetry about Wallada and Ibn Abdus, who replied by exiling him.

Then he became a Sad Man and wrote a famous love poem about missing her.

The poetic back-and-forth that followed, SOME SAY, was the inspiration for future genres of European romance lyrics, once the Europeans had stopped clubbing each other over the head with sticks for long enough to do a bit of writing. SOME SAY the works of Wallada and Ibn Zaydun, and the work produced in Wallada's salon, laid the literary foundations for works like the *Canterbury Tales*, the *Divine Comedy*, and *Tristan and Iseult*, and the Arthurian tales – particularly since Wallada was of a higher social status than Ibn 'Whiny Fuckboy' Zaydun, a staple theme of later chivalric tales.

Despite Cordoba's openness to literary salons filled with ~sensual wordplay~, there were of course haters who took issue with Wallada's general attitude, comportment, and habit of striding about town giving no fucks. Luckily, those haters have been cast into the dustbin of history, unlike Wallada and her poetic pals.

A hundred years after her death, the Andalusian writer Abu Al-Hasan Ibn Bassam described Wallada's influence on the Cordoban cultural scene. He called her 'a lighthouse in a dark night' and said that, 'The greatest poets and prose writers were anxious to obtain the sweetness of her intimacy, which it was not difficult to attain.'

Listen, readers. One of you is probably very clever. One of you will surely invent time travel in the next fifty years or so. Is it you? Yes. You there. You sitting on the train with the crisps. I can see you. When you have invented time travel, sweet and clever reader, please slide into my DMs and let me know. We can take a little trip to Wallada's literary salon together, listen to some anguished poetry, and take forbidden night walks in gardens with our new Andalusian lovers. Sound like a plan? Good. Now get inventing, please.

Until then, here's one more fact about Wallada before you go. On each sleeve of her robe, Wallada had embroidered a line of poetry. The lines in English differ a bit between translations, but here's the idea:

On one sleeve: 'I am, by God's will, fit for high positions! And I walk with pride along my own road.'

On the other sleeve: 'I let my lover touch my cheek, and gladly bestow my kiss on him who craves it.'

She bestowed those kisses gladly, friends! May you also bestow your kisses gladly, and walk with pride along your own road. And should you encounter a cheating asshole while on your way, just sleep with his political rival, exile him from your life, make fun of him through the medium of ~sensual wordplay~, and live your best life like Wallada did.

# 78

# Nell Gwynn

### 1650–1687

N ell Gwynn was one of the greatest hos of English history, and we should all pay our respects to her for this. She was born in 1650 to a ho mother who ran a house of hos, and then went to work in that great hotbed of hos, the theatre. England had just emerged from two decades of rule by the Puritan non-hos[24] who had won a bloody civil war between supporters of the Parliament hos and the monarchist hos, in which lots of people died, and so

---

24. Absolutely unrelated side note: here are some actual names that Puritans gave their children, as collected by Nell Gwynn's biographer and descendant Charles Beauclerk: Abstinence, Forsaken, Tribulation, Ashes, Lamentation, Fear-not, Weep-not, Kill-sin and Fly-fornication. Imagine it! 'Fly-fornication, if you've finished your prayers you must help Tribulation with his!' These are the people that had such a hard time with witches in the US. Maybe they should have focused their attentions on their incredibly shit names instead. OK side note over.

everybody was ready for a laugh. Nell Gwynn was just the ho that England needed to deliver that laugh. She worked her way up from the lowest rung of the theatre – the orange-selling wenches who had to spar daily with the ho men of the theatre pit – to a bonafide star. From there, she caught the eye of an even greater ho than she, King Charles II, the first king to attend the public theatre. For 17 years Nell became the ho king's favourite ho, and was beloved throughout the land, that land full of hos, England.

The 1660s diarist and confirmed messy bitch who lived for drama, Samuel Pepys, called Nell 'the most impertinent slut', which funnily enough was also my nickname in college. A critic of Charles II, Bishop Burnet, called her 'the indiscreetest and wildest creature that ever was in a Court,' which funnily enough was my other nickname in college. Women of the theatre were basically treated as pieces of meat by the genteel theatre-going hos of the Restoration period, and the actresses were paid less than the men (classic). Some theatres actually paid salaried whores to come and be professional hos for the theatre, to deflect the attentions of horny patrons away from the actresses so that they wouldn't get pregnant and leave.

Before finding her way to the theatre, Nell said she was 'brought up in a bawdy house to fill strong waters to the gentlemen.' I'm not sure what this means but it sounds pretty ho-y. Her rise to the top can't only be explained by the fact that Nell was a 10/10 babe – what really mattered was that she was a wit and a comedian. In all three settings of the bawdy house, the theatre, and the court, Nell set herself apart from all the other hos by being incredibly funny and quick, which is hard to believe, given that everybody knows women can't be funny. As an orange wench, she would have to stand in the pit and yell, 'Oranges! Will you have any oranges?' because apparently people didn't know about delicious crisps back then. They'd also earn tips by passing notes between all the men and women in the audience who loved to come to the theatre to get laid.

With her quick wit and swearing ability in the pit, Nell was the first orange wench to make it as an actress, though she wouldn't be the last. Nell became friends with the renowned playwright of the day, Aphra Behn, who was scandalously a woman and a professional writer. That's right: a GIRL wrote SCRIPTS in the SIXTEEN HUNDREDS. Nobody tell Hollywood that girls can write scripts or they'll get really stressed and confused and we wouldn't want to upset them.

Here's Sam Pepys again, who loved to go backstage because he was a big ho himself, describing what he saw there:

'Nell was dressing herself, and was all unready, and is very pretty, prettier than I thought . . .' But then he goes on: 'But Lord! To see how they were both painted would make a man mad, and did make me loathe them; and what base company of men comes among them, and how lewdly they talk!' And thus Pepys completed the full Tinder fuckboy repertoire of 'Wow ur cute,' to 'God you're such a slut I don't even think you're that good-looking,' to 'Um, I actually prefer girls who don't wear make-up.'

Anyway Charles II was a guitar-playing fucker who had more mistresses than would be possible to list in a book of this size. Charles' main ho before Nell came along was one Barbara Castlemaine, who apparently bit the penis off a dead bishop. Sounds like my ex-wife! But yes, Charles was the ho king, and did his ho-ing not just in his private chambers but out and about in the taverns and even eventually Nell's house, where he would sometimes receive foreign dignitaries. In fact, there's a chance Charles even visited Nell's mother's bawdy ho house. The point is, Charles was a big ho and they were a perfect couple.

The actual queen, Catherine, was never able to have a child, but Charles, the ho that he was, had *lots* of children by his fleet of mistresses, including Nell. She also got a sweet-ass house out of this arrangement. So don't despair, those who say they'll never be able to afford to buy a house in London: be a ho and a wit and everything will work out just fine.

We will end on an extract of a really shit poem that some rando admirer wrote for Nell:

> *She is pretty, and she knows it;*
> *She is witty, and she shows it;*
> *And besides that she's so witty,*
> *And so little and so pretty,*
> *Sh'has a hundred other parts*
> *For to take and conquer hearts.*

All love poetry should be banned.

# 79

# George Sand

1804–1876

The French novelist Amantine-Lucile-Aurore Dudevant was born in 1804 in Paris to parents who clearly had trouble deciding on a single first name. When she picked a pen name, however, Amantine-Lucile-Aurore came up with the polar opposite of her birth name: George Sand. A strong name, a sandy name, a name totally without hyphens. She published her first novel under this name in 1832, titled *Indiana*, about a woman who ditches her crap husband in search of good times – something that happened in George's own life.

After leaving her annoying husband in the French countryside, George moved to Paris to cultivate an artistic and literary network of male and female lovers, as one does in Paris. One of George's artsy toy boys was the composer Frédéric Chopin. When the pair broke up after about two years, George publicly dragged him in her novel *Lucrezia Floriani* by basing a sickly prince character on the frail composer. What's the point of writing novels if you don't get to parody your exes? Another of her lovers, the writer Alfred de Musset, described her as 'the most womanly woman', once again proving that men make poor writers.

George's novels featured love affairs that crossed class boundaries and, inspired by her upbringing in Normandy, were often set in the French countryside, among the fields of baguettes and rivers of Camembert, or whatever it is they grow in the French countryside. She scandalised the public by wearing men's clothing, citing the fact that it was cheaper and more practical. When will clothing companies learn that women just want pockets? She caused even more scandal by not only smoking tobacco, but doing so publicly, something forbidden to women by custom. George Sand didn't give a damn, and smoked giant cigars all over town while happily invading the private sanctums of men.

The super emo French poet Charles Baudelaire was not a fan of George and her various immortalities. He wrote: 'She is stupid, heavy and garrulous. Her ideas on morals have the same depth of judgement and delicacy of feeling as those of janitresses and kept women . . . The fact that there are men who could become enamoured of this slut is indeed a proof of the abasement of the men of this generation.' We can only assume from the above quote that Charles Baudelaire was a sad virgin, and also completely in love with George Sand.

In addition to her novels and her torrid affairs, George wrote political texts on the rights of women and working-class people, who often featured in her novels. Her most famous quote of all, though, is this incredibly French and Instagram-worthy line: 'There is only one happiness in life, to love and be loved.' Poor Baudelaire, who probably never got to feel such a thing.

# 80

# Lucy Hicks Anderson

1886–1954

Lucy Hicks Anderson was born in 1886 in Kentucky. When she was young, her parents took her to the doctor to find out why their child, who had been born a boy, had declared she was a girl called Lucy, and that she'd be wearing a dress to school. Her parents weren't sure what to do, but the doctor simply told them to raise Lucy as a girl, and that was that – they did.

Or at least, that should have been that. Lucy made it to middle age before she had to deal with any BS for being trans. In the meantime, she lived her life, and what a life it was.

Lucy left school to work as a domestic servant at age 15, got married at 34, and moved to settle in Oxnard, California to live her best Californian life. Lucy would host elaborate dinner parties for dozens of people and was a famously exceptional cook. Her soirées would make the society pages, and Lucy won all sorts of competitions for her cooking. She held rallies for the Democratic

Party and was an all-around star of Oxnard. Meanwhile, on the other side of town, Lucy ran a 'boarding house', a place to get illegal booze and women in the midst of Prohibition. She got in trouble for her side-hustle a few times, and fortunately was once bailed out of jail by a wealthy banker who was desperate for her to cater his dinner party that evening. This is why everyone needs at least one rich friend.

Life was going just fine when one day in 1945, a doctor came to inspect the women of Lucy's boarding house, where a venereal disease outbreak had been traced. Lucy was 59 years old and married to her second husband when the doctor insisted on examining her as well as the girls, resulting in a scandal that would embroil Lucy in court for perjury. Wait, what? Yes, Lucy was charged with 'falsifying marriage documents' (since two 'men' could not be married) and 'defrauding the government' (since she should therefore not be entitled to collect her husband's GI benefits).

Imagine 'defrauding the government' with your genitals. Because it would be just horrible if the government didn't know what your genitals looked like at all times.

And so Lucy went to court, the first trans person to have to do so to fight for her marriage. She argued that her gender identity had nothing to do with how she was born, and challenged the court:

I defy any doctor in the world to prove that I am not a woman.
I have dressed and acted as just what I am: a woman.

Nevertheless, the jury found Lucy guilty of impersonation and fraud. Her marriage was voided, and in a twisted interpretation of justice, the only way that Lucy would be allowed out of jail was if she wore men's clothing. There are so many cases in this book of women being the scandal of their times for wearing trousers. Lucy was scandalous because she didn't – and this after *decades* of nobody knowing or giving a damn about her gender history, and only worrying about whether or not they could book the famous socialite to cater their parties.

Imagine being that afraid of who does or doesn't wear trousers.

# 81

# Mercedes de Acosta

1893–1968

The writer Truman Capote used to play a game called International Daisy Chain. It was a bit like a sexy game of 'six degrees of separation', with the aim of getting from one random person to another in as few hook-ups as possible. He said that Mercedes de Acosta, the Cuban and Spanish American playwright, was 'the best card to hold' in this game. 'You could get to anyone from Cardinal Spellman to the Duchess of Windsor.'

Mercedes, you see, was a notorious seducer of the stars, known as 'that furious lesbian' and 'the greatest starfucker ever', and more innocently as a 'social butterfly'. It's not known if she ever uttered the perfect line attributed to her, 'I can get any woman from any man,' but whether or not she said it, it was quite true.

Mercedes was known for strutting through the streets of New York in the best possible way one can strut through the streets of New York: in manly trousers, with pointy, buckled shoes, a tricorn hat, and, of course, a cape. Why go for a walk around town if you're not even going to wear a cape?

Mercedes wrote her first play in 1916, which was never produced, possibly because it included powerful female characters who challenged the institution of marriage. Producers weren't keen to work with a strong-willed woman like Mercedes – and no doubt her work itself put them off. Luckily, today all plays and films feature lots of strong, relatable female characters!

Mercedes found most of her professional success as a writer in the 1920s and 30s. By age 35, Mercedes had had three poetry books and two novels published, and had four plays produced in a time when, as another female playwright who came before her, Marion Fairfax, put it: 'The best and first thing for an aspiring playwright to do is to be born a man.'

Making things even more difficult for Mercedes, in 1927 the New York state legislature passed a bill to prevent plays from being interesting. More specifically, plays 'depicting or dealing with, the subject of sex degeneracy, or sex perversion' would be banned. This was exactly the sort of thing Mercedes wrote about, though what was considered degenerate or perverted in the 1920s is the kind of thing you'll find within two minutes of searching Tumblr nowadays. And in the 1930s, when Mercedes tried her hand at scriptwriting for film, the Motion Picture Production Code of 1930 banned depictions of homosexuality, along with interracial sex and abortion.

In the following decades, things only got harder for a woman in showbiz, and especially for a queer woman who was uninterested in making herself palatable to mainstream homophobic culture. Mercedes was completely open about her sexuality, despite mounting suspicion of lesbians who many saw as having a mental health condition. One psychoanalyst, who frankly sounds like a virgin, helpfully explained in the 1950s that lesbians have 'only a surface or pseudo happiness. Basically, they are lonely and unhappy and afraid to admit it.' Yes. Yes, I'm sure that's what it is.

Mercedes had an incredibly glamorous older sister, Rita, who was known for a time as 'the most beautiful young woman in New York,' a title now held by my pal Shiva (hey Shiva!). At an opera premiere in 1910, Rita wore a plunging backless gown, and the composer Puccini himself promptly 'abandoned his seat and ensconced himself at the back of Rita's loge, where he remained transfixed on her provocative back'. Why are men like this?

As a child at school, Mercedes had passed notes between two nuns who were in love. When the nuns were discovered and separated, Mercedes got so upset that she ran through the corridors shouting 'I am not a boy and I am not a girl, or maybe I am both – I don't know . . . I will never fit in anywhere and I will be lonely all my life.' Mercedes did eventually marry a man, Abram Poole, a painter, but took with her on their honeymoon to Europe a bundle of love letters from her lover, the Broadway star Eva Le Gallienne – one to open each day of the trip. In fact, Eva ended up joining the happy couple in Europe.

Mercedes' most famous romance, however, was with the glamorous starlet Greta Garbo. Please enjoy this description of Garbo's legs by Mercedes: 'They were not tan or the sunburned color which is commonly seen, but the skin had taken on a golden hue and a flock of tiny hairs growing on her legs were golden too. Her legs are classical. She has not the typical Follies girl legs or the American man's dream of what a woman's legs should be. They have the shape that can be seen in many Greek statues.' Statue legs should be the new unachievable beauty craze.

As Mercedes and Greta's relationship progressed, Greta got spooked by the increasing publicity about her sexuality. The press said of Greta Garbo, 'The most talked-about woman in Hollywood is the woman no wife fears.' Mercedes was possessive, and they split up. She was devastated. But, in the manner of history's great seducers, she swiftly moved on to Marlene Dietrich, who wore top hats. Mercedes sent her so many flowers that Marlene said, 'I was walking on flowers, falling on flowers, and sleeping on flowers.'

As Hollywood became more conservative in the 1930s, things got harder for Mercedes, who could never recreate her successes of the 1920s. She suffered through several deaths in her family, including her beloved sister Rita, the most beautiful woman in New York. Mercedes grew depressed, and fell on hard times.

To help make ends meet, she wrote an autobiography in 1960 titled *Here Lies the Heart* which recounted her many exploits in showbiz – including veiled references to her affairs with the stars. Garbo was furious, and she and others thought the memoir was too close to outing her lovers. They cut her out of their lives. When Mercedes died, she had next to her a Bible in which she'd pasted pictures into the cover of Greta, whom she never fully got over. Because you wouldn't, would you?

# 82

## Gladys Bentley

1907–1960

One day in 1934, the police came to Midtown Manhattan's King's Terrace nightclub to padlock its doors shut. Their aim was to protect the innocent public from the lewd musical offerings of one 'masculine-garbed, smut-singing entertainer,' Gladys Bentley. 'The chief and filthiest offering of the evening,' said the offended patron who lodged a formal complaint to the police, 'is a personal tour of the tables by Miss Bentley. At each table she stopped to sing one or more verses of a seemingly endless song in which every word known to vulgar profanity is used.'

Imagine being the narc who complained to the police about that? It sounds amazing.

Here's an example of a Gladys ditty from the scandalous musical revue which the police commissar deemed too 'vile' to go on. It's called, 'It's a Helluva Situation Up at Yale':

*It's a helluva situation up at Yale.*
*It's a helluva situation up at Yale.*
*As a means of recreation,*
*They rely on masturbation.*
*It's a helluva situation up at Yale.*

Whether or not there was a helluva situation up at Yale is unclear. However, what is known is that Gladys Bentley, pianist, blues singer, and entertainer, was too much for Midtown to handle. She was a black working-class lesbian from Philadelphia who only wore men's clothes. Up in Harlem, however, things were different. While plays on Broadway got censored, Harlem hosted drag balls and all-night parties and Gladys's various inappropriate entertainments. She was a part of the fabric of the neighbourhood, drawing crowds of all races to experience her husky-voiced, innuendo-laden show.

Gladys Bentley got her start in the 1920s performing as a pianist at parties, then graduated to fancy nightclubs, and eventually toured the country with her one-of-a-kind performances. She'd wear a white tuxedo with her hair greased back, and sang with a group of dancing, effeminate men behind her. One picture shows her in front of six men dressed as sailors, kneeling behind her and captioned the 'Favorites of the King'. Gladys would rewrite popular songs to be naughty, and get her audience to sing along with them. She was big and butch and could sing jazz and blues standards with a voice that switches between a gravelly tenor, a bird-like falsetto and scatting. She sang the classics, but she also wrote and recorded original songs. She could sing a ballad that would bring a room to tears, or make an audience laugh so hard with her dirty jokes that the police would be left with no choice but to have the whole place shut down.

A 1931 Harlem guidebook entry for the Clam House, where she

performed regularly, called her a 'pianist and torrid warbler', noted the club was 'best after 1am', but warned the show was 'not for the innocent young'. The poet Langston Hughes, being a poet, described her with more style, saying how she could play the piano 'all night long, literally all night, without stopping . . . from ten in the evening until dawn, with scarcely a break between the notes, sliding from one song to another.' She was 'a large, dark, masculine lady, whose feet pounded the floor while her fingers pounded the keyboard . . .'

Her show was hers, all hers, and her style unforgettable: Gladys Bentley *invented* the white tuxedo. In a time when queer women performers could only allude to their sexuality in order to protect themselves, Gladys leaned into it, and built a career upon it. She even married a white woman, whose identity is unknown, in a New Jersey civil ceremony. Gladys was a star who packed houses and was beloved by her audiences no matter how loudly the critics disparaged her and her fellow performers as 'sexual perverts and double entendre jokes crackers'. She was the soundtrack to the Harlem Renaissance and all the poets and writers and composers who lived through it. Gladys was King.

The world isn't guaranteed to grow more open-minded and tolerant with time. When Gladys moved to LA in the 40s and 50s, she found there a much more conservative society than Harlem in the 20s and 30s. One club where she hoped to perform had to get a special permit to allow her to wear trousers. Whether it was a personal shift, or a natural reaction to living through the years of McCarthyism and its attendant anti-gay hysteria, Gladys took to the press to disown her previous life, presenting instead a respectable image of 1950s womanhood, all pearls and flowery dresses.

She even tried her hand at heterosexual marriage, taking one or possibly two husbands in a row, but kept a picture of her mysterious wife on display in her home, and ended up divorced.

But even once she had reformed to a life of straight domesticity, Gladys would recollect with fondness her style from a bygone age: 'tailor-made clothes, top hat and tails, with a cane to match each costume, stiff-bosomed shirt, wing collar tie and matching shoes'. Listen to Gladys' 'Worried Blues' and imagine her whole body tapping out the rhythm at the piano, dressed as splendidly as that.

# 83

# Coccinelle

1931–2006

Trans men and women get enough shit nowadays, so you can only imagine what it was like in the 1950s. Coccinelle was the stage name of Jacqueline Charlotte Dufresnoy, the French club singer who shot to fame across Europe and the world, and over the course of her life paved the way for the rights of future trans people in France.

Coccinelle – 'ladybug' in French – was not some obscure and unknown show girl, but a bona fide star who hobnobbed with some of the biggest names in showbiz. She was a blonde bombshell who looked like Brigitte Bardot, Marilyn Monroe and the other sex symbols of the era. She was given a flat at the height of her stardom overlooking Sacré-Coeur in Paris, as a gift by an admirer. (Where does one find such admirers? Asking for a friend.)

The journalist (and future second husband) who profiled her in 1959, Mario A. Costa, described her breathtaking glamour the first time he saw her: 'Suddenly she appeared, attracting every eye, impeccably dressed, dazzlingly elegant and overwhelming beautiful.' As all women are, but Coccinelle especially.

Coccinelle was born in 1935, and had a hard time once she was sent to an all-boys school at age 12, away from all her girlfriends with whom she felt most comfortable. 'If there is one word which sums up the early years of my existence and stands as their symbol it is that one: *loneliness*,' Coccinelle said. After years of bullying and harassment from her teachers, she was happy to leave school at 16 to become an apprentice for a celebrity hairdresser in the Champs-Élysées. She was learning under a master, and beloved by most of the fancy customers who came in, but one day, some stupid cow (sorry but she really was) was so offended by Coccinelle, who at the time presented as an effeminate man, that she launched into a tirade of verbal abuse. It didn't matter to her that Coccinelle was in the middle of bleaching her hair. Why would you be horrible to someone who had your hair in their hands? As I said, a stupid cow (not sorry).

Throughout her life, Coccinelle was never one to stand for disrespect and harassment. To this particular stupid cow (less sorry than ever before) she replied: 'Madame would certainly be more at home – and attract more attention – in the zoological gardens. Antonio [Coccinelle's boss] is a hairdresser, not a miracle worker!' Needless to say, the customer wasn't pleased. Coccinelle was heartbroken, however, when Antonio fired her, in the spirit of the customer always being right.

But once again, Coccinelle wasn't one to be trampled on. Years later, Coccinelle would return to get her revenge, resplendent in her elegant clothes, asking for an appointment with the famous Antonio, who was now suddenly anxious to please her and look after her long, thick blonde hair. After questioning if Antonio recognised her, Coccinelle revealed that she was his former assistant, stunning him completely. 'He had got rid of me. Now he was waiting on me, ready to obey and anxious to please me,' she remembered. 'I had just had a very sweet revenge . . .'

A lot had happened in between those two experiences at the hairdressers. Coccinelle first became aware of her true identity while walking around the Strasbourg–Saint-Denis neighbourhood of Paris one day at the age of 18, when she was accosted by five sex workers and brought into the hotel where they worked. There, they did Coccinelle's hair and make-up – one woman even lent her large fake breasts – and dressed her for the first time in women's clothing. 'She's the prettiest one of us all!' they declared, and became friends.

Coccinelle began going about town in the clothes and make-up of her new friends. On one such outing, Coccinelle saw her mother approaching on the street, who didn't immediately recognise her. She called out to her mother, who stopped and stared for a while before realising it was her child. Then, though, as Coccinelle recalled it, 'she came up to me and took my head and held it against her breast, comforting me and speaking with infinite gentleness as if she were soothing a little child. "I understand everything now, everything, Jacques my dear . . . Don't cry, things will be all right because I'll always be your mother . . ."'

Coccinelle came home and decided to destroy all photos and evidence of Jacques Dufresnoy. 'Oh, how I hated him, that creature of a sex that was not really mine!' Coccinelle remembered.

She worked as a switchboard operator for a while, where a close work friend suggested that she see about auditioning to perform in a cabaret. Coccinelle went to her sex worker friends to help her make her transformation, and wowed the cabaret owner. She was hired right away.

And so began Coccinelle's stardom. She performed in famous nightclubs like the Crazy Horse Saloon and Le Carrousel de Paris, and made her film debut in *European Nights* in 1959, which was rated 'X' by the British censor, proving that British people are less fun than the French. She took her act on tour, performed before sold-out crowds night after night, and became BFFs with the legendary Hollywood star Marlene Dietrich.

She also kept a farm in Normandy, and one day decided to bring her beloved farm animals back to Paris with her to live on her balcony. Her balcony pigs and chickens created quite a stir, but unfortunately, they had to go. The police got involved once animal droppings started landing on the heads of passers-by.

Despite her fame, and her celebrity friends, and her incredibly glam life, Coccinelle faced constant trouble trying to travel, as her passport stated that she was Jacques Charles Dufresnoy rather than Jacqueline Charlotte, with a picture of her as a man. Frustrating as it was, Coccinelle occasionally took the opportunity to mess with customs agents. She later recalled an instance when some border agents demanded to know why she didn't dress as a man, to which she replied: 'Dress as a male? With breasts like this? But that wouldn't be right. I would become a transvestite!'

More trouble came when Coccinelle received a draft notice to join the military. She arrived at the military offices in all her splendid glamour, where the officers would not accept that this was indeed the person they had called up for duty. And so she gave them a striptease – annoyed that she was normally paid to do so – and recalled their reaction: 'That day I found out that officers' faces always turned purple. Perhaps it was the fashion. Those military men, hardened warriors with years of service, accustomed to danger and the terrible sight of the dying and the dead, behaved like shy schoolboys when they had to deal with a man who had female hormones.'

They ended up marking her 'totally unfit for the French army', which was perfectly fine by her.

Coccinelle fought another kind of battle in her advocacy for the rights of trans people. She started a foundation called 'Devenir Femme' – to become a woman – which supported those seeking surgery, and helped establish another organisation to research sex and gender. When she married French journalist Francis Bonnet it was the first known marriage of a trans person in France, and so set a legal precedent for others to be married in future. It was a legal marriage carried out by the French Roman Catholic Church, who only said she had to be re-baptised as Jacqueline. She was given away by her father, and the wedding made front-page news.

She also underwent not the first, but certainly the most publicised sex reassignment surgery of her generation, travelling to Casablanca for the operation. 'Dr Burou rectified the mistake nature had made and I became a real woman, on the inside as well as the outside,' she recalled. 'After the operation, the doctor just said, "Bonjour, Mademoiselle," and I knew it had been a success.'

With the power of her celebrity and status as a beloved national icon, Coccinelle was recognised as a woman by the French state following her surgery. From her position as a national icon, she was able to campaign for trans rights. She was bold and fearless and didn't let people get away with bullshit. She took the privilege she had as a painfully hot woman – who happened to look like the blondest, most 'classically' European beautiful icons of her day – and used it for good. And so must we all use our privilege as incredibly hot people for good.

#

# 84

1898/1904–1975

*U*mm Kulthum was a legendary Egyptian mega-diva from the 1950s and 60s, who you can't properly understand without listening to some of her music first. Go. Listen. Search for a live performance like 'Enta Omri' on YouTube. Yes, her performances are about an hour of continuous, uninterrupted music, so you don't have to listen to the whole thing before continuing reading, since after all, you have that appointment you need to get to pretty soon.

What you'll hear in any live recording, though, is the sheer JOY of the crowd. The whistling and screaming and people just occasionally losing it and shouting out to God. There is a word in Arabic – *tarab* – which can be summed up by this reaction to Umm Kalthum's music, of ecstasy and trance and, I dunno, the classical Arabic musical equivalent of that feeling when the beat drops.

Another thing you'll notice is the, like, ten minutes of music that pass before she even starts singing. Things need to be set up just right, you know? You'll get her voice only when she's ready, when the orchestra is ready, when that guy in front has shut up. If you are a true diva, you will know exactly when to begin, and until then bless your audience with the very sight of you, with your big 1960s hair and your giant sparkling earrings and your silk scarf dangling from your hand for a bit of extra flair.

Umm Kulthum was born in either 1898 or 1904, and as we know, it would be rude to ask which. Her father was an imam who taught her to sing and how to recite the Qur'an, a skill which is credited as lending her great clarity of pronunciation of the formal Arabic in her music. From the age of 12, Umm Kulthum toured with her family ensemble, dressed as a boy at first in order to avoid the objections of haters. Her incredible singing ability led to her getting noticed by prominent Egyptian classical musicians. She moved to Cairo in the 1920s, met the city's most important composers, and shot to fame. While many elite musicians performed for small private audiences, Umm Kulthum was the people's singer, giving public performances and then monthly radio performances that would bring Cairo to a standstill.

For a mega-diva, Umm Kulthum was also incredibly private. She had grown up in humble circumstances, and stayed humble throughout her life, as we all must remember to do once we are rich and famous. She was an Egyptian nationalist and supporter of the country's first president, Gamal abdel Nasser – though it is the popular belief that more Egyptians turned out for her funeral in 1975 than his in 1970. Sorry Gamal! Umm Kulthum's songs still sell millions of records every year and she can be heard on the radio across the Arab world, spreading *tarab* long after her death.

# 85

# Josephine Baker

## 1906–1975

Where do I even start with Josephine Baker?

She lived a life so full, so paradoxical, and so complicated that it's almost unfathomable. Her story encompasses so many decades, so many tensions, and so many struggles of the 20th century that her life can be read as a sort of history textbook. If that sounds boring, I promise it isn't.

Here's the short version: Josephine was a rather scandalous American showgirl from St Louis, Missouri, who took Paris by storm in the 1920s and 30s. She spied for the French Resistance in World War II, and became a French national hero for her war service. She was an activist for civil rights in the US, and hoped to prove that racial harmony was possible by adopting children from all over the world to be raised together in her chateau in the French countryside.

Here's the long version:

Josephine Baker was many things at once. She was contradictory. She was American, but she was French. She was an artistic genius, and a tawdry clown. She danced topless, and aspired to be a respected actress. She was kind and selfless, except when she was arrogant and self-absorbed. She started out desperately poor, and later she dripped with diamonds. She grew up stealing coal from moving trains, and later in life wheedled jewels from wealthy men – and then sold those jewels to buy food and coal for the poor of Paris. In her later years, she was saddled with debts and bankrupted.

She slept with men and with women. She was funny, and she was completely mad. She slept all day and danced all night for as many shows as could fit into the hours of darkness. She'd go out in fur coats with nothing underneath.

She couldn't sing, but she wanted to, so she learned. She pretended not to be married when she was, and pretended to be married when she wasn't. She said that every man she ever loved was her husband (which was a lot of men). She loved fine clothes and extravagant fashions, but not as much as walking around the house naked (even when visitors came to call).

She ran a nightclub in Montmartre where her pet goat Toutoute, and her pig Albert, ran free among the motley crowd. She walked her cheetah, Chiquita, down the Champs-Élysées on a leash, and briefly had a pet gorilla whom she dressed up like a man.

She was once driving through Paris and crashed into a lamp post, got out of the car, calmly signed some autographs, then went home in a taxi.

She was a queen in Paris, but was refused entry to hotels in New York City for being black. America rejected her, and it broke her heart.

She performed in the 1930s in German and Austrian and Hungarian theatres while nationalists protested outside, calling her the 'indecent black devil'. She didn't care much for politics, but became a political activist, met with dozens of world leaders, and travelled to every corner of the globe.

She used people, and also lay down her life for others. She praised Mussolini, and then rejected fascism more completely and utterly than many French civilians during the war. She was an unreliable, unpredictable, uncensored type of woman, who also made a totally discreet, calm, and level-headed spy who carried secret messages pinned inside her bra and kept her cool under pressure. She secured false passports for Jews fleeing the Nazis, and sometimes claimed she was part Jewish (she wasn't).

She had an endless stream of lovers, but preached to American servicemen to stop sleeping with women while stationed in North Africa, in order to limit the spread of venereal disease.

She was terrified of loneliness, but so unafraid of bombing raids that she'd rather keep eating her ice cream than hit the ground. She was an absolute diva, but performed for soldiers outside in the freezing cold if there wasn't enough room for them all to see her perform indoors.

She sometimes performed in blackface and at home she bleached her skin. She played to racial stereotypes, and fought against racism. She spoke before 250,000 people at the March on Washington in 1963 with Martin Luther King.

She would announce her retirement from show business and then be back on tour. She decided to become a nun. Then she changed her mind after a week.

She loved children but she couldn't have them – so she adopted 12 children from around the world. She kept them in her enormous chateau, where visitors could come and observe the 'Rainbow Tribe' coexisting in racial harmony. She had good intentions, but sometimes they went very wrong.

She died after one last, exuberant show in 1975, at age 68.

To be honest, that wasn't even the long version. The actual long version of Josephine's story lasted 68 years and would probably take 68 years to do it justice.

She was the ultimate nasty woman, and lived too much life to fit into a short space. So read about her. Read her memoirs, which she filled with brazen lies, which you'll forgive her for because she's Josephine Baker and she's wonderful.

The trouble is, Josephine Baker lived with so much passion and spirit and elegance and obscenity and pain and pleasure that if you think about her for too long, you'll get a headache and possibly start to cry out of either joy and/or incredulousness, depending where you are on your menstrual cycle, if you have one. Find a performance of hers to watch online, and you'll see what I mean.

# Women who punched Nazis

## (metaphorically but also not)

# 86

# Sophie Scholl

## 1921–1943

*I* fear this is going to be a less fun chapter. If you were expecting to get a laugh out of every last tale in this book, I'm sorry to be the one to have to remind you: life is bad, the world is bad, history is mostly terrible, and once upon a time, there were Nazis.

Sophie Scholl's story is a unique combination of wildly inspiring and completely devastating. She and her brother Hans were leading members of the White Rose, a small group of young Germans, mostly students at the University of Munich, along with their curmudgeonly professor, who worked to resist Hitler during WWII. Together, they embody the height of youthful idealism and courage, and their eventual defeat reveals the depths to which a fascist regime will sink to maintain absolute control.

Sophie was born in Forchtenberg, in southern Germany, before moving with her family to nearby Ulm, where she grew up along with her siblings. Her family was incredibly close-knit and loving.

Their father, Robert, despised Hitler and the national socialists from the start, something that sounds like an obvious thing to do nowadays, but at the time was unusual. Even his children were swept up in the initial excitement of national socialism. Sophie's brother Hans joined the Hitler Youth before it was compulsory to do so, and Sophie joined the girls' equivalent – a source of tension in their household.

In 1936, however, Hans went to Nuremberg to represent the Ulm branch of the Hitler Youth at an enormous rally intended to incite ever more fervent nationalism among youth like Hans. Instead, he returned from the event completely disillusioned by what he'd seen.

When the war started, Sophie, too, grew more disillusioned with every piece of news she received from her friends fighting at the Eastern front, including her boyfriend, Fritz. In his letters she read of military failures and atrocities committed against the Jews which told a very different story to the state-sanctioned press reports at home. And so Hans and Sophie came round to their father's way of thinking, and their family dynamic returned to a peaceful and loving state. Sophie wrote to Fritz about her parents' love for their children: 'This love, which asks nothing in return, is something wonderful. It is one of the most beautiful things that has ever been given to me.'

Sophie was a great lover of nature and learning, and yearned to join Hans at the university in Munich. First, though, she had to complete her national service as a kindergarten teacher and factory worker, which she despised, knowing that she was contributing to the war machine. She also couldn't stand the other girls at the factory, who were only really interested in talking about boys and clothes, and who also happened to be a bunch of fucking Nazis.

Eventually, Sophie joined the university in 1942 to study

Philosophy and Biology. While there, she learned by accident that Hans and his friends had formed a group to resist Hitler. They had managed until that point to keep it secret from even their own families. She insisted upon joining.

The primary action of this group, which called itself the White Rose, was to distribute leaflets denouncing the regime across their university, across Munich, and across Germany. They created the leaflets in a secret atelier with a typewriter and a duplicating machine (an old-timey photocopier). These were their only weapons against an utterly ruthless state.

In the course of their underground work the group distributed six different leaflets, with earlier versions encouraging passive resistance to the regime, along with long interludes discussing philosophy and obscure, pretentious references – you know, the kind of thing every university student loves to talk about. As the months went on, and with the help of their professor Kurt Huber, the leaflets grew clearer and more urgent in tone.

The group had to have absolute trust in each other. For context, this was a society in which friends, neighbours, and even family members would report each other to the Gestapo, the German secret police, for having the wrong ideas about Hitler. Children were meant to report their own parents should they hear any anti-Nazi rhetoric at home. In 1939, a factory worker who spoke up in protest against the dismissal of Jewish workers was immediately shot to make an example of what would happen to those who disagreed, disobeyed, and disrupted the ideological work of the regime.

Creating leaflets was no easy task in 1942 Munich. White Rose members would buy small amounts of paper and a few stamps at a time in order not to raise suspicion about their need for these scarce and rationed resources.

Then, they would take suitcases full of their anti-regime leaflets – just about the most incriminating thing you could be found with in Nazi Germany short of a large banner saying 'Hitler is a wanker' – and travel alone on trains to different cities, always careful to sit in a separate part of the train from where they had left their suitcases in a luggage rack. Once in a new city, they would stuff postboxes with the letters to reach another part of the country. In this way, the Gestapo would not know where the letters were coming from. Along their incredibly dangerous journeys, they also managed to recruit small numbers of supporters in other cities and at other universities to begin leafleting work of their own. Sophie acted as the group's treasurer and helped to distribute the leaflets.

Living in constant fear of being caught, and in constant despair at the state of their country, the group had to keep up appearances of being quite relaxed about their lives. They took walks in the day, attended concerts in the evening, and printed their leaflets at night. Hans and the group's other young men were sent for a period to the Russian front to work as medics in the very war that they hated.

The sixth leaflet of the White Rose was written by their professor, Huber, who was more conservative than his protégés and hated the Nazis for what he saw as their misuse of the military, and their destruction of the German state that he loved. He wrote a fiery critique of the defeat of German forces at Stalingrad on February 3rd, 1943, an event that sent shockwaves through a people used to endless propaganda about victory after glorious German victory.

It would be their last leaflet.

On the morning of February 18th, Hans and Sophie went together to the University of Munich with a suitcase of these leaflets, and stacked them in piles outside classrooms and in corridors all around the main atrium of the university, shortly before classes were due to let out. They were just about to leave the scene when they realised they still had leaflets left in their suitcase that could incriminate them. They hadn't put any on the top floor of the atrium, so they climbed the stairs with the last of the leaflets.

Just at the moment the bell rang and students began to stream from their classrooms, Sophie pushed a pile of the papers from the top of the atrium so that they would flutter down onto the heads of their classmates and lecturers. In their conservative university, in a city where Hitler had received some of his earliest support, the inflammatory leaflets fluttered like so many white petals from a tree in spring.

Hans and Sophie, with their now-empty suitcase, tried to blend into the crowds of students who flooded the atrium and were shocked at what they'd found. Before they could make their escape, however, they were stopped by a janitor who claimed he'd seen them drop the flyers. The head of the university called the Gestapo, who at first could not believe that these calm, respectable-looking students could have had anything to do with such dangerous ideas.

Taken to police headquarters, Sophie and Hans were separated and interrogated. After initially denying everything, the Gestapo gained enough evidence to incriminate them, at which point each claimed that they and they alone were the White Rose, in order to protect their friends.

Sophie's interrogator tried to get her to confess that her actions were not her responsibility, but rather, she had been led astray by her brother. To claim this might have saved her life, but she denied it, and told her interrogator she expected to receive the same sentence as her older brother. 'I would do it all over again – because I'm not wrong,' she told him. '*You* have the wrong world view.'

At this point, Sophie and Hans' parents had no idea that they had been arrested, or even that their children had been organising resistance to the regime through the White Rose. Their children had lived up to their parents' ideals after all, and now it would cost them the ultimate price.

The details of Sophie's last days are known to us thanks to her cellmate, Else Gebel, a political prisoner who was roomed with Sophie in order to prevent her attempting suicide. Else said that Sophie remained totally calm throughout her interrogations and captivity, only breaking down at the news of the arrest of their fellow White Rose member, Christoph, who was a husband and a father. Christoph had warned the younger members of the group that they had been getting too reckless, employing increasingly bold resistance actions such as writing anti-Hitler graffiti across the city each night. Christoph was implicated in their activities when the Gestapo discovered a seventh leaflet written in Christoph's handwriting.

The day before the trial of Hans, Sophie and Christoph was sunny and warm. 'Such a beautiful sunny day, and I have to go . . .' Sophie said to Else.

On Monday, February 22nd, Hans, Sophie and Christoph appeared before one of the most cruel and terrifying of Hitler's judges, Roland Freisler, who was known to scream and shout tirades against defendants. The trial was planned by Himmler himself, who ordered a secret and quick execution of all three, rather than a public hanging, which he feared would create martyrs out of these young people whose leaflets had created a spark of fear in the heart of the regime. They had to disappear quietly.

One by one the three young people were brought before Freisler, and jeered by an audience of loyal party officials.

Having finally heard the fate of their children, Hans and Sophie's parents rushed to Munich and managed to force their way into the courtroom, where their father Robert cried out to the party loyals assembled to watch the proceedings: 'There is a higher justice! They will go down in history!' before being pushed outside to await the verdict.

The verdict was, as planned, death for all three. Christoph had begged for mercy as a father with a sick wife, and been denied leniency. Hans declared to Freisler and the courtroom: 'You will soon stand where we stand now!' Sophie was quiet and calm.

The three did not know that their deaths would come not in a few months' time – and not after a long enough time to give the Allies a chance to win the war. They would be executed that same afternoon, at 5pm, just three hours after hearing their fate.

On the wall of his cell, Hans wrote a line of Goethe: 'Despite all the powers closing in, hold yourself up.' Christoph wrote in a last letter to his wife, Angelika: 'I am dying without any hate.'

The guards, breaking the rules, allowed Hans and Sophie to see their parents one last time. To try and console her about the fact that her life was to be cut so short, Sophie said to her mother: 'What are those few years anyway?'

The guards allowed the three prisoners to share a cigarette before their execution.

As he went to the guillotine, Hans yelled: 'Long live freedom!' Sophie remained calm and poised till the end.

The janitor who had caught Hans and Sophie was rewarded with a promotion and 3,000 Reichsmark, the equivalent of about £13,000 today. This was the price of three lives – as well as the lives of the several other members of the White Rose who had fled, but were tracked down and arrested one by one. Roland Freisler, the judge, would die in an Allied bombing attack on the people's court in Berlin.

During her captivity, Sophie had said to her cellmate Else: 'What difference does my death make if our actions arouse thousands of people? The students will definitely rise up.'

But they didn't rise up. In fact, some students at the university of Munich held a rally in appreciation of the janitor who had caught them.

News of the White Rose's actions and murder would, however, reach the outside world. A White Rose leaflet smuggled out of the country made its way to the US and *The New York Times*. The Allies would end up dropping tens of thousands of copies of their sixth and final leaflet across Germany.

We will never know if we could have been as brave and good as the White Rose, because we can only hope that we will never have our courage tested in quite the same way. I told you this wouldn't be a fun chapter! My soul hurts now. Does yours? Nope, this wasn't a fun chapter at all.

There's not much else to say to help ourselves feel better about one of the greatest horrors history has ever known, but at the very least, we can try and make sure it never happens again.

# 87

# Hannah Arendt

1906–1975

annah Arendt was one of the greatest philosophers of the 20th century, today honoured by being one of the only women widely taught in university philosophy courses, if it is indeed an honour to be scrutinised by 18-year-old budding philosophers, who are known to be sweaty and tiresome.

Hannah was born in 1906 in Germany to a Jewish family. She studied in the 1920s under the famous philosopher Martin Heidegger, and when she was 19 and he was 36 (and married), the two embarked on a tumultuous romance. After about a year, Hannah cut things off, citing her need to focus on her philosophy career, one of the all-time most common reasons that girls dump boys. They kept up their correspondence as philosophy pals, however, for the rest of their lives. In the 1930s, things became awkward between them, to say the least, when Heidegger briefly became a bit of a Nazi, proving that brilliant philosophers are often also idiots. He later called his foray into the Nazi party 'the greatest stupidity' of his life, but didn't exactly apologise for it either. So if you think your ex is embarrassing, at least he or she was (hopefully) never a Nazi.

In the early 1930s Hannah worked gathering evidence of growing anti-Semitism, and in 1933, after an arrest by the Gestapo, she fled Germany for France. When France was occupied by the Germans, she was imprisoned at the internment camp in Gurs. She was released and escaped the country when her husband,

Heinrich Blucher, attained visas to the United States. Their US visas had been issued 'illegally' by Hiram Bingham IV, an American diplomat in France, whose father, grandfather, and great grandfather, the Hirams Bingham one through three, by total chance appear in two other women's stories in this book. What is up with this family? They get around. (Hiram Bingham number four is the best Hiram Bingham, clearly.)

Hannah taught in every prestigious American university you can think of. In 1959 she became the first female lecturer at Princeton, a place people go to say they've been to Princeton, and eventually ended up at the uncreatively named New School in Manhattan. Over the course of her career Hannah dealt with the most important issues of the century: totalitarianism, evil, and violence, among other such fun dinner party topics.

In 1951 Hannah wrote *Origins of Totalitarianism*, which analysed Stalin and Hitler's regimes as new forms of government distinct from previous breeds of tyranny. In 1958 her work *The Human Condition* sought to figure out the ways different political and social structures allow or prevent people from living good and happy lives. I made my clever friend Trevor explain the thesis of this book, because I am lazy and it's complicated: 'She pretty much writes a philosophical history of the entire world going back to antiquity, and then concludes that the basic condition of modern life is alienation, so philosophers spend all their time thinking about "the self". But she thinks the claim that the contemplative life is better than the active life is false and restricts access to "a good life" to lucky people who sit around thinking all day.' Thanks Trevor! (Trevor is one of those people who sit around thinking all day.)

In her 1963 work *On Revolution*, Hannah argued that the reason for the failure of most revolutions is that they simply replace one governing power with another governing power, instead of the much more YOLO strategy of *getting rid of power completely*. Just another thing to think about the next time you're feeling philosophical.

Hannah Arendt is perhaps most remembered, though, for *Eichmann in Jerusalem: A Report on the Banality of Evil*. The book, published in 1963, was based on her reporting for *The New Yorker* on the trial of Adolf Eichmann, who had managed the logistics of the deportation of Jewish people in the Holocaust. At the trial, she was struck by how very underwhelming this great monster of the century was. He sat inside a glass cage, with a bit of a cold, and defended himself as a simple administrator whose only aim was to follow the law and the command of the Führer. Hannah concluded that he was a fundamentally mediocre man, an idiotic 'clown' susceptible to cliché, and a bureaucrat – and that this fact was essential to understanding the nature of evil.

She wrote that 'evil comes from a failure to think'. It was this that had produced a man like Eichmann. 'The Israeli court psychiatrist who examined Eichmann,' she wrote, 'found him a "completely normal man, more normal, at any rate, than I am after examining him", the implication being that the coexistence of normality and bottomless cruelty explodes our ordinary conceptions and presents the true enigma of the trial.' Evil became normal in Nazi Germany: 'In the Third Reich evil lost its distinctive characteristic by which most people had until then recognized it. The Nazis redefined it as a civil norm.'

Hannah wrote in *Eichmann in Jerusalem* about the way the Nazi regime used often contradictory lies to maintain its grip on power and the effect of this mendacity on the German populace: 'The German society of eighty million people had been shielded against reality and factuality by exactly the same means, the same self-deception, lies, and stupidity that had now become engrained in Eichmann's mentality,' she wrote. 'These lies changed from year to year, and they frequently contradicted each other; moreover, they were not necessarily the same for the various branches of the Party hierarchy or the people at large. But the practice of self-deception had become so common, almost a moral prerequisite for survival, that even now, eighteen years after the collapse of the Nazi regime, when most of the specific content of its lies has been forgotten, it is sometimes difficult not to believe that mendacity has become an integral part of the German national character.'

The publication of *Eichmann in Jerusalem* sparked huge controversy. Less than two decades after the end of World War II, the public and the surviving European Jewish community were still figuring out how to talk about the war and the Holocaust. Some saw this philosophical take to be too cold, and too soon. The book also criticised those Jewish leaders who had collaborated, which Hannah's critics saw as victim-blaming. Others believed that in stating that Eichmann was not a madman, a psychopath, or even particularly clever, she was excusing him for his crimes – something she vehemently denied, but which led to her alienation from many of her friends. Nevertheless, the idea of evil as a banal thing provided a radical new framework to understand how it is born and spreads across a society as a normal and acceptable thing that 'can spread like a fungus over the surface of the earth and lay waste the entire world'.

*Eichmann in Jerusalem* ends with Hannah's clear and devastating reasoning of why Eichmann must die, addressing him directly:

And just as you supported and carried out a policy of not wanting to share the earth with the Jewish people and the people of a number of other nations – as though you and your superiors had any right to determine who should and who should not inhabit the world – we find that no one, that is, no member of the human race, can be expected to want to share the earth with you. This is the reason, and the only reason, you must hang.

# 88

# Noor Inayat Khan

## 1914–1944

**B**efore you get your hopes up, this chapter has another sad ending. But don't worry, first you get to hear about some old-school spying, some grit and survival against all odds, and more than one unbelievable escape from the Gestapo. This is the story of Noor Inayat Khan, the WWII secret agent who earned one of Britain's highest honours, the George Cross, for her brave work from behind enemy lines in German-occupied Paris.

The Special Operations Executive, or SOE, was set up in the summer of 1940 to create a network of spies with the task, in Churchill's words, to 'set Europe ablaze!' They would do so by spying on and sabotaging the German war effort, funnelling weapons, money, and materials to resistance forces in occupied countries, and setting things on fire.

Not just anyone could be an SOE agent. To survive behind enemy lines in the SOE's French section, an agent had to be perfectly fluent in the language. This didn't just mean being able to convincingly ask, *'Où est la bibliothèque?'*, though that's a good start, but rather to be an expert in all French mannerisms and customs. You had to speak on the phone like a French person, dress like a French person, and even comb your hair like a French person. How do you comb your hair like a French person? I don't know, that's why I'm not a spy. *(Or am I?)*

Noor perfectly fitted the bill. Though she was born in Moscow, and lived some years in England, she spent most of her life in Paris with her family. France was home. Her father was a Sufi teacher descended from Indian Muslim nobility, and her mother a white American who converted to Islam. Their home in Paris was a centre of religious and musical gatherings, and when her beloved father died, Noor and her siblings took care of their broken-hearted mother. Noor became a published children's author, and was quiet, musical, and sensitive. When Germany invaded France, Noor and her family escaped to England, but Noor was determined to return to France to help her country. She was perfectly fluent in French, and presumably could comb her hair in the mysterious French fashion, whatever that means. She was, however, told off a few times in SOE training and in the field for making tea the English way, milk first, instead of the French way, milk second – a trivial thing that English people like to have long, pointless arguments about,[25] but which in the field could be a life-or-death distinction.

The cover story of an SOE agent headed behind enemy lines had to be completely bulletproof. Agents had to learn an entire backstory to their fake identity, which usually hailed from towns whose

---

25. The correct answer is milk first when AND ONLY WHEN you're brewing the tea in a pot, but second when you're making it with a teabag directly in the cup.

records had been destroyed in the war, so that the Germans couldn't check if they really existed. Agents had to invent entire extended families and know their details off by heart, which is especially impressive considering how hard I find it to remember my first cousins' names. An agent was given a fake name (Noor's was Jeanne-Marie Renier) as well as a code name (Madeleine). Noor's true identity was also hidden under yet another name: Nora. She'd applied to work for the war effort as Nora rather than Noor, since the British apparently had trouble with 'foreign' names, bless them and their ignorant ways.

Noor was recruited to the SOE for her French background and the strength of character she had shown in her work in other areas of the war effort. Over a year of training, Madeleine aka Jeanne-Marie aka Nora aka Noor learned the art of spy craft in its entirety, from complicated codes, to spotting and interpreting hidden messages that would be sent to them via programmes on the BBC French service, to physical combat. Noor was to learn to be a radio operator, responsible for sending coded messages between agents in the field and the SOE headquarters in Baker Street in London. She would be the first female radio operator sent to occupied France. It was one of the deadliest roles an agent could have, as the job required lugging around 30 pounds of radio equipment in a heavy suitcase, whose purpose would be obvious to any Germans or sympathisers. Even worse, the Germans were constantly searching for the direction of intercepted radio signals. A radio operator had to search for new locations every day to set up her equipment, which included a 70-foot aerial, and had to keep her communications as brief as possible before leaving the area. In Paris, the Germans only needed a half hour to track down a transmission.

Some instructors had doubts if the 5'3" Noor, such a gentle, quiet young woman, would cut it as an agent. While a highly skilled telegraphist, she had reacted with great stress under some of the SOE's training exercises, such as when instructors would burst in on trainees' sleeping quarters in the middle of the night to subject them to a mock Gestapo interrogation. Another worry was that she was too beautiful to be able to blend in (same). 'If this girl's an agent, I'm Winston Churchill,' one instructor had said. Over the course of her service, however, Noor would prove those who doubted her wrong. She never questioned that she was the right person for the job, and fully understood her service would likely result in her death. The average radio operator in occupied Paris lasted six weeks before capture – Noor would break this grim record by a long way. Nevertheless, each time an agent died the position would have to be immediately replaced, as radio operators were the only link between agents and the French Resistance and London.

Knowing the danger that awaited her, Noor set out for France. A friend recalled Noor's excitement a few days before she left: 'She had stars in her eyes. She wanted to go.' Vera Atkins, an SOE official who saw off the agents from London, sent Noor away with four pills: a sleeping pill to slip to someone if needed, a stimulant pill should she need to stay alert for hours or days at a time, a pill to give herself a fake stomach illness, and finally, a suicide pill.

Nearly as soon as Noor arrived in France, things went wrong. The very agent who received her aircraft in a field in France in the early hours of the 17th of June, 1943, later turned out to be a double agent giving information to the Germans. The bad luck would only continue. Noor was arriving into a circuit of spies that had already been compromised by the capture of two Canadian agents whose parachute drop had gone wrong. The Gestapo had arrested the pair and discovered on them the code names and addresses of other spies in the network. One by one, members of the so-called Prosper circuit were arrested by the Gestapo – as well as the French families who had helped and hidden them.

As the network collapsed, the SOE's headquarters in Baker Street asked Noor to return to London. The circuit was busted, and it was simply too dangerous for her to remain. Noor, however, said she would stay in Paris. She was the only radio operator left, and wanted to try and rebuild the spying network. For the next three months, often completely alone and left to her own wits, Noor managed to evade the Gestapo who were constantly hunting the elusive Madeleine. She used her incriminating transmission equipment to arrange deliveries of money and equipment as the French Resistance prepared for the long-awaited Allied invasion of France. She planned the successful escapes of other agents to safety, got false papers for spies, and managed the escape of 30 Allied airmen who had been shot down in enemy territory. She transmitted messages both to the SOE headquarters and to Charles de Gaulle from his exiled Free French headquarters in London. She had to move location constantly to evade capture, relying on her old friends from her more innocent days in Paris as a student, musician and children's author, who couldn't believe the daring agent she had become. She was able to send letters back to her family in Britain – letters that unbeknownst to her were being photocopied by that double agent prick and shared with the Germans.

You already know how this ends, but first we can enjoy the times that Noor escaped arrest despite absurd odds.

One time, Noor was pressed for time and left with no choice but to set up her giant aerial out of her own window. She lowered it from her window, then went out into the street in order to arrange it in a tree without being spotted. To her horror, a German officer saw her and asked, 'May I help you?' Instead of fainting, screaming, running away, or any of the other reactions she might have reasonably decided upon, Noor simply said, why yes, she'd be ever so grateful if he would. Imagining Noor to be a pretty lady trying to set up a radio antennae to listen to some music, the German officer *helped her set up her actual spy equipment* and then went on his merry way, probably pleased at himself for gallantly assisting such a delightful young Frenchwoman.

Another time, Noor was riding the metro with her equipment, a dangerous daily task since the Gestapo frequently checked the luggage of anyone on public transport. She noticed she was being watched by a pair of German soldiers, but couldn't get off at the next stop without appearing suspicious. When the Germans approached her to ask what she was carrying, she kept cool once again, and told them it was a 'cinematographic apparatus'. She opened her suitcase just a bit to point out to them the various components of her *cinematographic apparatus*, and the soldiers, not wanting to admit that they didn't know a thing about what a *cinematographic apparatus* should look like, believed her, because of course, of *course* that thing in her suitcase is a *cinematographic apparatus*, only idiots don't know what a *cinematographic apparatus* looks like. 'We thought it was something else,' they said, and left her alone with her giant suitcase filled with exactly the thing they thought it was.

Here's the bit that really, really sucks: after managing to keep working for three months on the run, dying her hair, always changing her location, and staying alive, Noor was betrayed by the sister of a resistance member who went to the Gestapo and demanded money in exchange for the address of a British agent. The Gestapo offered her 100,000 Francs, about a tenth of what a British agent would normally fetch. Noor was just a few days shy of her replacement's arrival. She was meant to head home at last on the 14th of October. Instead, on the 13th, she was captured and taken to the Gestapo headquarters on Avenue Foch.

Mistakes were made. Noor had misunderstood her instructions from London to carefully 'file' her messages. London meant 'file' in the journalistic sense – to carefully transmit her messages. She thought they meant 'file' as in keep them. And so, when arrested, her codes and old messages were seized with her, as well as her radio equipment, which the Germans then used to send fake messages to London requesting arms, money and agents directly into the Germans' hands.

London made mistakes too. When Noor sent a distress code under German watch, to communicate that she had been captured – a special key that was exactly 18 letters long – they assumed she had made a mistake, even though she never made mistakes in her codes. They didn't realise she had been captured for months. She didn't reveal anything in interrogations, but the Germans were able to inflict great harm on the Allies using their 'radio games'.

Even in captivity, Noor wasn't done trying to escape the Gestapo. As soon as she arrived, she demanded to take a bath. She was so stubborn and so absurd in asking for it, that they just let her, and even shut the door when she demanded privacy. As soon as she was alone, Noor crawled out the window and onto the roof. She was quickly caught and brought in through another window.

She hadn't given up yet, however. Knowing there were inmates in the cells around her, Noor tapped in Morse code on the wall, and managed to make contact with two other captive agents. Noor and the two men hatched a plan to escape through the barred windows at the tops of their cells by passing notes and a pilfered screwdriver hidden in the toilet between them. One night, on the 25th of November, the three finished loosening the bars on their skylights with the screwdriver, and escaped onto the roof.

Unfortunately for them, an RAF attack soon set off air-raid sirens, and their captors discovered their escape and set up a cordon for the area. They swung into the window of a neighbouring house, but once inside, were trapped. They made a run for it, and were captured yet again. (It's possible that Noor then made a THIRD escape from the Gestapo, but if she did, the Germans didn't record it, probably out of embarrassment.)

The three escapees were offered a declaration to sign that would promise their captors they would not try to escape again. One did sign it, and survived the war to tell the story of what had happened at Avenue Foch. But Noor did not, and was sent to Pforzheim prison, classified as a highly dangerous detainee, kept in isolation, tied in chains, and given only the lowest rations to eat. She was the first British agent sent to Germany during the war. Despite her total isolation, Noor passed messages with a group of French political prisoners in Pforzheim prison by scratching short communications onto the prison's food bowls, which would take a few days to circulate round the prisoners before reaching the correct person. The women kept each other's spirits up by scratching overheard news of Allied victories.

Noor passed her contact information in this way to one of the French women, Yolande. It was thanks to this, and Yolande's efforts to track her down after the war, that we know what happened to her in the end: Noor was transported from Pforzheim to Dachau concentration camp in September 1944, where she was beaten, shot, and cremated. As Germany began to realise its impending loss in the war, Himmler had given an order to kill all captured secret agents because they knew too much about the Nazis. Just seven months after Noor died, the Allies liberated the camp. It wasn't until two years after the war's end that her former colleagues and her family discovered her fate.

343

Sixteen women agents of the French SOE section died in the war. President Eisenhower said that the SOE's work shortened the war by six months. Noor was awarded medals for her bravery by the French and the British, who noted her insistence on staying in Paris under grave danger, the many lives she saved through her work, and the fact that she didn't betray anyone under extreme pressure while imprisoned and tortured. Today, there is a statue of Noor in Russell Square in London. In the springtime, it's surrounded by little purple crocus flowers.

# 89

# Nancy Wake
1912–2011

*Y*ou've already heard a bit about the SOE, since you're reading this book straight through in one sitting, as books ought to be read. If you aren't, you're a terrible person, but here's the tl;dr: the Special Operations Executive was a spy agency set up by Winston Churchill, British prime minister famous for leading Britain through WWII and being a bit of a prick, with the aim of 'setting Europe ablaze' through sabotage and other secret spying things.

Men and women SOE agents were the stuff of James Bond films, though everyone knows that it would be impossible nowadays to cast a female James Bond, because if women appear in an action film for longer than it takes to whip their tops off, they become terribly ill and die. Best not to risk it.

Anyway. Nancy Wake was born in 1912 at Roseneath, in Wellington, New Zealand, but moved to Australia and grew up in the Sydney suburb of Neutral Bay, a place known to be very neutral. Nancy was a rebellious teen, as teens are wont to be, and ran away at 16 to work as a nurse and support herself under a made-up name, which in retrospect was a pretty spy-y thing to do. In 1932, she left Australia and ended up training as a journalist in London, before moving to Paris and getting a job and a hot French husband, Henri. She was living the dream, but then the war began and fucked up her life, along with everyone else's.

Nancy and Henri immediately went to work assisting the French

Resistance after France's invasion by Germany in 1940. Nancy worked as a courier and a guide for as many as 1,000 Allied airmen seeking to escape via the Pyrenees mountain range into neutral Spain. The Gestapo was aware of her activities but could not track her down. They called her 'White Mouse'. She was impossible to catch, often flirting her way past guards, as she explained in an interview with the *Australian News* in 2011, just before she died:

'I'd see a German officer on the train or somewhere, sometimes dressed in civvies, but you could pick 'em. So, instead of raising suspicions I'd flirt with them, ask for a light and say my lighter was out of fuel . . . A little powder and a little drink on the way, and I'd pass their posts and wink and say, "Do you want to search me?" God, what a flirtatious little bastard I was.'

In 1942, with the German occupation of southern (Vichy) France and her resistance network betrayed, not to mention a five-million-franc reward on her head, things got too dangerous and Nancy escaped on foot over the Pyrenees and from there to England. Her husband stayed behind – and was captured and killed by the Germans the next year. He had refused to reveal anything to them about who Nancy was or where they could find her. She would not discover his fate until the end of the war.

Once in England, Nancy was not finished fighting the Germans. She joined the SOE and impressed her instructors with her wide set of spy skills. One instructor noted that 'she enjoys life in her own way, drinks and swears like a trooper.' Vera Atkins, the intelligence officer organising the French section of the SOE from London, described her as 'a real Australian bombshell. Tremendous vitality, flashing eyes.'

Ready for action, Nancy parachuted into France at the end of April 1944. As Nancy liked to tell the story, her parachute got stuck in a tree, and some smug Frenchman meant to receive her party made a remark about how he wished all trees bore such beautiful fruit. She replied with her trademark charm, 'Don't give me that French shit.' Listen up, gentlemen of the world! Don't give ladies that French shit unless it has been explicitly requested.

Nancy's job in France was to assist a spy network and resistance forces in the mountainous Auvergne region in the centre of the country. Nancy's war exploits were frankly ridiculous. Not only did she directly participate in battles, but she recruited 3,000 'Maquis' guerrilla soldiers to join the resistance, eventually leading 7,000 fighters who worked to sabotage and distract German forces in the lead-up to the 1944 invasion of Normandy on D-Day.

Once, while attacking an arms factory, Nancy murdered a German soldier with her bare hands: 'They'd taught this judo-chop stuff with the flat of the hand at SOE, and I practised away at it. But this was the only time I used it – whack – and it killed him all right. I was really surprised.'

I mean you would be surprised, wouldn't you?

When Nancy returned to England, the governments of France, Britain and New Zealand threw medals at her. She married again and moved to Australia, where she unsuccessfully ran for parliament a few times as a candidate for the Liberal party.

Nancy spent her last decade living at the Stafford Hotel in Piccadilly, London, where she drank gin and tonics and told war stories to any and all who would listen. Once her money ran out, Prince Charles picked up the bill, because no one wants to be the jerk to kick a 98-year-old woman out of a hotel bar, let alone the most decorated woman war hero of WWII. Not only would it be rude, but also, Nancy once successfully killed a man with a single judo chop.

# 90

# Dorothy Thompson

1893–1961

The American journalist Dorothy Thompson was the first foreign correspondent to be kicked out of Nazi Germany, in 1934, because she'd offended Hitler with her reporting. In 1931 she had been the first foreign journalist to interview him, and he probably didn't like this description:

> He is formless, almost faceless, a man whose countenance is a caricature, a man whose framework seems cartilaginous, without bones. He is inconsequent and voluble, ill-poised, insecure. He is the very prototype of the Little Man. A lock of lank hair falls over an insignificant and slightly retreating forehead . . . The nose is large, but badly shaped and without character. His movements are awkward, almost undignified and most un-martial . . . The eyes alone are notable. Dark gray and hyperthyroid – they have the peculiar shine which often distinguishes geniuses, alcoholics, and hysterics.

He had told her in the interview how he planned to come to power: 'I will get into power legally. I will abolish this parliament and the Weimar constitution afterward. I will found an authority-state, from the lowest cell to the highest instance; everywhere there will be responsibility and authority above, discipline and obedience below.'

She did not believe he could do it: 'Imagine a would-be dictator setting out to *persuade a sovereign people to vote away their rights*,' she wrote. When Hitler came to power the next year, she admitted she had made a grave error of judgement and set about reporting on his early years in power with her forthright style until she was at last expelled from Germany. One book critic, who doesn't matter, complained how in her writing, Dorothy's 'emotions gain the upper hand over her logical reasoning,' the most male-critic thing ever said. If you can't be emotional about 1930s Germany, what can you be emotional about?

When she returned to the US, Dorothy only stepped up her criticisms and warnings about the unprecedented danger posed by Hitler. She wrote a thrice-weekly column for the *New York Tribune* read by millions and was a radio presenter for NBC, and broadcasted anti-Hitler propaganda directly to Germany that was later compiled into a book called *Listen, Hans*. In 1939, *Time* magazine called her the most influential American woman after only Eleanor Roosevelt thanks to her compelling style, prolific output, and enormous following. 'Dorothy Thompson is the US clubwoman's woman,' the magazine said. 'She is read, believed and quoted by millions of women who used to get their political opinions from their husbands, who got them from Walter Lippmann.' The Nazi propaganda chief Joseph Goebbels, meanwhile, called her 'the scum of America'.

In 1935, Dorothy imagined what it would look like if and when a dictator came to power in the United States. Here's what she said, as quoted in a 2006 book by Helen Thomas, *Watchdogs of Democracy? The Waning Washington Press Corps and How it Has Failed the Public*:

No people ever recognize their dictator in advance. He never stands for election on the platform of dictatorship. He always represents himself as the instrument [of] the Incorporated National Will . . . When our dictator turns up you can depend on it that he will be one of the boys, and he will stand for everything traditionally American. And nobody will ever say 'Heil' to him, nor will they call him 'Führer' or 'Duce'. But they will greet him with one great big, universal, democratic, sheeplike bleat of 'OK, Chief! Fix it like you wanna, Chief! Oh Kaaaay!'

# 91

# Irena Sendler

1910–2008

*I*rena Sendler did not want to be remembered as a hero. 'Heroes do extraordinary things,' she said in her old age. 'What I did was not an extraordinary thing. It was normal.' What Irena did was save at least 2,500 Jewish children from the Warsaw Ghetto in World War II Poland. Was this normal?

On the one hand, no. It wasn't. Ninety per cent of Poland's Jews were killed over the course of the war. Fifteen per cent of Poland's entire population died in these years. The penalty for helping a Jewish person was instant death, for you and also for your family. Only about 5,000 out of one million Polish Jewish children survived the war. Irena and the network that she cultivated saved thousands of these children. For six years Irena Sendler woke up each morning and made a choice to risk her life on behalf of others. So, sorry, Irena, if you look at the numbers, that's not normal, that's pretty heroic.

On the other hand, it should be normal, right? It should be 'normal' to want to save lives, to use what privileges you have in order to help the victims of unimaginable horrors. Was it normal for Warsaw residents to enjoy an Easter carnival in 1943 so close to the walls of the Ghetto that they could see, safely from the top of the ferris wheel, the German forces crushing the Jewish uprising within? *That's* what shouldn't be normal.

We won't call Irena a hero, in any case, because the term bothered her. 'Let me stress most emphatically that we who were rescuing children are not some kind of heroes,' she said. 'Indeed, that term irritates me greatly. The opposite is true – I continue to have qualms of conscience that I did so little.'

Perhaps this is just the mindset of the social worker, and Irena was, by trade, a social worker. She was born in 1910 to a father who had been the same way, a civic-minded doctor happy to treat Jewish patients in a time when most Catholic doctors wouldn't. Because of this, Irena grew up enmeshed in the Jewish community of the village of Otwock, speaking Yiddish with her friends though she herself was Catholic.

Irena attended Warsaw University, and wanted to become a lawyer, but was discouraged from pursuing this unfeminine profession by her department, so studied literature and became a teacher instead. She found her true calling, however, when she went to train as a social worker at the Polish Free University. It was here in the early 1930s that Irena built a close-knit friendship circle under their professor, Dr Helena Radlinska, that would form the backbone of her future resistance network. In the years Irena was at university, the Polish far right grew ever more emboldened, beating people on campus and forcing Jewish students to sit apart from their classmates at lectures. But things were about to get worse.

Hitler's forces invaded Poland in September 1939, and within the first year of the occupation of Warsaw, Irena and her circle of social worker friends had set up an underground network to illegally provide social services to Jewish families by forging paperwork and funnelling food, money and clothing to them.

In early 1941, when Warsaw's Jews were forced to move into the 73 rundown streets that would comprise the walled-in Warsaw Ghetto, Irena and her network were ready to assist once more. Jewish refugees from across German-occupied territory were sent to the Ghetto, and the enclosed area would at its peak contain over 400,000 people. Families crowded into single rooms, suffered from poverty and disease, and subsisted at first on rations of 184 calories per person per day.

As a social worker, Irena was able to obtain a pass to allow her in and out of the Ghetto on the premise of helping to control epidemics and prevent their spread outside its walls. Irena could not look away from the agony of those inside. 'I knew the suffering of the people rotting away behind the walls, and I wanted to help my old friends,' she later said. These Jewish friends included her boyfriend, Adam, and other classmates from the Polish Free University including Ala Golab-Gryberg, who became the chief nurse of the Warsaw ghetto.

As the situation became more dire inside the Ghetto – and the consequences for helping Jewish people more severe – Irena expanded her operations to provide whatever social services she could to its inhabitants. Passing through the German-controlled checkpoints, she smuggled food, dolls for children, and typhoid vaccinations, sometimes in her bra. (It's a recurring theme among women who resisted Nazis – hiding forbidden information or materials inside their bras. Bras may be uncomfortable, but they've served anti-fascist purposes in the past.)

Irena's office also handled blank copies of the documents such as birth certificates that Jewish families would need to escape the Ghetto and the Germans under false, non-Jewish identities. In the summer of 1942, the Germans began the process of deporting the Jews of the Warsaw Ghetto to the Treblinka extermination camp, though they said the train carriages would merely take them somewhere else to be 'relocated'. Terrified parents inside the Ghetto increasingly made the heartbreaking decision to part with their young children, entrusting them to the care of Irena and her network, who would smuggle them out and place them in hiding under new identities with forged documents.

Meanwhile Irena's friend Ala saved hundreds of people from deportation by pretending to have permission to set up a medical clinic at Umschlagplatz, the square in the Ghetto from where the trains departed. She played along with the German ruse that the deportation was merely a resettlement, insisting to them that some were too ill or sick to travel. Of course the Germans did not care who was too ill – but for a few weeks they let her divert some 'sick' people from the trains to her hospital. Once there, she and her fellow nurses had to break the legs of otherwise healthy patients before inspections to prove they were unfit to travel. Ala became known in the Ghetto as 'the good fairy'.

And so Irena and her most trusted friends smuggled children and babies out by increasingly inventive means. They hid children under rags and in coffins moving in and out of the Ghetto under the legitimacy of Irena's epidemic control passes. Babies, carefully tranquillised by Ala so that they would not make a sound, were smuggled out in burlap sacks and toolboxes and in briefcases. Tunnels dug by children, buildings with secret doors on either side of the Ghetto's perimeter, and toxic sewers provided dangerous escape routes. If they made it out, they would be met by Irena or one of her network on the other side.

Once they were out, though, the children were in more danger than ever. To be Jewish and caught outside the Ghetto walls was an instant death sentence. The first port of call for an escaped child would be one of Irena's safe houses. If he or she was old enough to understand what was going on, they had to memorise Catholic prayers and sometimes undergo makeovers to appear more 'Aryan'. Toddlers, though, couldn't understand what was happening and were prone to speak Yiddish and accidentally reveal their identities, and so were among the riskiest to rescue. Three-year-olds, you'll know if you've ever met one, don't generally do what they're told. Yet Irena carried on, developing new escape routes and safe havens on the outside. Their former social work professor from the Polish Free University, Dr Radlinska, herself born Jewish, helped coordinate the work of several secret operations like Irena's from her hiding place in a convent.

In the spring of 1943, 750 men and women of the Warsaw Ghetto rose up in armed resistance against the Germans. Eighty five per cent of the Ghetto's population had already been deported, and those who remained were hunted where they hid. Those young people who remained and decided to fight only had revolvers, home-made bombs and a few smuggled rifles, but on their first day of fighting managed to take the Germans by surprise and force their retreat. Ala was still inside, and set up a medical facility for wounded fighters, while Irena was able to sneak in and out of the Ghetto and rescue more children in the chaos of the battle.

The uprising lasted about a month – as merrymakers at the Easter fair outside the Ghetto looked on. The furious Germans called in reinforcements and completely destroyed the Ghetto with bombs and fire. Ala and most of the other resistance fighters were discovered in their hiding places and arrested. Ala was sent to the Poniatowa labour camp, but her resistance was not over: she set up a secret youth circle and medical clinic at the camp, and led an uprising of the prisoners in which she was killed. Ala fought, resisted, and helped people until the very end.

Irena's network were being arrested and killed, but her list of rescued children continued to grow from several to dozens to hundreds to thousands of names. She was careful to maintain meticulous records, written in a fine pencil on cigarette paper, which she guarded with her life. These records included each child's true identity and the address of the family that had taken them in. Irena needed this information in order to direct funds and clothing and other supplies to the children, but it was also necessary, Irena said, 'so that we could find them after the war'. Only Irena knew the content of the lists and could connect the dots between the children's old and new identities, but she knew that if she was captured and killed by the Gestapo – which could happen at any moment – this information was too precious to be lost with her. And so she wrote their names down and hid the papers in her apartment.

In the fall of 1943, the Gestapo did come and take Irena away on suspicion of her activities with the Polish resistance group Zegota. The group had been founded by two women in 1942, and had brought Irena's network into their fold. When the Germans took Irena, however, they didn't know how important a resistance leader they had captured – the Germans had been hunting for the mysterious woman codenamed 'Jolanta' for years, but didn't know it was Irena. She was taken to the Pawiak Prison and tortured, but she never revealed her work saving children or any other facts about the resistance. She merely said she was a simple social worker. Ironically, it would be her lists of children that would save her: Zegota members on the outside knew that she had been taken, but not where those vital lists were hidden, and so they gathered funds to pay a huge bribe to secure Irena's release. The task of delivering the bribe fell to a 14-year-old girl in the resistance, who carried the equivalent of nearly £80,000 in today's money in her school backpack to meet a German guard in secret.

One morning at the prison, when Irena's name was called for execution, the bribed German led her another way from the firing squad and allowed her to escape. First, though, he punched her in the face, lest anyone down the line be tempted to think of him fondly, or believe he was acting on the right side of history in letting Irena go. Nope, just a Nazi taking a bribe!

When the Gestapo realised Irena had not in fact been executed that morning as planned, she shot to the top of their most-wanted list. Knowing she could be captured at any moment, Irena took care to bury the precious lists in empty glass soda bottles under an apple tree in her friend's garden. It was the winter of 1944. Irena had to miss her own mother's funeral in order to avoid capture – but only after ingeniously smuggling her out of the window of the hospital where she was being treated so that they could be together when she died. Again and again Irena Sendler managed to outwit the Nazis.

Even in hiding, Irena continued to direct the resistance, handling huge sums of money on behalf of Zegota, and managing an incredibly complex network of supporters and social workers and medics and, of course, children in hiding. In 1944, a 'Home Army' of Polish resistance fighters included 300,000 fighters, men and women. The 40,000 fighters in Warsaw, including 4,000 women, rose up on August 1st of that year.

By this point, Himmler had ordered German troops to kill *all* the residents of Warsaw, Jewish or not. No one got to be normal in the end, watching someone else's misery from the top of a ferris wheel. The Germans' reaction to the uprising was to flatten the entire city. Even then, under bombs and vicious street fighting,

Irena, Adam, and their friends set up a field hospital to treat the wounded. When their operation was discovered, they successfully bribed another German to spare them from deportation. But instead of fleeing, they set up *another* field hospital.

By the end of the war, the city was destroyed, and millions of civilians were dead. Irena's lists were now buried deep under rubble, never to be found. Irena did manage to reconstruct them as best she could from memory, but for most of the children whose true identities were hidden on the lists, there were no families left to find them.

Irena and Adam, who survived when all odds say that they shouldn't have, remained in Poland, got married and had children of their own, as well as taking in two Jewish foster daughters. (And then they got divorced, but hey, that's life.)

After the war, Irena would be imprisoned again, this time by the new communist secret police, for her connection to the resistance movement and the Home Army, which was at odds with the communists. Because of this political tension, Irena's story remained largely unknown until the 1990s, though she did receive recognition from Yad Vashem (the Holocaust memorial in Jerusalem) in 1965. Before Irena died in 2008 at the ripe old age of 98, she received awards and recognition from around the world for her wartime bravery, including a Nobel Peace Prize nomination and a letter from the Pope.

Can we stop here, and just reflect on the fact that World War II was not that very long ago? Maybe your grandparents were alive when this happened. Maybe your parents were. Or maybe, if you're old, you were alive for all of this. (Hello, older readers: I'm sorry about the swearing.)

What lesson can we take from Irena's story? It seems impossible to try at all. Her courage was too superhuman. The forces she resisted too unfathomably evil. Irena said it was normal for her to do everything she did – and this short telling of her life misses out more examples from the seemingly infinite supply of stories about the bravery of Irena, her friends, and other Polish resistors. In later years, Irena would always stress that what she did was only possible thanks to a small number of people who agreed that it was normal to risk their lives to rescue children. 'I want everyone to know,' Irena said, 'that, while I was coordinating our efforts, we were about twenty to twenty-five people. I did not do it alone.' So there's a lesson. To do good things, you need good people you can trust.

When you read about horrors, and especially the great horrors that cause people to say generations down the line that such horrors must never be forgotten or allowed to happen again, you may come to feel uneasy that the people who did those horrors, or who let those horrors happen while watching from the top of a ferris wheel, are not so different from people today. It can feel as though the only divide between a society which accepts and participates in great horrors, and one that rejects and resists them, is as fragile as a piece of cigarette paper.

Speaking of what's normal, it's normal to feel like garbage after reading all of this. Take a break, have a rest, and yes, feel like garbage, because history is terrible, and you mustn't forget it. We can only hope that there are more Irenas than not-Irenas out there, and that we ourselves can be more Irena than not-Irena, always.

Your new revolutionary
role models

# 92

# Olympe de Gouges
## 1748–1793

On the 5th of October 1789, 6,000 angry French women marched on Versailles armed with knives, sticks, clubs, pikes, and cutlasses. The French Revolution was in full swing, the Bastille had been stormed, things were on fire in the countryside, and somewhere in the distance the revolutionary future Jacobins were cheerfully sharpening their guillotines.

It all began with a bit of a riot in the marketplace in Paris, due to the fact that there wasn't any bread – and everyone knows that bread is pretty much the entire point of Paris. That and cheese. And looking bored in cafés.

At the end of their 12-mile march, King Louis XVI received six of the angry bread women, and promised them yes, there would be bread for Paris. Delicious, fluffy baguettes. (Or whatever type of bread they used to eat in 1789. It was probably gross.)

Just for good measure, the marchers stuck around till morning, when they stormed the bit of the palace where Marie Antoinette herself lived, and 'accompanied' the King and Queen back to Paris to sort out the bread situation. The royals were likely not terribly keen on taking this journey, though it was arguably rather merry. Some women handed out blue, white, and red ribbons to onlookers, some rode the cannon they'd pilfered along the way like so many cowboys – and others carried the heads of Versailles guards on sticks. The French Revolution was a confusing time.

But was it good for women? Well, much of history is just people disagreeing about things, writing books about those things, and getting mad at other people who disagree with those books, and writing books about how the other books are bad. The argument about the role of women in the French Revolution, and how much they benefited or suffered because of it, is no different.

Simone de Beauvoir wrote in 1949 in *The Second Sex* that the Revolution was basically trash for women. But in prettier, French-ier words. Another historian, Joan Landes, sums it up thusly: 'The Republic was constructed against women, not just with them.' And one more hot take from another modern academic, Catherine Silver: 'The women of France rioted, demonstrated and struggled in the cause. However . . . women received no substantial benefit from the redistribution of rights after the destruction of the aristocracy.'

Beyond rioting and marching with heads on pointy sticks, women took other direct actions as a means of engaging in politics. Women participated in something called the 'grocery riots' in 1793, which was a bit like shopping in a Sainsbury's on a Sunday afternoon, if everyone shopping in a Sainsbury's on a Sunday afternoon was angrily demanding price controls, an end to hoarding and profiteering off food, as well as social equality, democracy, and rights for women. And the ingredients for a nice Sunday roast.

Enter Olympe de Gouges, stage left. This is a great joke about her politics, and the fact that she was a playwright. Frankly, reader, I just nailed it. Anyway, Olympe de Gouges was born with the much less cool name, Marie Gouze, in 1748, in the south-west of France. She moved to Paris after the death of her underwhelming husband (RIP) and began building up her reputation as a *femme de lettres*, a lady-writer who did lady-writer things such as writing plays and pamphlets, corresponding with other fancy writerly types, hob-nobbing with important intellectuals in salons, getting in fights with troupes of actors for delaying the performance of her plays, and presumably staring wistfully out of Parisian windows, as the French are known to do.

She wrote her most famous play, *Zamore et Mirza*, a comedy about a shipwreck, in 1784, but by 1789 had reworked it into an anti-slavery play, *L'Esclavage des Noirs*. She began to build a reputation not only for her abolitionism, but for her revolutionary zeal, and as an advocate for women's rights.

All of this culminated in her most important work, the 1791 pamphlet, *Declaration of the Rights of Women and the Female Citizen*, which she addressed to Marie Antoinette. 'Woman is born free,' the declaration begins, 'and remains equal to man in rights.'

De Gouges wrote her *Declaration* in response to her great disappointment in the revolutionary constitution of 1791, which included a *Declaration of the Rights of Man and of the Citizen*, and had made women 'passive' citizens of France. This meant that while they were technically citizens they couldn't vote or do other citizen-y things. Thanks boys!

The constitution drew from the Enlightenment ideals of reason, rationality, and objectivity – but only applied them to secure justice for dudes. De Gouges loved the revolution, and was super into reason and rationality, but alas, like many men, the revolutionary leaders had turned out to be trash in the end. Or a prettier, French-ier version of trash.

And so De Gouges wrote in her *Declaration* that women – whom she described as 'the sex that is superior in beauty as in courage' (a true statement) – deserved all the same rights as those offered to men in the constitution.

In a postscript to the declaration she added that 'marriage is the tomb of confidence and love,' which may also be true, I'll get back to you in, say, 20 years' time. De Gouges was in favour of sex outside marriage, and attached a sample marriage contract to her declaration. It wasn't terribly romantic, but then again, marriages weren't particularly romantic before the revolution, either. The contract called for the equal status of men and women in marriage, and also called for equal rights for legitimate and illegitimate children. (Olympe believed herself to be the illegitimate daughter of a fancy man.)

After the execution of Louis XVI in 1793 (RIP) the Jacobins churned out a few more constitutions extending the right to all men, but no women, which makes sense because if women tried to vote, their big poofy skirts would just get stuck in the voting booths and hold up the democratic process.

By the time France's littlest fuckboy Napoleon turned up on the scene and enacted the Napoleonic law code of 1804, all the worst things about the pre-revolutionary old regime patriarchy were brought back and entrenched. Husbands could imprison wives for adultery but not the other way round (of course), women couldn't make contracts or own property without their husband's consent, and fathers could even imprison their children for disobedience. Which is all quite shit.

Olympe herself fell victim to the Terror, i.e. the bit of the Revolution from about 1792 to 1794 that was extra guillotine-y. She had opposed the execution of Louis XVI, and was a bit of a fan of Marie Antoinette despite her revolutionary ideals. In 1793, she proposed that the French people should have a plebiscite to decide what kind of government they wanted. For this, for her defence of the King, and for writing a play seen as too 'sympathetic' to royalists, (though she denied this), she was arrested and imprisoned for three months. The Jacobins sentenced her to death on November 3rd 1793 for supposed sedition and counter-revolutionary activity, and she was led to the scaffold the next day.

An anonymous witness at Olympe's execution described the way 'she approached the scaffold with a calm and serene expression on her face.' How must it have felt to be killed by the same revolution of which you considered yourself a driving force, through your writings and your radicalism? Probably not great, to be honest.

In her *Declaration*, De Gouges wrote one of her most famous lines: 'A woman has the right to mount the scaffold. She must possess equally the right to mount the speaker's platform.' If a woman can be executed, she also deserves the right to be heard. Perhaps to say, 'Please don't execute me, you absolute cunts.'

De Gouges has become something of a hero to those modern feminists who consider her the 'first French feminist'. She now has a Place named for her in Paris, where people can go and contemplate Olympe and the 40,000 others killed in the French Revolution, while eating some delicious bread.

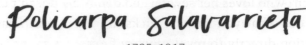

# 93

# Policarpa Salavarrieta

1795–1817

Being underestimated is pretty central to many women's lives in history (and also in an office where I once worked), but for Policarpa Salavarrieta, it was exactly what she needed to do her job. In the early 19th century, the Spanish King Ferdinand VII sought to reconquer those bits of South America that had got a bit too independent for Spanish tastes in the years when he had been distracted by Napoleon invading Iberia, which would be pretty distracting if you think about it. One of the places he sought to reassert control was New Granada, including what is now Colombia. Policarpa was one of those who wasn't going to let him.

Policarpa, known as 'La Pola' to her buds, was a spy for revolutionary, pro-independence forces, and in 1817 snuck into Bogotá, which was loyal to old man Ferdinand, using a forged passport. Once in Bogotá, Policarpa became 'Gregoria Apolinaria', an innocent seamstress and housekeeper only interested in mending your socks, and definitely not listening in on your sensitive discussions, no siree, nothing to see here. Just a relaxed, simple girl who loves her sewing and definitely doesn't care about finding out what you royalist fucks are up to and relaying that information directly to revolutionary forces, ha ha, no, girls hate stuff like that.

With her brothers and her *gentleman friend* fighting on the revolutionary side, Policarpa was ready to do her bit. Other than her totally innocent work as a seamstress for royalist families, Policarpa also recruited revolutionary sympathisers among the royalist troops, convincing them to defect with that golden combination of flirting and bribery. She also raised money and hid soldiers and weapons. She even sewed uniforms because, after all, she was merely an innocent seamstress.

Nobody suspected her until one day, some guys who clearly sucked at spying were captured with documents proving her association with the rebels. She was arrested and sentenced to death, but spent her 15 minutes of gallows fame wailing against the Spanish, cursing them with such wild abandon that they had to get their drummer to ramp it up a notch to try and drown her out, while a Spanish officer shouted, 'SHE'S CRAZY, DON'T LISTEN!' Yeah man, some girls are just crazy.

Policarpa's last words, remembered by the 19-year-old future Colombian president José Hilario Lopez who was in the crowd, were: 'Assassins! My death will soon be avenged!' Well, everyone knows the best way to get vengeance on your enemies is to be put on currency, and until they replaced them all recently, Policarpa Salavarrieta appeared on a Colombian bill[26], like a

---

26. Fun fact from my pal Laura: When the Colombian government replaced all the money with new designs (of both men and women celebs, some

10,000 peso 'Fuck you' to her executioners. That's only worth about $3, or £2.50, but still, her executioners didn't get to be on money, did they?

goodies and some baddies) the new bills didn't fit in the cash machines and they had to redo them all, lol.

# 94

# Sofia Perovskaya

1853–1881

*L*isten up, girls! There will be times in your life when MEN tell you that you can't achieve your dreams. I know, right? You will be UNDERESTIMATED in your abilities and it will be TOTALLY UNFAIR because you are STRONG and GORGEOUS and you can succeed in WHATEVER you want to do, whether it's raising a family, or painting beautiful art, or running a MARATHON, or thriving in BUSINESS, or ASSASSINATING THE TSAR OF RUSSIA.

This is exactly what happened to Sofia Perovskaya in the 1870s and 80s. SOME people – who were *men* – thought that *just because she was a woman,* she couldn't follow her *socialist revolutionary dreams* and *become a terrorist* and *organise a successful plot to kill the hated Alexander II* and *be the first woman in Russia to be executed for a political crime.* Men are always underestimating women – but Sofia sure proved them wrong!

Before the 1860s, Russian socialist radicalism was a bit of an old boy's club. As things got more radical in the 60s, though, the women took revolutionary matters into their own hands. They started gathering with their gal pals to talk about girly things, like securing housing and employment, having a bit of a moan about the fact that women couldn't work or move about without the permission of their husbands and fathers, and assassinating the tsar. You know, just girly stuff. In fact, some of what they talked about was so girly that they occasionally banned men from attending their gatherings. Sometimes men just don't *get* assassinating the tsar.

These radicals were still ladies, though, weren't they? So naturally, they also loved a bit of fashion! To get the 1860s #feminist #look, you had to trade in your fancy gentlewoman clothes for a plain dark wool dress, ditch your male chaperone, flee your oppressive family, wear blue glasses, smoke publicly, talk too loudly, and sacrifice your very life in the name of revolution. Men just HATE it when women talk too loudly and assassinate the tsar!

In the 1870s, Sofia joined the Tchaikovsky Circle of medical student revolutionaries, who spread socialist propaganda among their classmates, in factories and in villages. They also held night classes for workers to learn about why they were being screwed, and began to build up a workers' organisation for the first time ever in Russia. The Circle was made up of seven women and 23 men, men who understood that chicks dig revolutions.

Sofia's Tchaikovsky group wasn't the only revolutionary circle – another one, the Fritsche group, was made up of 13 young Russian women attending university in Zurich, just hanging out, studying hard, and plotting for the coming socialist revolution. They were having a great time until in 1873 the Russian government decreed that they all had to stop studying abroad and come home, accusing them of fomenting political unrest, sleeping around, and giving each other abortions. You know how college girls are with their abortions! So they came back to Russia and, much to the consternation of the Russian government, became labourers and carried on their fomenting.

Anyway, the 70s went on in a frenzy of revolutionary fervour, with feminists focusing on the ways in which women were exploited by the economic fuckery of their country. It was the tsarist rule that made things terrible, so it would be the tsar who had to go.

A split in the circle ended up producing a new group keen on a bit of violence and terror, the Narodnaia Volia, or 'People's Will'. Their plan was to assassinate the tsar, which, as we know, was kinda Sofia's *thing*. Here she was, the daughter of a family of the wealthy landed gentry, ready to fuck shit up and suffer the consequences.

Sofia wasn't to be the first plucky female to succeed in the Russian assassination game. Every guerilla warfare fightin' girl needs a good role model, right? Hers was Vera Zasulich, from south Russia, who shot the governor of St Petersburg in January 1878, a man who had once beaten up a political prisoner for not removing his hat in his presence. Men, right? Anyway she tried but failed to kill him and got away with it.

By the time it was Sofia's turn to have a go, there had already been FIVE failed attempts to assassinate Alexander II. Sometimes it takes a woman's touch to get it right, in life, in business and in murderous plots. She watched his movements, organised her agents, and gave the signal for the exact moment that the bombs should be lobbed at the tsar's passing horse and carriage. These are the kind of leadership skills every girl needs to learn!

Sofia rejected the leniency that she might have received for being a woman, instead choosing to *lean in* and be hanged along with four other men in on the plot, proving that women really can have it all.

So don't forget, girls – you gotta live, laugh, love, and never, EVER listen to anyone who tells you that just because you're a woman, you can't assassinate the tsar.

# 95

# Alexandra Kollontai

## 1872–1952

You probably know of International Women's Day as the day that brands mark each year by selling women clothing, pharmaceuticals and financial services via the medium of empowering ads. But did you know that you can trace the origins of this important annual marketing tradition to long before Nike wanted us to buy their trainers and chase our dreams? It's hard to imagine, but it's true: the original International Women's Day was nothing less than a *communist plot*. And nobody does a communist plot like the Russians.

In 1913, the Duma, the Russian parliament, reluctantly designated International Woman's Day to be the official girl version of Labor Day: socialism, but pinker and frillier. The idea had originated at the 1910 International Socialist Conference in Copenhagen, the culmination of several years of Russian feminism on the march. Women of different political bents and social classes (though mostly posh ladies, as these things often started out) gathered to discuss women's suffrage and create the League for Women's Equality. The first Women's Day march took place in 1913, and included a contingent of Bolsheviks, whom we'll hear more about shortly.

Alexandra Kollontai was born in St Petersburg in 1872 to a wealthy family, but would grow up to be the most important Bolshevik feminist, and one of the first female ambassadors anywhere in the world. For Alexandra, the only way to improve the status of women was to grant them economic independence and power. Russia before the revolution was a largely peasant society. It was shit to be a peasant, and even shittier to be a peasant woman, and so Alexandra worked to organise poor working women and develop a feminist iteration of Marxism. (If you don't know much about Marxism, just go to your nearest university, find a house party, and ask the first man you see with glasses and a beard to tell you more. He'll explain it.)

Russian feminist women wanted a change to repressive divorce laws. They wanted equality in education and work and the law, and access to birth control. These were radical ideas at the time, but thankfully, 100 years later, nobody denies that women should have access to whatever birth control they need! Glad we sorted that one out. But the Bolshevik platform for women wasn't just 'everybody gets divorces and birth control!' They wanted to radically overhaul the family unit itself. Only by destroying the family would women be free to work and be educated and thus empowered. Social childcare and communal kitchens would free working women from the unpaid labour of home.

For Alexandra Kollontai, the struggle for women's rights was a 'struggle for bread', as she said. Many, but not all male Bolsheviks (#NotAllMaleBolsheviks for those following along on Twitter) thought that women were too politically backward and too uneducated to be able to really understand Marxism, socialism, and the revolutionary ideal. (If you did make it to that house party and found the guy with the glasses and the beard, you may find yourself running into the same trouble.)

Russian women would prove those bearded glasses-wearers wrong, however, and how else, but by starting the Russian Revolution itself in 1917. On International Woman's Day in 1917, masses of women textile workers called a general strike. It was March 12th, or February 7th by the Russian calendar, and so is known as the February Revolution. The tsar abdicated in the wake of the mass protests, and a provisional government took charge and granted women the right to vote – the first major power in the world to do so. (Sorry, New Zealand, I know you gave women this right in 1893, but you're just so little and far away.)

When the provisional government dragged its feet about pursuing women's issues, still convinced women were too ignorant to do socialist politics, Alexandra Kollontai told them off: 'But wasn't it we women, with our grumbling about hunger, about the disorganisation in Russian life, about our poverty and the sufferings born of the war, who awakened a popular wrath?' she asked them. 'Didn't we women go first out to the streets in order to struggle with our brothers for freedom, and even if necessary to die for it?' Yes, Alexandra, but don't be so naggy, *God*.

Alexandra Kollontai also advocated for a sexual revolution. She saw romance itself as a trap set by men to assert their ownership of women, but understood that women still wanted and needed to have sex and so they may as well have it. She said that having sex should be no more shocking or significant than 'drinking a glass of water'. To be promiscuous was to be revolutionary; to be prudish was to be bourgeois. But 'if love begins to enslave' women, Alexandra wrote, 'she must make herself free; she must step over all love tragedies and go on her own way.' Jealousy between women must be overcome to achieve true sisterhood, and she wrote novels which explored these radical ideas. Some of her books were so sexually explicit that they were banned or censored, including one which may or may not have been about an affair that Lenin may or may not have had.[27]

Alexandra also would have written great Valentine's Day cards: 'Monogamy is a bourgeois construct,' the outside would say, and on the inside it would just say, 'I slept with your friend Pavel.'

Anyway, after *another* revolution – the October Revolution by the Russian calendar – the Bolsheviks came to power, and Alexandra became the first commissar of social welfare. Between the two revolutions, the more radical socialists had struggled with the quite bourgeois provisional government. But by December 1917, the Bolsheviks had repealed existing marriage and divorce laws, and decreed that the clergy no longer had the power to carry out marriages, and that only civil marriages were valid. Women could no longer be fired for getting pregnant, and would receive paid maternity leave and breaks to breastfeed. New laws mandated that men and women should be paid the same for equal work, another radical concept that thankfully 100 years later has been totally sorted out all over the world.

In October 1918, a new Family Code declared that children born in or out of wedlock were equal before the law. To divorce, either party simply had to say that they didn't want to be married any more. Adoption was abolished. Why? I don't know, it was a crazy

---

27. He did. It was with another prominent Bolshevik woman, Inessa Armand, and the Bolsheviks were so embarrassed by the whole thing that when Lenin died they tried their darndest to erase her from history. Yet here we are, having a dalliance with the sexy past in a footnote.

time, maybe a man with glasses and a beard can explain the hindrance of adoption to an equal society. Alexandra and other more ~extremist feminist socialists~ went so far as to say that all children should be nationalised. As I said, crazy times. But after the shocking destruction of a tsarist society in which women were the property of men, there were no bad ideas.

Well, until there were. In the summer of 1918, a devastating civil war broke out between the Bolsheviks and a strange alliance of liberals and monarchists and peasant rebels and foreign interventionists and proto fascists – a war that would claim 13 million lives out of a population of 136 million. Things got bad for Russians, and worse for Russian women, living under a state of practical anarchy in which soldiers on all sides raped women of both sides and justified it with whichever ideology they happened to support. Instead of fighting for reforms, women were fighting to stay alive.

After the civil war ended in a Bolshevik victory, the new Soviet Union under Vladimir Lenin tried to revive the cause of women and equality between the sexes. Lenin said that women should run for election, and that 'every cook must learn to rule the state'. The head of education, Anatoly Lunacharsky – whose official title was the 'Commissar of Enlightenment' – said that, 'A true Communist stays home and rocks the cradle,' while his wife goes out to evening classes or party meetings, a line that all modern wives ought to employ. As for Alexandra Kollontai, she headed up the new *Zhenotdel*, the Women's Department, which was tasked with the cause of educating children, and organising women workers and peasants, often representing them against shitty male managers in workplace disputes. By the middle of the 1920s, half a million women activists were travelling the country to indoctrinate, educate, and support women. When Alexandra eventually opposed Lenin, he made her ambassador to Norway to get rid of her. After Lenin's death in 1924, Joseph Stalin rose to power, and in 1930 he dissolved the *Zhenotdel*. Alexandra became a supporter of Stalin, but you kind of had to in order to stay alive.

The lesson we can learn from all of this, in any case, is that in order to properly mark International Women's Day, instead of staring slack-jawed at an emotionally stirring ad for shoes, we must nationalise Nike and redistribute its trainers among the masses. We must nationalise Forever 21. We must nationalise all the brands, and then nationalise them some more, and then we must ban love. It's what the original Women's Day marchers would have wanted.

# 96

# Juana Azurduy

### 1781–1862

Juana Azurduy de Padilla was born in what is now Bolivia in 1781, and would become famous as a fighter in the struggle for independence from Spain that began in 1809. Juana was orphaned early on, the daughter of an indigenous mother and a Spanish father, and went to live in a convent. She began her training as a nun at age 12, but was expelled at 17 for being too rebellious, which would later literally be her job, so the joke's on those boring nuns. Juana then met a dreamy soldier, Manuel Padilla, and so Jesus lost another bride to an IRL man. Sorry, Jesus! You can't have all the girls.

Juana and her boo fought together against Spain from 1809, and joined an army sent from Buenos Aires in 1811. When they lost and Spain regained control of the region, the family's lands were confiscated, and Juana and her children were captured by the royalists. Dreamy Manuel rescued them, however, and they all went into hiding from where they recruited 10,000 soldiers to fight a guerilla war. They enjoyed a few victories against the royalists, but also suffered the deaths of their four children from malnourishment while in hiding. Juana later became pregnant again, though, and even carried on fighting the Spanish while carrying her fifth child.

Juana was made a lieutenant colonel by the rebel government after she led a number of successful battles. Manuel died in 1816 (RIP), and she gave birth to their daughter in the middle of fighting a military campaign, which has long been considered among the worst ways to give birth. But hey, she was in charge of 6,000 men who weren't going to command themselves.

Bolivia became independent in 1825, and Juana retired from her fightin' days to live in her home city with her daughter. But the newly independent Bolivia would not return the lands that the Spanish had taken from her and her husband and so she lived in poverty, probably pretty fucking pissed off. The famous liberator of South America Simón Bolívar once paid her a visit, felt guilty, and arranged for her to start receiving a pension. He also told a fellow independence leader that, 'This country should not be named Bolivia in my honour, but Padilla or Azurduy, because it was they who made it free.' In the end, however, he must have been like, 'Just kidding definitely call it Bolivia lol,' as that's what it's called today.

# 97

# Rosa Luxemburg

## 1871–1919

This book is very innocent. It contains no secret political agenda. If this book DID contain a secret political agenda, it most certainly wouldn't be for all the girls of the world to grow up to be radical leftist revolutionaries who, inspired by the tales of heroic women who came before them, take it upon themselves to overthrow capitalism. That would be absurd!

If you happen to know somebody who MIGHT want to overthrow capitalism, however – perhaps your friend who goes to another school – you should refer them to the life and works of Rosa Luxemburg for tips.

Rosa was born in 1871 in Poland, which was then part of the Russian Empire, and moved with her family to Warsaw when she was little. She became politicised from a very young age, devoting her free time to mastering the works of Marx, as all little girls love to do. Rosa and her family were Jewish, and lived through anti-

Jewish pogroms that swept Russia in the 1880s. At age 14, she saw four socialists hanged from the Warsaw citadel. Instead of thinking, 'better not be a socialist, then', Rosa launched herself into left-wing politics. She was denied an award at school for being a good student because she had such ~rebellious tendencies~. By 19, she had to leave Poland out of fear of arrest for her underground revolutionary activities.

Women weren't allowed to attend university in Tsarist Russia, because of course, girls are known to be icky and have cooties, so instead she went to Zurich in Switzerland to continue her studies. Rosa ended up in Germany working with the left-wing branch (naturally) of the Social Democratic Party. She was a brilliant commentator and a gifted public speaker who could command great crowds despite being about three inches tall.[28] And above all else, she wrote and wrote and wrote, both for the public in pamphlets and articles, and in long letters to her gal pals to swap ideas about revolution.

One of Rosa's most important intellectual feats was to come up with a theory about something called the *accumulation of capital*. How can an ever-increasing amount of commodities be sold in the same market in order to sustain the growth of capitalism? Can we just buy more and more and more shit we don't need forever? My bedroom says yes.

Of course we buy shit all the time. For instance, you had to buy this book, instead of being issued a copy by the state, which is a shame. Well, unless you're in a library. Or you're a thief. Or borrowed it from your pal Roz. Or maybe you live many years from now in the Utopian Socialist Republic of Larkmenia on the faraway

28. According to my clever friend Trevor, she would wear giant hats so that people could see where she was.

planet of Ogg, where money has been replaced with the free exchange of warm, tender hugs. In which case, welcome, and thank you to whoever thought to bring this humble book along with them on the Thousand Years' Journey, when all Earth's surviving beings fled the planet to seek refuge from the Great Dronesmog of 2051.

Anyway, Rosa theorised that in order to survive and carry on growing forever, capitalism would have to embark on an imperial project, rampaging across the globe and penetrating new markets in new countries and filling them up with its shit, until the whole world is fucked and the environment has been destroyed and everyone's dead from war.

This is exactly how she saw World War I: an imperial project that would set workers against each other in war when really they should be standing together in international solidarity. She embarked on a speaking tour against the war, calling for workers to sabotage the state in protest, for instance by participating in strikes to halt transportation and industry. The state was not having this, and she was arrested. She was still in prison when the war was lost and the Kaiser deposed.

The Social Democrats took power. But Rosa and her fellow far-lefties such as Karl Liebknecht, with whom she co-founded the Communist Party of Germany, were far from satisfied with the Social Democrats' actions once in power. They were mostly unhappy about what they *didn't* do: they didn't reform the economic system, as they had in Russia, though they had created a parliamentary democracy.

Another important Rosa theory was about the spontaneity of revolution. She believed that you could not orchestrate a revolution, or direct it once it's happening, without destroying it entirely. This was one of her critiques of Lenin's handling of the 1917 Russian Revolution – that and the use of state terror.

A second revolution began sweeping Germany in 1919, started by some rogue elements in Rosa's party. It was, in her opinion, far too soon for another revolution. But, of course, what was started could not be controlled, and she realised she had to go along with it. The Social Democratic leadership under Friedrich Ebert set about destroying this revolution, and did so by unleashing a citizen's militia known as the Freikorps against them. Both Rosa and Karl Liebknecht were beaten and killed by the Freikorps, and Rosa's body was thrown into a canal. She was 47.

Ironically, the Freikorps were basically an early form of the Nazi party, who, in the next generation, would then turn against the Social Democrats, and give us Hitler. Two thumbs down, Friedrich.

Historians will tell you that you're not supposed to speculate about how history would have turned out differently if this or that event had never happened.[29] Luckily, I'm not a real historian. What if Rosa hadn't been killed? What else would she have done? Her murder would tear the German left apart for years to come – could a more unified left have prevented the rise of national socialism? Am I saying that Rosa Luxemburg could have stopped the Nazis? No, I'm not committing to that argument because I'm ending all of these sentences with a question mark? Good.

In any case, there's a lot to learn from Rosa Luxemburg. Not that you or I are planning anything. No siree! Nothing to see here!

---

29. I am told by historians that historians actually love to do this, even though it's naughty. Or perhaps *because* it's naughty.

# 98

# Constance Markievicz

## 1868–1927

nybody who knew the Irish revolutionary Constance Markievicz as a child would not have expected her to live the life she did. She was born in 1868 to the aristocratic Gore-Booth family, and was a member of the wealthy landowning Anglo-Irish elite. In the tenant farming system of the time, farmers paid rents to rich landlords who sometimes didn't even live in the country. To be Irish and Catholic meant being a second-class citizen in your own country, in a poor and precarious situation. Constance, on the other hand, grew up in her family's beautiful home of Lissadell Court in County Sligo, which had 48 rooms.

Constance learned all the things a young lady of a high station should learn from her governess, nicknamed Squidge. She was beautiful and tomboyish and daring, and loved to ride horses, hunt, and sketch. She was clever and vivacious and happy and bold. Once, at a dinner given at her home, some important man or another, whose name we can happily ignore, put his hand on her leg under the dinner table. She picked it up, held it in the air, and announced to the assembled guests: 'Just look at what I have found in my lap!' We can only assume that the man then died on the spot. RIP, you old perv.

The poet W.B. Yeats, who would visit his relatives in the town near Lissadell, wrote that Constance 'had often passed by on horseback going or coming from the hunt and was the acknowledged beauty of the county.' He wrote a poem comparing her to a wild bird (in a good way). Years later, she would have lunch with Yeats in London, but a man at a neighbouring table, overcome by her beauty, would steal Yeats' thunder by writing a sonnet dedicated to her on his tablecloth and cutting it out to present to her as he left. (And Yeats would be held responsible for the damage to the tablecloth.)

Constance moved to Paris for a while to study art, and started wearing a ring to show that not only did she love art, but she was actually married to it, which is an incredibly 'art student' thing to do. Despite this marriage, she also met a dishy Polish count in Paris, Casimir Dunin Markievicz, who was tall and broody and had black hair and blue eyes, and so she married him too, and became the Countess Markievicz.

By all accounts, that could have been that for her life. She could have been hot and clever and funny and rich. But Constance was destined to be remembered for a lot more than being an annoying art student and the wild bird in a Yeats poem.

From the 1890s on, Constance was becoming interested in two things: women's suffrage and Irish nationalism. She began attending meetings of Sinn Féin after its creation in 1908. Sinn Féin's goal was to make Ireland independent of British rule. Constance and other nationalist women founded a women's newspaper called *Bean na h-Eireann*, 'Woman of Ireland', 'advocating militancy, separatism and feminism'. Just like women's mags today.

The aims of the suffragists and the nationalists were often at odds. Suffragists criticised nationalist organisations for not taking their women members seriously, and nationalists criticised those suffragists who wanted to participate in the British parliament that they believed should have no say over the governing of an independent Ireland. Constance believed in both movements, but thought the fight for an independent Ireland should come first. So she especially wasn't a fan of those suffragists who bloody loved the empire.

In a 1909 lecture to the Students' National Literary Society, Constance rallied the students to her way of thinking: 'Arm yourselves with weapons to fight your nation's cause. Arm your souls with noble and free ideas. Arm your minds with the histories and memories of your country and her martyrs, her language, and a knowledge of her arts, and her industries. And if in your day the call should come for your body to arm, do not shirk that either.' Needless to say, giving speeches like these put Constance on the British authorities' radar.

In those years Constance also founded a pro-independence boy scout troupe, took them camping, and taught them to shoot. She dropped her Countess title, preferring to be known as the *much* less formal Madame Markievicz, and began to abandon her society obligations and pleasures. Her elite friends didn't mind to see her go, now that she was so involved in the unseemly realm of politics, working side by side with the poor, providing food for striking families in 1913, and generally getting her hands dirty in a way they thought an elegant lady should not.

On Easter Sunday, 1916, Constance, her nationalist pals, and an army of volunteers prepared for revolution. Constance was the first person to publicly proclaim the new Irish Republic, reading the text of its Proclamation to gathered onlookers on the steps of Liberty Hall in Dublin on the eve of the revolution. The document declared that the new republic would include equal suffrage. However, it was only signed by men, because unfortunately women were unable to write their names until the pen-maker Bic invented the 'Bic For Her' pen in 2012.[30]

At midday the next day, Constance and her company of the Citizen Army took St Stephen's Green, asking the park-goers on that sunny day if they could please vacate the park because it was needed for an uprising. Constance's branch of the nationalist movement had thought that the timing of the revolution, during World War I, would mean the British would not direct their full military might to quash an uprising. Boy, were they wrong! British troops arrived and fought the rebels, who were vastly outnumbered, into submission.

Constance took part in the fighting, at one point exchanging fire with British officers who had been having a nice lunch at a hotel overlooking the park when the revolution kicked off under their noses. They tried to shoot her, but she kept popping out from behind a tree to shoot back at them, which is a pretty annoying thing to happen when you're trying to have a nice lunch. In later years, Constance would also be accused of shooting a constable dead – however it's unclear if she was even present at the green when he was hit.

Constance was second-in-command of her battalion. At the end of a week's standoff and full-on trench warfare, it retreated into the College of Surgeons, where they would get word that the

---

30. Good news, ladies! This is not a figment of my wild imagination but a real pen you can buy.

leaders of the uprising had surrendered. Defeated, Constance emerged from the college, kissing her gun before she handed it to the waiting British captain in surrender. The Captain offered her a lift to the prison, as she was a lady, but she refused, and marched with her fellow revolutionaries – both men and women – to her own imprisonment.

Constance was the only woman to stand trial for the uprising, in a secret military tribunal before a judge whom she described as 'a fuzzy little officer with his teeth hanging out to dry'. She recounted the experience in a letter to her sister: 'I told the Court that I had fought for the independence of Ireland during Easter Weekend and that I was ready now to die for the cause as I was then.' She was found guilty and sentenced to death by being shot – but this was commuted to penal servitude for life because she was a woman. Devastated as her fellow revolutionaries were executed one by one, she told her captors: 'I wish you had the dignity to shoot me.'

Over the decade following the Easter Rising, Constance would be imprisoned and released by the British three times, as the tides of revolutionary fervour and Irish politics ebbed and waned. In 1918 she became the first woman elected to the House of Commons, though as a member of Sinn Féin she never took up her seat. At times Constance was reviled by her contemporaries, and at others, held up as an unparalleled national hero. She was bitterly disappointed when in 1921 the Irish Republic she had been fighting for since 1916 was replaced with the Irish Free State, which tied Ireland to the British Commonwealth along with countries like Canada and Australia. Constance wanted the whole British Empire to burn, and the new consensus was unsatisfying to her as a radical.

But in 1927, sick and reaching the very end of her life, Constance would see clearly the support she had gained from the Irish people when they came to sing and pray outside her hospital room. 'It is so beautiful to have had all this love and kindness before I go,' she said. When she died, thousands lined the streets to watch her funeral procession.

# 99

# Luisa Moreno

## 1907–1992

*E*verything good you have in this life you only have because of somebody else. You may think you have pulled yourself up by your own bootstraps, without a single person to help you, but somebody had to invent those bootstraps, and somebody had to make them in a factory, and somebody had to organise the people who worked in that factory so that they'd be paid fairly and not be killed on the job. Yes, I know that logic doesn't fully make sense, but the idea of pulling yourself up by your bootstraps never made any physical or metaphorical sense to begin with, and anyway my point is we all owe our well-being to the work of people like Luisa Moreno. 'One person can't do anything,' she once said. 'It's only with others that things are accomplished.'

Luisa Moreno was born in 1907 in Guatemala into wealth and privilege. Her father was a powerful coffee grower, and her mother had that elusive job of wealthy women everywhere: a socialite. When Luisa was of the age to take up higher education, she was furious at the rulings preventing women from attending university. So she gathered up her fellow wealthy and influential girlfriends to lobby the government, foreshadowing her long life of rabble-rousing.

Before launching into a successful labour-organising career, though, Luisa would have to get her aimless poet years in, as we all must. She ran away to Mexico City at the age of 19 to live her best bohemian life and consort with artists like Diego Rivera and Frida Kahlo. She wrote poetry, supported herself as a journalist, lived a dreamy life, then married a painter (red flag, ladies!) who in later years would prove to be a bit of a shit. Luisa got pregnant, and the couple moved to New York City in 1928, to fulfil Luisa's wish that her baby would be a 'Latin from Manhattan', a rhyme worth moving country for.

Once in New York, Luisa and her underwhelming man found themselves belonging to an entirely different station to that which they enjoyed in their hobnobbing days in Mexico City, and their fancy socialite days before that in Guatemala. They lived in a tenement in Spanish Harlem, and had money trouble. Luisa got a job as a seamstress to support the whole family. Living and working in poor conditions, broke and trying to raise a newborn baby, the natural course of action, from Luisa's point of view, was to join the Communist Party, get her co-workers together and launch a union. Some people make good organisers, others crumble at the idea of arranging their own birthday party. Luisa was a good organiser. While the women seamstresses led the negotiations and lobbying of their employer, their husbands did the husband jobs of organising fundraisers and weekly dances in support of the union, and looking handsome at dinner parties. Behind every strong woman is a handsome, helpful boy!

Luisa's natural talent as an organiser caught the attention of the wider American labour movement, and she soon got a job for the American Federation of Labor, the AFL. The AFL at this time was organising workers across the country, but it was afraid to work in Florida because of the intimidation of labour activists by that most embarrassing set of racists, the KKK. Thankfully this organisation of grown men who like to dress up as ghosts and murder people has since been eradicated, and in no way, shape or form supports a sitting president, because that would be absurd and the American people wouldn't stand for it.

Despite knowing the threat that would face her, and because they were too chicken to go themselves, the AFL sent Luisa to Florida. She left her husband behind, who had since revealed himself to be an abusive drifting piece of river garbage, and set about mobilising the Latino and African American cigar-rolling workers of Florida. Luisa had left the Communist Party by then, but was more devoted than ever to organising workers. She negotiated a contract for more than 13,000 workers in Florida, then went and did the same in several more states across America. As we think back on what these negotiations must have looked like between the under-five-foot-tall Luisa and furious captains of industry, we can only hope she entered the meetings, put her feet up on the bosses' desks, calmly lit a cigar and began, 'Look here mister, this is how it's gonna be . . .' This fact cannot be historically verified, and therefore cannot be assumed to be untrue.

Over the next few decades, Luisa travelled the country, forsaking her own right to a pleasant and settled family life in order to improve the conditions of literally hundreds of thousands of American working-class people. She ended up in Los Angeles organising cannery workers primarily composed of Mexican and Jewish women, fighting discriminatory hiring practices and winning the women better pay and hours and even on-site day-care, and earning herself the nickname of the 'California Whirlwind'.

While in California, Luisa joined a group of community organisers working to expose the racism of the Los Angeles criminal justice system. They called themselves the Sleepy Lagoon Defense Committee, organised in response to the LAPD's arrest of hundreds of young Latino men in a trumped-up reaction to the murder of a young man, José Díaz, whose body had been found in the Sleepy Lagoon reservoir. It was the biggest mass conviction in California history, and an obvious attempt to harass and imprison young people of colour in Los Angeles rather than prosecute a crime. The police never even questioned the two men last seen with José. Amid racial tensions raised around the case, the so-called Zoot Suit Riots broke out, a series of white attacks on mainly Mexican American men and others seen wearing zoot suits, which supposedly took up more fabric than was acceptable to use during wartime. The police allowed this violence to go unchecked, and even got involved themselves – all while the white-run press cheered the white gangs along, and deemed the Sleepy Lagoon Defense Committee 'communists' and 'trained rabble-rousers'. Which, yeah, they were, so what? As Luisa joined with leaders from other communities to fight discrimination, the police and the FBI attempted to divide and conquer.

Eventually, it would be the accusation of communism amid the rising Red Scare in 1940s America that led to the end of Luisa's American career. In 1950, Luisa was deported after being declared a 'dangerous alien' by the House of Representatives' incredibly-named 'Un-American Activities Committee'. It's funny what gets to be called American and un-American, given that the United States was literally founded by 'trained rabble-rousers'. And so Luisa, the first Latina elected to a high-ranking position in the American labour movement and who would probably have made a great president, was instead deported to Guatemala with her husband.

'They can talk about deporting me,' Luisa said defiantly, 'but they can never deport the people that I've worked with and with whom things were accomplished for the benefit of hundreds of thousands of workers – things that can never be destroyed.'

And that, friends, is where your damn bootstraps come from.

# Jayaben Desai

### 1933–2010

*Y*ou are a man, a clever man, a clever business man. You have cleverly earned yourself some money, or cleverly inherited the money that your father so cleverly made, or perhaps his father, and that is why you cleverly opened a factory in the 1960s. Now, it's 1970s Britain. The youths are listening to all manner of alarming musical genres and their hair has grown long and threatening, and it is of your opinion that they should cut their hair and get a job and contribute to this country, the disco-dancing scroungers.

Your lovely factory in north-west London is a fine place to work. You develop the film of people's photos by mail order. It's a perfect system, and you turn a tidy profit.

And your employees! How they love you. They are mostly of South Asian origin, and you call them 'my ladies' and they can't get enough of it. Sure, they have to ask permission to use the toilet, and yes, it's true, if they don't work fast enough you *may* threaten to fire them – but after all, you're the boss, and how else will they learn? They should just be happy to be there! If they don't like it, they can leave and work in someone *else's* factory, or maybe they can be clever enough to open a factory of their own.

One day, you tell an employee she has to work overtime. She says she won't do it. You say she *has* to – you're the boss, after all, and you make the rules, because you are very clever and deserving. You call her and her friends 'chattering monkeys', and this 4'10" woman tells you:

'What you are running is not a factory, it is a zoo. But in a zoo there are many types of animals. Some are monkeys who dance on your fingertips. Others are lions who can bite your head off. We are those lions, Mr Manager.'

That woman is Jayaben Desai, and she's about to make your life very difficult for the next two years.

Jayaben Desai was born in Gujarat, India in 1933, and after marrying her husband Suryakant in 1955, moved to what is now Tanzania. The pair lived comfortably off Suryakant's income as the manager of a tyre factory, but with the persecution of Asians in East Africa in the 1970s, the couple eventually moved to London.

In London, the couple and their two children found themselves suddenly on the bottom rung of society. Jayaben's husband worked as an unskilled labourer, and she sewed in a sweatshop before taking work at the film processing plant of Grunwick. After two years of working there, she had had enough of the gruelling conditions and in August 1976 stood up to her bosses. Although she wasn't part of a union, she walked out, and in the days that followed led a walkout of a hundred of her colleagues. They were fed up with long hours and low wages and demanded the right to be members of a recognised union and to negotiate better conditions for themselves. She told her bosses: 'I want my freedom.'

In the weeks that followed, Jayaben's walkout developed into a strike backed by trade unions and supporters from around the country. The Grunwick management would not budge, and nor would the women, who were offered reinstatement to their jobs if they dropped the whole union thing. Police arrived at the picket lines; more than one person was struck by a manager in a car on his way into work.

The mostly white, male postal workers in the local Cricklewood sorting office decided to join the 'strikers in saris', refusing to deliver Grunwick's post, which was a pretty crippling move for a company that operated by mail order. 'You don't say "no" to Mrs Desai,' one postal worker explained. This tiny woman, who stood on the picket line with her handbag under her arm, was truly a force of nature.

The women seemed on the verge of a victory when a group stepped in to oppose them called the National Association for Freedom, or NAFF, a slightly unfortunate acronym. The Grunwick dispute had captured the attention of the entire nation, and was taken up on one side by the unions in support of the protesting women, and on the other by Conservative politicians in Westminster under the leader of the opposition, Margaret Thatcher, in defence of Grunwick's management. NAFF organised the delivery of Grunwick post across the country to break the postal workers' ban on its mail. Meanwhile the Labour government, under much pressure, appointed an inquiry to look into the situation, which found that the women should get their jobs back and be allowed a union. The Grunwick management, however, ignored the inquiry's findings.

Jayaben was determined to carry on, even as the Trades Union Congress and other backers began to distance themselves. Once a cause célèbre of the left, now the backers saw the impossibility of victory and were nervous about negative national attention. 'Would Ghandi give up?' Jayaben asked the workers.

But with the end of TUC support and the Grunwick management's complete intransigence in the face of rulings and recommendations that the women should be allowed a union, the dispute ended in defeat for the women in 1978.

In the election of 1979, which brought Margaret Thatcher to power, Grunwick became the centre of debates raging through a changing Britain. A new brand of Conservatives pointed to the conflict to argue that the unions had too much power. Meanwhile, Jayaben had been left disillusioned with the unions. A few years before she died, she said, 'Trade union support is like honey on the elbow; you can see it, you can smell it, but you can never taste it!'

She did not, however, regret the day she walked out of her job demanding better treatment for herself or her co-workers, or the two years that followed in which she travelled the country rallying support from all sectors of British society. Speaking after the defeat of their effort, Jayaben reminded the strikers of what they had accomplished:

'We have shown that workers like us, new to these shores, will never accept being treated without dignity or respect.'

They had shown that they would not simply be grateful for whatever they were given. They had shown that they could win the support of white workers. They were poor, and small, and female, and immigrants, but they were powerful and unafraid to demand they be treated as such. Britain could not simply expect a cheap, replaceable and submissive source of workers from its former empire – at least not on Jayaben's watch. While people older than millennials (they exist!) may remember seeing the Grunwick strike on the news, most don't remember the name of Jayaben Desai, who stood up to extremely powerful forces without fear.

'They wanted to break us down,' Jayaben told the strikers, 'but we did not break.'

# Conclusion

Many of the women in these pages couldn't be more different from each other. They are, after all, separated by their backgrounds, their politics, vast oceans and thousands of years.

If they all gathered together in one place it could make for a very awkward dinner party. Julie D'Aubigny would stab Mercedes de Acosta with a sword as they both tried to flirt with Hedy Lamarr, who would just ignore them because she was excitedly talking about maths with Emmy Noether and Hypatia. Josephine Baker and Coccinelle would get naked and dance on the table while Nana Asma'u and Hildegard von Bingen blushed furiously and muttered prayers under their breath.

Ida B. Wells and Frances E.W. Harper would greet each other as old friends and excuse themselves to the kitchen because they had a *lot* of gossip to catch up on. Sappho and Ulayya bint al-Mahdi would languish in a corner on some cushions, whispering dirty poems and cackling to each other. Noor Inayat Khan would swap spy stories with Policarpa Salavarrieta, and Rosa Luxemburg would be hiding in a closet plotting the downfall of capitalism with Alexandra Kollontai and Luisa Moreno. Everyone would avoid Qutulun as she kept challenging people to wrestle, except Lozen, who'd distract her then steal one of her horses and gallop away into the night.

Sojourner Truth would make a rousing speech that brought the room to tears, and Susan La Flesche Picotte would kindly invite Margery Kempe to go upstairs for a cup of tea and a medical check-up to try and find a cure for her incessant wailing. Wáng Zhēnyí would be getting her mind blown by Annie Jump Cannon and Cecilia Payne-Gaposchkin filling her in on 200 years of astronomy. Lucy Hicks Anderson and Pancho Barnes would produce the smuggled liquor, and Gladys Bentley would play the piano all night while Miriam Makeba sang. Annie Smith Peck would climb up on a cabinet and refuse to come down, shouting about how she held the altitude record for the party. Tomoe Gozen would accidentally almost murder someone, and the whole thing would be shut down by the cops when Zenobia, Ching Shih and Artemisia of Caria tried to invade the next-door neighbour's house. Nellie Bly would write a tell-all memoir about the whole disastrous evening.

Actually, that sounds like the greatest party ever.

So yes, they are a diverse bunch. But before you get to know these women as individuals, and learn their battles and their theories and their hopes and their dreams, you first have to know that they existed at all. Women have been there all along. They've been there, and they've been doing things! They've been relentlessly doing stuff, whether you knew about it or not!

This book is full of women who conquered, and flourished, and enjoyed their lives too much for the comfort of those around them. But it's also full of women who failed. Who tried to make change, and couldn't. Who had to admit defeat and adapt to the dangerous world which rose to crush them, change them, or even kill them.

But other than, well, the ancient murderers I've included for the fun of it (shout-out to my girl Empress Wu) they were fundamentally good and smart and brave. We might not have known their stories before now because their goodness and their smartness and their bravery either wasn't valued or was too threatening to win the recognition of history's conquerers.

So should you find yourself on the receiving end of the disapproval of someone more important or more powerful or supposedly smarter than you, stop and wonder what their motive might be.

You may find you're more powerful than you think.

# Old People Glossary

Welcome, old(er) readers! I am so happy that you have joined us. Despite the infinite wisdom of your many years, you may have found yourself at a loss when faced with some of the more *youthful turns of phrase* in these pages. Not to worry! I have collected some of my repeat offences against language to try and explain them to you. You'll note that the entries in this glossary appear in no particular order, because the universe is random and life is ultimately meaningless, and I hoped to reflect that. Also I accidentally wrote it this way and was too lazy to rejig it to be alphabetical. Classic millennials! Anyway, here you are. Go ahead and bookmark this page for future reference, you old scoundrels!

**Boo** (n.) – Your husband or wife or boyfriend or girlfriend or partner or person you drunkenly snogged once in your teens and later thought back on with at least a little fondness.

*'Come to brunch with me tomorrow! Bring your boo.'*

**Side boo** (n.) – The person *other* than your husband or wife or boyfriend or girlfriend or partner with whom you have a romantic, usually illicit dalliance. Shame on you!

*'Sorry, I can't bring my boo to brunch because he found out about my side boo and dumped me, lol.'*

**Lol** (abbr.) – Lol means 'laughing out loud'. It does NOT mean 'lots of love', despite what every dad in the world seems to think. An all-caps 'LOL' might mean you have actually made a small noise of delight, whereas 'lol' means you have merely smiled in your mind but not on your face, or possibly that you are furious with the person you have said it to. If it is a complete sentence with a full stop – 'Lol.' – there is an added level of self-aware childishness or irony, perhaps following an inside joke, or a sex joke. Lol.

*'Lolololol.'*

**Messy bitch** (n.) – A messy bitch is a person who delights in scandal, as embodied by Joanne Prada or 'Joanne the Scammer', a character on Twitter invented by Brenden Miller who is known for being 'THE messy bitch who lives for drama.' If this explanation has only made you more confused, I am sorry. You get to own property, and millennials get Joanne the Scammer. That's the deal.

*'George Osborne is a messy bitch who lives for drama.'*

**Sick burn** (n.) – An excellent insult. To deliver a truly sick burn, you must cut deeply into someone's ego using your superior, brutal wit. Onlookers to your sick burn will either go 'Ohhhh!' or suggest your victim applies ice to their burn, which is a terrible turn of phrase because you should NEVER put ice on a physical burn.

*'Sick burn, bro.'*

**Meme** (n.) – The word 'meme' was unfortunately coined by that great bell-end of our time Richard Dawkins to signify a piece of information or concept that spreads across society. Nowadays it's easiest to understand a meme as a viral Internet joke. Sometimes memes are funny, sometimes they are not funny, sometimes they are racist, and sometimes they mean absolutely nothing and go viral anyway.

*'I don't understand this meme with the pigs and the oats, can a young person please explain it to me?'*

**Lit** (adj.) – When something is lit, it's lively, it's happening, it's kicking off, it's the place to be.

*'Twitter is gonna be lit when the nukes get fired.'*

**Tbh** (abbr.) – This stands for 'to be honest', but for whatever reason, has a slightly different *feel* to it when in its abbreviated form. It can be placed at the beginning of a sentence as if to introduce a confession or guilty thought, or at the end to signify something that everyone obviously already thinks, though these are not strict rules.

*'You should quit your job tomorrow tbh.'*
*'Tbh I should. I just want a million pounds tbh is that so much to ask?'*
*'You deserve it tbh.'*

**IRL** (abbr.) – This stands for 'in real life'. In our modern, high-tech, fast-paced, high-fallutin' world, it is necessary to have a quick way to distinguish things that have happened on the Internet from things you saw and touched and spoke to in the real, living, breathing, terrible world.

*'Hahaha I just did an IRL lol.'*

**Tinder** (n.) – This does not refer to wood that you burn in a wholesome snowy cabin, but rather, a phone application where people decide if they want to have sex with each other based on a few photos and whatever few lines they have used to describe themselves in their 'bio'. Misguided gentlemen use the app to send photographs of their penis to people they've never met.

*'If Romeo and Juliet met on Tinder instead of IRL things probably would have turned out a lot better for them tbh.'*

**Dragged** (v.) – If you are being dragged, or receiving a dragging, you are being criticised publically for poor behaviour, and you probably deserve it.

*'Drag him! DRAG HIM!'*

**Buzzkill** (n.) – Something which has suddenly changed your mood from light-hearted and cheerful to miserable about the bitterness of life and the horrors of the world.

*'I was reading this funny book about women in history when suddenly there was a whole bit about Nazis and it was such a buzzkill tbh.'*

*'Nazis are the worst kind of buzzkill tbh.'*

**Lean In!** (a command by a rich woman) – The phrase *Lean In* was coined by a Facebook executive, Sheryl Sandberg, who made it the title of her book about how ~career ladies~ can best fight their way to the top of corporations to achieve unfathomable riches and glossy hair. On the one hand, as a concept, *leaning in* can put a lot of pressure on women to change their behaviours to better suit a sexist workplace, and is only really relevant to the top socio-economic echelons of society. On the other hand, it's fun to imagine yelling at a woman who has been dead for a thousand years for murdering her enemies.

*'Lean in, Empress Wu!'*

*'Lean in, Ælfthryth!'*

*'I tried to lean in and ask for more money but instead I got fired, lol.'*

**~putting these things around stuff~** (punctuation) – This cannot be properly explained, it is simply an ~aesthetic~. It can be used to note your self-awareness at employing a phrase that is either hackneyed or ~fancy~ or both.

*'My friend Harriet travels a lot for work because she's a very glamorous ~career woman~.'*

**Amirite?** (abbr.) – An abbreviation of 'Am I right?', to be read in the style of a slightly sleazy stand-up comic who has run out of things to say. Amirite? Yeah, I am!

*'Sounds like my ex-wife – amirite fellas?! The guy in the back, he gets it!'*

**Narc** (n.) – Literally a narcotics agent, but can really mean anyone who takes your drugs away. A person who is a buzzkill.

*'I can't believe some narc called the cops on my bitchin' party.'*

**NBD** (abbr.) – This stands for 'no big deal'. It usually means that something was a HUGE deal to you, but you're trying to pretend you're chill about it.

*'Yeah, my tweet got like 15 likes, nbd.'*

**Slide into DMs** (v.) – To send someone a direct message rather than tweeting them publically. Implies lustful intent. Can also be used metaphorically for offline scenarios.

*'Romeo slid into Juliet's DMs like: "My name, dear saint, is hateful to myself, because it is an enemy to thee; Had I it written, I would tear the word."'*

**Bants** (n. or adj.) – Short for banter. A thing can be bants, a person can be bants, or a person or thing can reveal a distinct lack of bants, which is always a great disappointment. A person may decide to do something foolish 'for the bants', which is almost never a good idea.

*'And Juliet replied, "What man art thou that thus bescreen'd in night so stumblest on my counsel? If you're going to slide in my DMs like this you'd better bring the bants."'*

**Emo** (adj. or n.) – Emo is both a genre of super-emotional music, and a ~way of being~. If you are emo, you feel things deeply. You are not OK. Nobody understands you. You probably have lots of eyeliner and/or black hair straightened into a colossal fringe and I dated you when I was 16.

*'Who among us did not experience an emo phase?'*

**Metal** (adj.) – Like emo, but with metal music. Can be used to mean that something is hardcore. If you have never heard heavy metal, go into your kitchen and drop all your pots and pans on the floor while screaming. That's what it sounds like.

*'Holy crap Izzy my period was so metal this month.'*

**Fake news!** (n.) – Though some people and presidents believe any media attention that casts them in a poor light to be 'FAKE NEWS!', the phrase actually refers to an article someone has written that they *know* to be made up, in order to generate traffic to their website or for other nefarious reasons.

*'I read an article I disagreed with and therefore deem it to be FAKE NEWS!!!'*

**Woke bae** (n.) – A gentleman who is both attractive and attuned to the social justice issues of the day. Perhaps he is attractive *because* he is attuned to the social justice issues of the day. Or perhaps he became interested in the social justice issues of the day merely because he wanted people to be attracted to him, in which case his status as a true woke bae is called into question.

*'Sooo I thought Steve could be my woke bae but then he got mad when I joked that his dog had white male privilege.'*
*'Told you that guy was a prick.'*

**WhatsApp** (n.) – A popular text-messaging service before which no human communication was possible.

*'How did people even talk before they had WhatsApp voice notes? Idk.'*

**Idk** (abbr.) – Short for 'I don't know'.

*'Idk man, I'm kind of freaked out by hang-gliding.'*

**YOLO** (abbr.) – Short for YOU ONLY LIVE ONCE, as coined in 2011 by the musical artist Drake. While it should imply that you ought to live your life very carefully and never risk damage to life and limb, it is in fact a thing you yell before you do something incredibly stupid, dangerous, or expensive.

*'Come on man, just think how much chicks dig hang-gliding! You can put a pic on your Tinder profile it'll be awesome. YOLO man!!'*
*'Yeah, OK, fine, YOLO let's do it!'*
*[They both die in a terrible hang-gliding accident.]*

**Ho** (v. or n.) – An expression for a *loose woman or man* that is usually derogatory but in this book is used warmly.

*'Why shouldn't people in the 17th century get to ho it up a bit? Everyone's always been a big ho. YOLO.'*

**BS** (abbr.) – Short for bullshit. The shit that comes out of a bull, as opposed to a horse, which is called horseshit.

*'My boo told me he was working late but I'm pretty sure it was BS.'*

**A lad** (n.) – A person who likes a bit of banter and often does legendary things like drinking 12 cans of beer and placing their bare bum against the window of a bus.

*'St Brigid of Kildare was a lad.'*

**An absolute lad** (n.) – A lad but more.

*'St Brigid of Kildare was an absolute lad.'*

**Tl;dr** (abbr. or n.) – Short for 'too long; didn't read'. Can also mean the shortened, summarised version of something. Often used if someone has sent you an article over 300 words.

*'Hey did you read my book??'*
*'Sorry tl;dr.'*

# Acknowledgements

It turns out that writing a book makes you a pretty awful person. The amount of whining you do and how self-centred you become is truly astounding. (And by you, I mean me. See what I mean?) To make things worse, all of this whining happens as a result of having received an incredible opportunity – to write a damn book, with a lot of help from a lot of people. What I'm saying is, thank you and I'm sorry to everyone who came into contact with me and supported me in the short but intense period of my life spent creating this wild she-beast of a book.

First of all, thank you to my agent Charlie Viney of The Viney Agency, for reaching out to me in 2016 to see if I wanted to write a book, which it turns out I did. As a first-time author with little to no understanding of how the world works, I will always be grateful for your guidance, your good humour, and your belief in me and this project.

Thank you to Hannah Black at Hodder & Stoughton, not only for your wise editing, but for your kindness in delivering me much-needed praise at the very moments when I was ready to set fire to my computer. (Great name btw.) I am also grateful to Ian Wong at Hodder for doing *literally everything*, particularly the nitty-gritty gruelling bits of making a book not suck. Thank you to Caitriona Horne, Heather Keane, and Rebecca Mundy for your marketing and PR work, as well as your top Twitter bants. Thank you to Claudette Morris and Susan Spratt for turning a miserable-looking Word doc into a real live book, and to Lesley

Hodgson for getting all the wonderful photos you see in these pages – they add so much to the work, and were not always easy to find. In fact, everyone at Hodder did an incredible amount of work in a very short amount of time, and I hope it didn't make you sick of historical ladies. It's not their fault, it's mine.

Guess what: there are lots of others who worked on this book even though it wasn't even their damn job to do so. Before I even get to them, I want to direct all my readers to the bibliography. This book depended on the work of Real Historians™, who do meticulous hard work for not much reward. Please have a look especially at the biographies I read for this project – these authors dedicated years to researching the details of these women's lives that bring their stories to life. They did the hard part and I got to have the fun, so please support your local historians and buy their excellent books.

Speaking of Real Historians™ (and other varieties of Real Academics™), this book was made 100 times better by the edits and suggestions of a whole army of clever PhD types, many of whom I quoted in these pages. Thank you to Joseph Kellner for having a look at my Russians, and to Eoghan Ahern and Timothy Wright for taking on my medieval babes. Thank you to Julia Wambach for sharing your expertise on my French and WWII-era chapters, to Melissa Turoff for your invaluable suggestions on my South Asian chapters, and to Maha Atal for your edits on my African chapters. Thank you to Trevor Jackson for looking in on my philosophers and revolutionaries – you, too, are a philosopher and a revolutionary. Thank you to Kelly Oakes for checking my scientists, you are not only a super smart scientist but also a brilliant writer and editor and I can't wait to read YOUR book. And thank you times a million to Laura Gutiérrez for not only editing multiple sections, but for being the best cheerleader a girl could ever want throughout this whole process.

But wait – THERE'S MORE. Thanks to Sam Stander for your perfect edits on my introduction, and to Bim Adewunmi for editing multiple chapters and for being a mentor, a friend, an advocate, and all-around top gal. Thank you to Gena-mour Barrett and to Tom Phillips, who did both normal editing and crucial banter checks. You are the funniest writers in the world, no offence to all other writers. I received so many great suggestions of women to include from friends and strangers – thank you in particular to Margaret Wetherell, Hattie Soykan, and Harry Kennard for going out of their way to find me excellent women in history. Thanks, I guess, to Dan Dalton for giving me a shitty old laptop to write the book with. Every time the 'e' key fell off, which was often, I cursed your name. Thanks to all my former colleagues at BuzzFeed UK for creating the environment of creativity and weirdness that incubated me as a writer over three years, you're all hilarious geniuses and I miss you guys.

Throughout my time spent writing and editing this book I was hosted by a number of fine and attractive people in their fine and attractive homes. Thank you to Maggy van Eijk and her family in Amsterdam, the perfect place to kick off the writing. Thank you Philippa and Flo Perry for hosting me in your splendid country home, where we worked hard but also took ample breaks for food, wine, and painting. Thank you Dee and Gordon Chesterman for being my surrogate parents while I worked in my very favourite place, your house in Ely. Sorry, Uncle Gordon, that you didn't get to letterpress-print the whole book. Maybe next time. Thank you also to Felicity Taylor and Harriet Williams for letting me stay with you so often in your house, my other favourite place, which happens to be the cultural and political heart of London. It was a home away from home, and also my banking address. Thank you to my brother and sister-in-law Simeon and Amy Jewell, their daughter and future remarkable woman Hazel, and Amy's parents Devra and John Harris, for looking after me in the dire last moments of writing and editing.

I wouldn't know any of the Real Historians™ above if it weren't for my boyfriend Sam Wetherell, the realest historian of all. Thank you Sam for being the first person to read and comment on every single chapter, for supporting me in my most extravagant moments of self-doubt, and most of all for making me delicious soups. You may not know how to put a duvet cover on, but you're very good at history, and I continue to learn so much from you.

And finally, I wouldn't even EXIST if it weren't for my parents, Jane and Chris Jewell, who not only made me a human person, for which I am very grateful, but raised me to be curious about the world, to care about other people and to not take myself too seriously. If the book does well, I promise to put you in an above-average retirement home some day. I love you both.

# Bibliography

**Ælfthryth**

Rabin, Andrew, 'Female Advocacy and Royal Protection in Tenth-Century England: The Legal Career of Queen Ælfthryth', *Speculum* 84, no. 2 (2009): 261–8.

**Æthelflæd**

Rank, Melissa and Rank, Michael, *The Most Powerful Women in the Middle Ages: Queens, Saints, and Viking Slayers, From Empress Theodora to Elizabeth of Tudor* (CreateSpace Independent Publishing Platform, 2013).

**Alexandra Kollontai**

Bridenthal, Renate, Koonz, Claudia and Mosher Stuard, Susan, *Becoming Visible: Women in European History* (Houghton Mifflin, 1987).

Míeville, China, *October: The Story of the Russian Revolution* (London; Brooklyn, NY: Verso, 2017).

**Annie Jump Cannon**

'Annie Jump Cannon: American Astronomer', *Encyclopedia Britannica*. Accessed July 29, 2017; https://www.britannica.com/biography/Annie-Jump-Cannon.

Greenstein, George, *Portraits of Discovery: Profiles in Scientific Genius*, 1st edition (New York: Wiley, 1997).

Julie, Des, *The Madame Curie Complex: The Hidden History of Women in Science* (The Feminist Press at CUNY, 2010).

### Annie Smith Peck

Kimberley, Hannah, *A Woman's Place Is at the Top: A Biography of Annie Smith Peck, Queen of the Climbers* (New York: St. Martin's Press, 2017).

### Artemisia Gentileschi

'Artemisia Gentileschi' *The Art History Babes*. Accessed July 29, 2017; http://www.arthistorybabes.com/podcast/2016/8/4/artemisia-gentileschi.

Danto, Arthur C., 'Artemisia and the Elders', *The Nation*, March 21, 2002; https://www.thenation.com/article/artemisia-and-elders/.

### Artemisia I of Caria

'Artemisia I of Caria', *Ancient History Encyclopedia*. Accessed July 29, 2017; http://www.ancient.eu/Artemisia_I_of_Caria/.

### Beatrice Potter Webb

Nolan, Barbara E., *The Political Theory of Beatrice Webb* (New York: AMS Press, 1988); http://webbs.library.lse.ac.uk/628/.

Seymour-Jones, Carole, *Beatrice Webb: Woman of Conflict* (London: Allison & Busby, 1992).

Webb, Beatrice, *The Co-Operative Movement in Great Britain* (London: Sonnenschein & Co, 1899).

Webb, Beatrice, *Beatrice Webb's Diaries,1912-1924*, 1st edition (Longmans, Green Co, 1952).

### Brigid of Kildare

Kennedy, Patrick, *Legendary Fictions of the Irish Celts* (Cornell University Library, 1866).

'Saint Brigid of Ireland | Biography & Facts', *Encyclopedia Britannica*. Accessed July 29, 2017; https://www.britannica.com/biography/Saint-Brigit-of-Ireland.

### Cecilia Payne-Gaposchkin

Greenstein, George, *Portraits of Discovery: Profiles in Scientific Genius*, 1st edition (New York: Wiley, 1997).

Julie, Des, *The Madame Curie Complex: The Hidden History of Women in Science* (The Feminist Press at CUNY, 2010).

**Ching Shih**

'6 Lady Pirates', *Encyclopedia Britannica*. Accessed July 30, 2017; https://www.britannica.com/list/6-lady-pirates.

'Ching Shih (Fl. 1807–1810) – Dictionary Definition of Ching Shih (Fl. 1807–1810) | Encyclopedia.com: FREE Online Dictionary', Accessed July 30, 2017; http://www.encyclopedia.com/women/encyclopedias-almanacs-transcripts-and-maps/ching-shih-fl-1807-1810.

Cordingly, David, *Pirates: Fact & Fiction* (Artabras, 1992).

**Coccinelle**

Costa, Mario A., *Reverse Sex . . . The Life of Jacqueline Charlotte Dufresnoy. With Portraits,* Translation by Jules J. Block (London: Challenge Publications, 1961).

**Constance Markievicz**

'BBC – History – 1916 Easter Rising – Profiles – Countess Markievicz'. Accessed July 29, 2017; http://www.bbc.co.uk/history/british/easterrising/profiles/po10.shtml.

Haverty, Anne, *Constance Markievicz: An Independent Life* (London: Pandora, 1988).

**Dorothy Thompson**

Sanders, Marion K, *Dorothy Thompson: A Legend in Her Time* (Houghton Mifflin, 1973).

Thompson, Dorothy, *Dorothy Thompson's Political Guide: A Study of American Liberalism and Its Relationship to Modern Totalitarian States* (New York: Stackpole Sons Publishers, 1938).

Thomas, Helen. *Watchdogs of Democracy?: The Waning Washington Press Corps and How It Has Failed the Public,* 1st edition (New York: Scribner, 2006).

Thompson, Dorothy, *I Saw Hitler* (Farrar & Rinehart, Inc., 1932).

Thompson, Dorothy, *Listen Hans* (Houghton Mifflin, 1942).

**Elizabeth Hart**

Ferguson, Moira, Hart Gilbert, Anne and Hart Thwaites, Elizabeth, *The Hart Sisters: Early African Caribbean Writers, Evangelicals, and Radicals* (University of Nebraska Press, 1993).

Lightfoot, Natasha, 'The Hart Sisters of Antigua: Evangelica Activism and "Respectable" Public Politics in the Era of Black Atlantic Slavery', in *Toward an Intellectual History of Black Women* (Chapel Hill, North Carolina: UNC Press Books, 2013).

**Emmy Noether**

'Emmy Noether, Mathematics Trailblazer', *Stuff You Missed in History*, September 7, 2015; http://www.missedinhistory.com/podcasts/ emmy-noether-mathematics-trailblazer.htm.

Mack, Dr Katie, 'Dr Katie Mack On Emmy Noether', *The Laborastory (Podcast)* on Player FM. Accessed July 29, 2017; https://player. fm/series/the-laborastory/dr-katie-mack-on-emmy-noether.

**Empress Theodora**

Rank, Melissa, and Rank, Michael, *The Most Powerful Women in the Middle Ages: Queens, Saints, and Viking Slayers, From Empress Theodora to Elizabeth of Tudor* (CreateSpace Independent Publishing Platform, 2013).

**Empress Wu**

Clements, Jonathan, *Wu: The Chinese Empress Who Schemed, Seduced and Murdered Her Way to Become a Living God* (London: Albert Bridge Books, 2014).

**Ethel Payne**

Morris, James McGrath, 'Ethel Payne, "first lady of the black press," asked questions no one else would', *Washington Post*. Accessed July 29, 2017; https://www.washingtonpost.com/opinions/ethel-paynefirst-lady-of-the-black-pressasked-questions-no-one-else-would/2011/08/02/gIQAJloFBJ_story.html.

Morris, James McGrath, *Eye on the Struggle: Ethel Payne, the First Lady of the Black Press* (New York: Amistad Press, 2015).

**Fanny Cochrane Smith**

Clark, J., 'Smith, Fanny Cochrane (1834–1905)', in *Australian Dictionary of Biography* (Canberra: National Centre of Biography, Australian National University, n.d.); http://adb.anu.edu.au/biography/smith-fanny-cochrane-8466.

**Fatima al-Fihri**

Glacier, Osire, *Political Women in Morocco: Then and Now*, 1st edition (Trenton, NJ: Red Sea Press, US, 2013).

**Frances Ellen Watkins Harper**

Field, Corinne T., 'Frances E.W. Harper and the Politics of Intellectual Maturity', in *Toward an Intellectual History of Black Women* (Chapel Hill, North Carolina: UNC Press Books, 2013).

**Funmilayo Ransome-Kuti**

Bishop, Moe, 'Coffin for Head of State', *Vice*, 2011. Accessed August 1, 2017. https://www.vice.com/en_us/article/znqen3/Wasted-Life-Coffin-for-head-of-state.

Byfield, Judith A., 'Feeding the Troops: Abeokuta (Nigeria) and World War II', *African Economic History*, no. 35 (2007): 77–87.

Byfield, Judith A., 'From Ladies to Women: Funmilayo Ransome-Kuti and Women's Political Activism in Post-World War II Nigeria', in *Toward an Intellectual History of Black Women* (Chapel Hill, North Carolina: UNC Press Books, 2013).

Byfield, Judith A., 'Taxation, Women, and the Colonial State: Egba Women's Tax Revolt', *Meridians* vol. 3, no. 2 (2003): 250–77.

Soyinka, Wole, *Aké: The Years of Childhood* (New York: Random House, 1981).

**Gabriela Brimmer**

Brimmer, Gabriela, and Poniatowska, Elena, *Gaby Brimmer: An Autobiography in Three Voices* (University Press of New England, 2009).

Mandoki, Luis, *Gaby: A True Story*, VHS, Sony Pictures Home Entertainment, 1987.

**George Sand**

Jack, Belinda, 'George Sand: A Woman's Life Writ Large', *New York Times*. Accessed July 30, 2017; http://www.nytimes.com/books/first/j/jack-sand.html.

'George Sand | French Novelist', *Encyclopedia Britannica*. Accessed July 30, 2017; https://www.britannica.com/biography/George-Sand.

**Gladys Bentley**

Wilson, James F., *Bulldaggers, Pansies, and Chocolate Babies: Performance, Race, and Sexuality in the Harlem Renaissance* in *Triangulations* (Ann Arbor, Mich.: London: University of Michigan Press; Eurospan distributor, 2010).

**Hannah Arendt**

Arendt, Hannah, *Eichmann in Jerusalem: A Report on the Banality of Evil* (London: Faber and Faber, 1963).

Arendt, Hannah, *On Revolution* (London: Faber & Faber, 1963).

Arendt, Hannah, *The Origins of Totalitarianism*, 2nd enlarged edition (Meridian Books, MG15, New York: Meridian Books, 1958).

Arendt, Hannah, and Canovan, Margaret, *The Human Condition: Second Edition*, 2nd revised edition (Chicago: University of Chicago Press, 1998).

Trotta, Margarethe von, *Hannah Arendt* (Zeitgeist Films, 2013).

**Hatshepsut**

'Hatshepsut | Ruler of Egypt', *Encyclopedia Britannica*. Accessed July 29, 2017; https://www.britannica.com/biography/Hatshepsut.

'Hatshepsut' *In Our Time*, BBC Radio 4. Accessed July 29, 2017; http://www.bbc.co.uk/programmes/b04n62jx.

**Hedy Lamarr**

'Hedy Lamarr | Austrian-Born American Actress', *Encyclopedia*

*Britannica*. Accessed July 30, 2017; https://www.britannica.com/biography/Hedy-Lamarr.

'Star Wars Episode III: Hedy Lamarr (YMRT #29)', *You Must Remember This*. Accessed July 29, 2017; http://www.youmustrememberthispodcast.com/episodes/youmustrememberthispodcastblog/2015/1/14/star-wars-episode-iii-hedy-lamarr-ymrt-29.

**Hildegard von Bingen**

'Hildegard Von Bingen', Series 25, *Great Lives*, BBC Radio 4. Accessed July 29, 2017; http://www.bbc.co.uk/programmes/b014q00c.

**Hypatia**

'Hypatia Biography'. Accessed July 30, 2017; http://www-groups.dcs.st-and.ac.uk/history/Biographies/Hypatia.html.

Zielinski, Sarah, 'Hypatia, Ancient Alexandria's Great Female Scholar', *Smithsonian*. Accessed July 30, 2017; http://www.smithsonianmag.com/history/hypatia-ancient-alexandrias-great-female-scholar-10942888/.

'Hypatia | Mathematician and Astronomer', *Encyclopedia Britannica*. Accessed July 29, 2017; https://www.britannica.com/biography/Hypatia.

**Ida B. Wells-Barnett**

Giddings, Paula J., *Ida: A Sword Among Lions: Ida B. Wells and the Campaign Against Lynching*, Reprint edition (New York: Harper Paperbacks, 2009).

Giddings, Paula J., *When and Where I Enter: The Impact of Black Women on Race and Sex in America* (New York: W. Morrow, 1984).

Wells-Barnett, Ida B., *Southern Horrors: Lynch Law in All Its Phases*, 1892; http://archive.org/details/southernhorrors14975gut.

**Irena Sendler**

Mazzeo, Tilar J., *Irena's Children: The Extraordinary Story of the Woman Who Saved 2,500 Children from the Warsaw Ghetto*, Reprint edition (New York; London; Toronto: Gallery Books, 2017).

**Jang-geum**

'Jungjong of Joseon – New World Encyclopedia'. Accessed July 29, 2017; http://www.newworldencyclopedia.org/entry/Jungjong_of_Joseon.

Myung-ho, Shin., 'Annals of the Joseon Dynasty Brought to Life by the Digital Era', *Koreana: A Quarterly on Korean Art & Culture*, 2008; http://koreana.kf.or.kr/pdf_file/2008/2008_AUTUMN_E022.pdf.

**Jayaben Desai**

Dromey, Jack, 'Jayaben Desai Obituary', *Guardian*, December 28, 2010; http://www.theguardian.com/politics/2010/dec/28/jayaben-desai-obituary.

'Grunwick: Chronology of Events | Striking Women: Voices of South Asian Women Workers from Grunwick and Gate Gourmet'. Accessed July 29, 2017; http://www.leeds.ac.uk/strikingwomen/grunwick/chronology.

'Jayaben Desai', *WCML*. Accessed July 29, 2017; http://www.wcml.org.uk/our-collections/activists/jayaben-desai/.

**Jean Batten**

'Jean Batten | NZHistory, New Zealand History Online'. Accessed July 29, 2017; https://nzhistory.govt.nz/people/jean-batten.

'Jean Batten – The Garbo of the Skies | Television | NZ On Screen'. Accessed July 29, 2017; https://www.nzonscreen.com/title/jean-batten-the-garbo-of-the-skies-1988.

Taonga, New Zealand Ministry for Culture and Heritage Te Manatu, 'Batten, Jean Gardner' web page. Accessed July 29, 2017; /en/biographies/4b13/batten-jean-gardner.

**Jean Macnamara**

Zwar, Desmond, *The Dame: The Life and Times of Dame Jean Macnamara, Medical Pioneer*, 1st edition (South Melbourne: Macmillan, 1984).

## Jind Kaur

Matthew, H. C. G., and Harrison, B., eds. Bance, Bhupinder Singh, 'Jind Kaur (1817–1863)', First Published 2004; Online Edition, Jan 2006, 854 Words, in *The Oxford Dictionary of National Biography* (Oxford: Oxford University Press, 2004).

## Josephine Baker

Baker, Jean-Claude, *Josephine Baker: The Hungry Heart* (New York: Cooper Square Press, 2001).

## Jovita Idár

Gonzalez, Gabriela, 'Jovita Idár: The Ideological Origins of a Transnational Advocate for La Raza', in *Texas Women: Their Histories, Their Lives* (Athens, Georgia: University of Georgia Press, 2015).

## Juana Azurduy

'Azurduy de Padilla, Juana (1781–1862) – Dictionary Definition of Azurduy de Padilla, Juana (1781–1862) | Encyclopedia.com: FREE Online Dictionary'. Accessed July 29, 2017; http://www. encyclopedia.com/women/encyclopedias-almanacs-transcripts-and-maps/azurduy-de-padilla-juana-1781-1862.

## Julia de Burgos

Pérez Rosario, Vanessa, *Becoming Julia de Burgos: The Making of a Puerto Rican Icon* (Urbana: University of Illinois Press, 2014).

## Julie D'Aubigny

Gardiner, Kelly, 'Swordswoman, Opera Singer, Runaway: "Goddess" Chronicles A Fabled Life', *NPR.org*. Accessed July 29, 2017; http://www.npr.org/2015/10/03/445032371/swordswoman-opera-singer-runaway-goddess-chronicles-a-fabled-life.

## Khayzuran

Mernissi, Fatima, *The Forgotten Queens of Islam*, Translated by Mary Jo Lakeland (Cambridge: Polity Press, 1993).

**Kosem Sultan**

Rank, Melissa, and Rank, Michael, *The Most Powerful Women in the Middle Ages: Queens, Saints, and Viking Slayers, From Empress Theodora to Elizabeth of Tudor* (CreateSpace Independent Publishing Platform, 2013).

**Lakshmibai, Rani of Jhansi**

Mukhoty, Ira, *Heroines: Powerful Indian Women of Myth and History* (Aleph Book Company, 2017).

**Laskarina Bouboulina**

'Bouboulina, Laskarina (1771–1825) – Dictionary Definition of Bouboulina, Laskarina (1771–1825) | Encyclopedia.com: FREE Online Dictionary'. Accessed July 29, 2017; http://www.encyclopedia.com/women/encyclopedias-almanacs-transcripts-and-maps/bouboulina-laskarina-1771-1825.

Gammell, Caroline, 'Greek Woman "Sets Fire" to Briton's Genitals: Laskarina Bouboulina the Heroine', *Telegraph,* August 7, 2009; http://www.telegraph.co.uk/news/worldnews/europe/greece/5989510/Greek-woman-sets-fire-to-Britons-genitals-Laskarina-Bouboulina-the-heroine.html.

**Laura Redden Searing**

Luck, Jessica Lewis, 'Lyric Underheard: The Printed Voice of Laura Catherine Redden Searing', *Legacy: A Journal of American Women Writers*, 30, no. 1 (2013): 62–81.

**Lilian Bland**

Bol, Rosita, 'Lilian Bland, the First Woman to Fly an Aircraft in Ireland', *The Irish Times*. Accessed July 30, 2017; http://www.irishtimes.com/life-and-style/people/lilian-bland-the-first-woman-to-fly-an-aircraft-in-ireland-1.2765782.

McIlwaine, Eddie, 'Journalist, Photographer, Crackshot and the First Woman to Fly an Aeroplane . . . the Amazing Lilian Bland', *BelfastTelegraph.co.uk*. Accessed July 30, 2017; http://www.belfast

telegraph.co.uk/life/features/journalist-photographer-crackshot-and-the-first-woman-to-fly-an-aeroplane-the-amazing-lilian-bland-28552187.html.

'Women's Museum of Ireland | Articles | Lilian Bland'. Accessed July 30, 2017; http://womensmuseumofireland.ie/articles/lilian-bland.

**Lillian Ngoyi**

Freeman, Cathy L. *Relays in Rebellion: The Power in Lilian Ngoyi and Fannie Lou Hamer* (Georgia State University, 2009); http://search.proquest.com/openview/71a114e383d1d4aac5cc517ea60de12e/1?pq-origsite=gscholar&cbl=18750&diss=y.

Joseph, Helen, *Tomorrow's Sun: A Smuggled Journal from South Africa* (Hutchinson, 1966).

Möller, Pieter L., 'They Also Served: Ordinary South African Women in an Extraordinary Struggle: The Case of Erna de Villiers (Buber)', 2010; http://repository.nwu.ac.za/handle/10394/5227.

**Lotfia Elnadi**

Cooper, Ann, 'Lotfia El Nadi – The First Woman Pilot in Egypt', *Ninety-Nine News: Magazine of the International Women Pilots*, November 1991, Vol. 17, No. 9 edition.

**Louisa Atkinson**

Chisholm, A. H., 'Atkinson, Caroline Louisa (1834–1872)', in *Australian Dictionary of Biography* (Canberra: National Centre of Biography, Australian National University, n.d.); http://adb.anu.edu.au/biography/atkinson-caroline-louisa-2910.

Clarke, Patricia, *Pioneer Writer: the Life of Louisa Atkinson: Novelist, Journalist, Naturalist* (Allen & Unwin, 1990).

**Louise Mack**

Phelan, Nancy, *The Romantic Lives of Louise Mack* (St. Lucia, Qld.: University of Queensland Press, 1991).

**Lozen**

Aleshire, Peter, *Warrior Woman: The Story of Lozen, Apache Warrior and Shaman* (St. Martin's Press, 2015).

Ball, Eve and Kaywaykla, James (narrator) *In the days of Victorio: Recollections of a Warm Springs Apache* (Tucson: University of Arizona Press, 1970).

**Lucy Hicks Anderson**

'Lucy Hicks Anderson', *We've Been Around* website. Accessed July 29, 2017; http://www.wevebeenaround.com/lucy/.

**Luisa Moreno**

Johnson, Gaye Theresa, 'Constellations of Struggle: Luisa Moreno, Charlotta Bass, and the Legacy for Ethnic Studies', *Aztlán: A Journal of Chicano Studies* 33, no. 1 (2008): 155–72.

Ruiz, Vicki, 'Una Mujer Sin Fronteras', *Pacific Historical Review* 73, no. 1 (2004): 1–20.

**Margery Kempe**

Kempe, Margery, *The Book of Margery Kempe* (DS Brewer, 2004); https://books.google.co.uk/books?hl=en&lr=&id=LypF-lv_ ZXgC&oi=fnd&pg=PR6&dq=margery+kempe&ots=GNk-TQe1xas&sig=_j1wq6Av80JEVww65jrxSj5pRZk.

Temple, Liam Peter, 'Returning the English "Mystics" to Their Medieval Milieu: Julian of Norwich, Margery Kempe and Bridget of Sweden', *Women's Writing*, 23, no. 2 (2016): 141–58.

Tuthill, Janet, 'Margery Kempe: A Mirror of Change in Late-Medieval England' (State University of New York at Stony Brook, 2016); http://search.proquest.com/openview/2ad6495aad62d5f57511c 35da5865277/1?pq-origsite=gscholar&cbl=18750&diss=y.

**Marie Chauvet**

Glover, Kaiama L., '"Black" Radicalism in Haiti and the Disorderly Feminine: The Case of Marie Vieux Chauvet', *Small Axe* 17, no. 1 40 (March 1, 2013): 7–21; doi:10.1215/07990537-1665407.

Glover, Kaiama L., 'Daughter of Haiti: Marie Vieux Chauvet', in *Toward an Intellectual History of Black Women* (Chapel Hill, North Carolina: UNC Press Books, 2013).

**Mary Wollstonecraft**

Gordon, Charlotte, *Romantic Outlaws: The Extraordinary Lives of Mary Wollstonecraft and Mary Shelley* (London: Hutchinson, 2015).

Taylor, Barbara, 'Wollstonecraft, Mary (1759–1797)', *Oxford Dictionary of National Biography* (Oxford University Press, 2014).

**Mercedes de Acosta**

Schanke, Robert A., *'That Furious Lesbian': The Story of Mercedes de Acosta*, Theater in the Americas (Carbondale, Ill.; London: Southern Illinois University Press; Eurospan, 2003).

**Mirabal Sisters**

Robinson, Nancy, 'Women's Political Participation in the Dominican Republic: The Case of the Mirabal Sisters', *Caribbean Quarterly*, 52, no. 2–3 (June 1, 2006): 172–83; doi:10.1080/00086495.200 6.11829706.

'The Assassination of the Mirabal Sisters', *Witness*, BBC World Service. Accessed July 29, 2017; http://www.bbc.co.uk/programmes/p04h454t.

**Miriam Makeba**

Allen, Lara, *Remembering Miriam Makeba: (4 March 1932–10 November 2008)* (Taylor & Francis, 2008); http://www.tandfonline.com/doi/pdf/10.2989/JMAA.2008.5.1.6.789.

Bordowitz, Hank. *Noise of the World: Non-Western Musicians in Their Own Words* (Brooklyn, NY: Soft Skull Press, 2005).

Ewens, Graeme, 'Obituary: Miriam Makeba', *Guardian*, November 11, 2008; http://www.theguardian.com/music/2008/nov/11/miriam-makeba-obituary.

Kaurismäki, Mika, *Mama Africa*, Documentary, 2011; http://www.imdb.com/title/tt1543029/.

## Murasaki Shikibu

'Beyond The Tale of Genji: Murasaki Shikibu as Icon and Exemplum in Seventeenth- and Eighteenth-Century Popular Japanese Texts for Women', *ResearchGate*. Accessed July 29, 2017; https://www.researchgate.net/publication/279315379_Beyond_The_Tale_of_Genji_Murasaki_Shikibu_as_Icon_and_Exemplum_in_Seventeenth-_and_Eighteenth-Century_Popular_Japanese_Texts_for_Women.

'Murasaki Shikibu | Japanese Courtier and Author', *Encyclopedia Britannica*. Accessed July 29, 2017; https://www.britannica.com/biography/Shikibu-Murasaki.

## Nana Asma'u

Azuonye, Chukwuma, 'Feminist or Simply Feminine? Reflections on the Works of Nana Asmā'u, a Nineteenth-Century West African Woman Poet, Intellectual, and Social Activist', *Meridians: Feminism, Race, Transnationalism*, 6, no. 2 (2006): 54–76.

Dangana, Muhammad, 'The Intellectual Contribution of Nana Asma'u to Women's Education in Nineteenth-Century Nigeria', *Journal of Muslim Minority Affairs* 19, no. 2 (1999): 285–90.

## Nancy Wake

Bailey, Roderick, 'Wake, Nancy Grace Augusta (1912-2011)', *Oxford Dictionary of National Biography* (Oxford University Press, 2015).

Leech, Graeme, 'Fearless Matriarch of Resistance', *The Australian*, August 8, 2011; http://at.theaustralian.com.au/link/04b8b68e-785a9578e2db9dd19d17b702?domain=theaustralian.com.au.

Stafford, David, 'Nancy Wake Obituary', *Guardian*, August 8, 2011; http://www.theguardian.com/world/2011/aug/08/nancy-wake-obituary.

## Nell Gwynn

Beauclerk, Charles, *Nell Gwyn: A Biography* (Thistle Publishing, 2015).

**Nellie Bly**

Bly, Nellie, *Ten Days in a Mad-House* (New York, NY: CreateSpace Independent Publishing Platform, 2011).

'Nellie Bly | American Journalist', *Encyclopedia Britannica*. Accessed July 29, 2017; https://www.britannica.com/biography/Nellie-Bly.

**Njinga of Angola**

Heywood, Linda M., *Njinga of Angola: Africa's Warrior Queen* (Cambridge, Massachusetts; London, England: Harvard University Press, 2017).

**Noor Inayat Khan**

Basu, Shrabani, *Spy Princess: The Life of Noor Inayat Khan*, 1st edition (New Lebanon, NY: Omega Publications, Inc., 2007).

**Olympe de Gouges**

Brown, Gregory S., 'The Self-Fashionings Of Olympe De Gouges, 1784-1789', *Eighteenth-Century Studies*, 34, no. 3 (20010301): 19.

Gouges, Olympe de, *Déclaration des droits de la femme et de la citoyenne* (Autrement, 2011); http://www.cairn.info/combats-de-femmes-1789-1799--9782746703971-page-223.htm.

Mousset, Sophie, *Women's Rights and the French Revolution: A Biography of Olympe de Gouges* (Transaction Publishers, 2011).

Rivas, Joshua, 'The Radical Novelty of Olympe de Gouges', *Nottingham French Studies*, 53 (2014): 345–58.

**Pancho Barnes**

Japenga, Ann, 'Pancho Barnes: An Affair With the Air Force: Ex-Socialite, Stunt Pilot, Club Owner Had the Right Stuff', *Los Angeles Times*, November 17, 1985; http://articles.latimes.com/1985-11-17/news/vw-6714_1_pancho-barnes.

Tate, Grover 'Ted', *The Lady Who Tamed Pegasus: The Story of Pancho Barnes* (Aviation Book Co, 1984).

**Phillis Wheatley**

Carretta, Vincent, *Phillis Wheatley: Biography of a Genius in Bondage* (University of Georgia Press, 2014).

431

Frund, Arlette, 'Phillis Wheatley, a Public Intellectual', in *Toward an Intellectual History of Black Women* (Chapel Hill, North Carolina: UNC Press Books, 2013).

Wheatley, Phillis, *The Collected Works of Phillis Wheatley* (Oxford University Press, 1988).

**Policarpa Salavarrieta**

Adams, Jerome R., *Notable Latin American Women: Twenty-Nine Leaders, Rebels, Poets, Battlers, and Spies, 1500-1900* (McFarland, 1995).

**Queen Liliuokalani**

Borch, Fred L., 'The Trial by Military Commission of Queen Liliuokalani', *Army Lawyer*, August 2014.

**Queen Nanny of the Maroons**

Gottlieb, Karla, *The Mother of Us All: A History of Queen Nanny, Leader of the Windward Jamaican Maroons* (Trenton, NJ: Africa World Press, 1998).

**Qutulun**

May, Timothy, *The Mongol Empire: A Historical Encyclopedia*, (ABC-CLIO, 2016).

**Raden Ajeng Kartini**

Kartini, Ibu, *On Feminism and Nationalism: Kartini's Letters to Stella Zeehandelaar, 1899-1903*, Translated and with an Introduction by Joost Coté (Clayton, Vic.: Monash Asia Institute, 1995).

Wargadiredja, Arzia Tivany, 'Kartini Was a Feminist Hero. So Why Is Her Holiday All About Beauty Pageants and Cooking Classes?' *Vice*. Accessed July 30, 2017; https://www.vice.com/en_id/article/aem7zp/kartini-was-a-feminist-hero-so-why-is-her-holiday-all-about-beauty-pageants-and-cooking-classes.

**Rani Chennamma**

Wodeyar, Sadashiva S., *Rani Chennamma* (National Book Trust, India, 1977).

**Rosa Luxemburg**

Evans, Kate, *Red Rosa: A Graphic Biography of Rosa Luxemburg*, Edited by Paul Buhle (Brooklyn, NY: Verso Books, 2015).

'Rosa Luxemburg', *In Our Time*, BBC Radio 4, Accessed July 29, 2017; http://www.bbc.co.uk/programmes/b08lfc77.

**Sappho**

Mendelsohn, Daniel, 'How Gay Was Sappho?', *The New Yorker*, March 9, 2015; http://www.newyorker.com/magazine/2015/03/16/girl-interrupted.

**Seondeok of Silla**

'Jungjong of Joseon – New World Encyclopedia', Accessed July 29, 2017; http://www.newworldencyclopedia.org/entry/Jungjong_of_Joseon.

Myung-ho, Shin, 'Annals of the Joseon Dynasty Brought to Life by the Digital Era', *Koreana: A Quarterly on Korean Art & Culture*, 2008; http://koreana.kf.or.kr/pdf_file/2008/2008_AUTUMN_E022.pdf.

**Sofia Perovskaya**

Bridenthal, Renate, Koona, Claudia and Mosher Stuard, Susan, *Becoming Visible: Women in European History* (Houghton Mifflin, 1987).

Porter, Cathy, *Fathers and Daughters: Russian Women in Revolution*, 1st edition (London: Virago Press Ltd, 1976).

**Sojourner Truth**

Smiet, Katrine, 'Post-Secular Truths: Sojourner Truth and the Intersections of Gender, Race and Religion', *European Journal of Women's Studies* 22, no. 1 (2015): 7–21.

'Sojourner Truth | American Evangelist and Social Reformer', *Encyclopedia Britannica*. Accessed July 29, 2017; https://www.britannica.com/biography/Sojourner-Truth.

'Sojourner Truth's Original "Ain't I a Woman" Speech', *The Sojourner*

*Truth Project*. Accessed July 29, 2017; https://www.thesojourner-truthproject.com/.

Truth, Sojourner, *Narrative of Sojourner Truth* (Penguin, 1998); https://books.google.co.uk/books?hl=en&lr=&id=pt0vYON-VXx4C&oi=fnd&pg=PT24&dq=sojourner+truth+narra-tive&ots=OiVCu2TVAA&sig=mDKl__hBZzFLu53nQA-3sZ7mlC8o.

Voices of a People's History of the United States, 'Kerry Washington reads Sojourner Truth', online video clip, YouTube; https://www.youtube.com/watch?v=yg3AYiRT4no

**Sophie Scholl**

Newborn, Jud and Dumbach, Annette, *Sophie Scholl and the White Rose*, Rev. ed. (Oxford: Oneworld, 2006).

*Sophie Scholl – The Final Days*, Zeitgeist Films, 2006.

**Sor Juana Inés de la Cruz**

Yugar, Theresa A., *Sor Juana Inés de La Cruz: Feminist Reconstruction of Biography and Text* (Wipf and Stock, 2014).

**Sorghaghtani Beki**

Allsen, Thomas, 'The Rise of the Mongolian Empire and Mongolian Rule in North China', *The Cambridge History of China*, 6 (1994): 321–413.

**Subh**

Glacier, Osire, *Political Women in Morocco: Then and Now*, 1st edition (Trenton, NJ: Red Sea Press, US, 2013).

Mernissi, Fatima, *The Forgotten Queens of Islam*, Translated by Mary Jo Lakeland (Cambridge: Polity Press, 1993).

**Susan La Flesche Picotte**

'Changing the Face of Medicine | Susan La Flesche Picotte', Accessed July 29, 2017; https://cfmedicine.nlm.nih.gov/physicians/biography_253.html.

Starita, Joe, *A Warrior of the People: How Susan La Flesche Overcame*

*Racial and Gender Inequality to Become America's First Indian Doctor* (New York: St Martin's Press, 2016).

**Tarabai Shinde**

O'Hanlon, Rosalind, *A Comparison between Women and Men: Tarabai Shinde and the Critique of Gender Relations in Colonial India.* (Madras; Oxford: Oxford University Press, 1994).

**Te Puea Herangi**

King, Michael, *Te Puea: A Life*, 4th edition (Auckland: Reed, 2003).

**Tomoe Gozen**

Brown, Steven T., 'From Woman Warrior to Peripatetic Entertainer: The Multiple Histories of Tomoe', *Harvard Journal of Asiatic Studies*, 58, no. 1 (1998): 183–99.

**Ulayya bint al-Mahdi**

Al Udhari, Abdullah, *Classical Poems by Arab Women* (London: Saqi Books, 1999).

Segol, Marla, 'Representing the Body in Poems by Medieval Muslim Women', in *Medieval Feminist Forum*, 45:12, 2009; http://ir.uiowa. edu/cgi/viewcontent.cgi?article=1773&context=mff.

**Umm Kulthum**

Goldman, Michal, *Umm Kulthum: A Voice Like Egypt* (AFD, 2007).

**Wallada bint al-Mustakfi**

Segol, Marla, 'Representing the Body in Poems by Medieval Muslim Women', in *Medieval Feminist Forum*, 45:12, 2009; http://ir.uiowa. edu/cgi/viewcontent.cgi?article=1773&context=mff.

Shamsie, Kamila, 'Librarians, Rebels, Property Owners, Slaves: Women in Al-Andalus' in *Journal of Postcolonial Writing*, 52, no. 2 (20160303): 178–88.

**Wáng Zhēnyí**

Bennett Peterson, Barbara and Zhang, Guangyu, *Notable Women of China: Shang Dynasty to the Early Twentieth Century* (Armonk, NY: MESharpe, 1999).

**Whina Cooper**

Bruce, Bryan, *Whina – Te Whaea O Te Motu*, (Red Sky Film & Television Limited, 1992).

King, Michael, *Whina: A Biography of Whina Cooper* (Auckland: Penguin, 1991).

**Wŭ Méi**

'Ng Mui', *International Wing Chun Academy*. Accessed July 29, 2017; https://www.wingchun.edu.au/the-academy/lineage/ng-mui.

'The History of Wing Chun', *Wingchun Masters*. Accessed July 29, 2017; http://wingchunmasters.com/history.

**Yaa Asantewaa**

McCaskie, Thomas C., 'The Life and Afterlife of Yaa Asantewaa', *Africa* 77, no. 2 (2007): 151–79.

**Zabel Yesayan**

*Finding Zabel Yesayan*, directed by Lara Aharonian and Talin Suciyan, Part 1 English Language, *Vimeo*. Accessed July 29, 2017; https://vimeo.com/160420509.

**Zenobia**

Zahran, Yasmine, *Zenobia, Queen of the Desert*, 2nd edition (London: Gilgamesh Publishing, 2013).

# Picture Acknowledgements

© Werner Forman / Universal Images Group / Getty Images: p. 9; © Fine Art Images / Heritage Images / Getty Images: p. 13, 44; © Biblioteca Statale, Lucca, Italy / Werner Forman Archive / Bridgeman Images: p. 25; © Asian Art & Archaeology, Inc. / CORBIS / Corbis via Getty Images: p. 48; © Musee Guimet, Paris, France / Archives Charmet / Bridgeman Images: p. 58; © Science History Images / Alamy Stock Photo: p. 66; © Art Collection 2 / Alamy Stock Photo: p. 80; © Collection Nationaal Museum van Wereldculturen. Coll. no. TM-10018776: p. 83; © Dame Jean Macnamara © attributed to Donovan / National Portrait Gallery, Canberra / Gift of Merran Samuel (nee Connor) / Donated through the Australian Government's Cultural Gifts Program: p. 93; © Photo Researchers / Mary Evans Picture Library: p. 96; © PF-(bygone1) / Alamy Stock Photo: p. 102; © Eric Carpenter/John Kobal Foundation/Getty Images: p. 106; © Lebrecht Music and Arts Photo Library / Alamy Stock Photo: p. 121; © Museo de America, Madrid, Spain / Bridgeman Images: p. 126; © Universal History Archive / UIG via Getty Images: p. 135; © Granger / Bridgeman Images: p. 155; © Anthony Phelps: p. 163; © Paul Fearn / Alamy Stock Photo: p. 167, 234; © Private Collection / Prismatic Pictures / Bridgeman Images: p. 181; © Prints & Photographs Division, Library of Congress, LC-USZ62-118946: p. 188; © adoc-photos / Corbis via Getty Images: p. 203;

## An invitation from the publisher

Join us at www.hodder.co.uk, or follow us
on Twitter @hodderbooks to be a part of
our community of people who love the very
best in books and reading.

Whether you want to discover more about a book
or an author, watch trailers and interviews, have the
chance to win early limited editions, or simply browse
our expert readers' selection of the very best books,
we think you'll find what you're looking for.

And if you don't, that's the place to tell us what's missing.

**We love what we do, and we'd love you to be a part of it.**

www.hodder.co.uk

 @hodderbooks

HodderBooks

HodderBooks